Toomey, Donald F.
The spell of
California's Spanish col
2001.
33305202127332
cu 09/18/21

THE

SPELL OF CALIFORNIA'S

SPANISH COLONIAL MISSIONS

BY

DONALD FRANCIS TOOMEY

SANTA FE

© 2001 by Donald Francis Toomey. All rights reserved.

Printed and bound in the United States of America. No part of this book may be reproduced in any form or by any electronic or mechanical means including information storage and retrieval systems without permission in writing from the publisher, except by a reviewer who may quote brief passages in a review.

Sunstone books may be purchased for educational, business, or sales promotional use. For information please write: Special Markets Department, Sunstone Press, P.O. Box 2321, Santa Fe, New Mexico 87504-2321.

FIRST EDITION

10 9 8 7 6 5 4 3 2 1

Library of Congress Cataloging-in-Publication Data:

Toomey, Donald F.
The spell of California's Spanish colonial missions / by Donald Francis I Toomey.—1st ed.
p.cm.
Includes index
ISBN: 0-86534-329-2 (pbk.)
1. Spanish mission buildings—California—Pictorial works. 2. Spanish mission buildings—California—guidebooks. 3. Spanish mission buildings—California—History. 4. Franciscans—Missions—California—History. 6. California—History—to 1846. 7 California—Pictorial works. 8. California—Guidebooks. I. Title.

F862.T66 2001
918.9404'54—dc21

2001020705

Photography by Donald Francis Toomey
Edited by Fr. Thomas J. Steele, S.J.
Designed by Vicki Marie Singer
Production by Vicki's Graphic Designs; Ted Singer, Vice President

Published by SUNSTONE PRESS
Post Office Box 2321
Santa Fe, NM 87504-2321 / USA
(505) 988-4418 / *orders only* (800) 243-5644
FAX (505) 988-1025

On the Cover Reredos of the recreated Santa Bárbara Presidio chapel.

TABLE
OF
CONTENTS

View of the unique church facade of Mission San Antonio de Padua; note bronze statue of Father Junípero Serra founder of the mission in 1771.

PREFACE
and
ACKNOWLEDGMENTS

SAINTS ALONG THE COASTLINE

Donald Toomey has done a major favor to each visitor to any one of the missions of California. These missions — all of them without exception – are historic, venerable, and handsome, but they are also profoundly instructive. Don Toomey has assembled all the basic historical facts of each mission, tracing each site from its late-eighteenth or early-nineteenth-century origin through its various disasters (fires and earthquakes predominate) and its various renovations up to the end of the twentieth century. He outlines each mission's success at achieving its purpose, and he expertly conveys to his reader his own deep appreciation of the Provincial Baroque architecture, art, and church life on the raw frontier. Why did these long-dead Franciscan missionaries live and labor as they did, gladly giving their lives for an ideal?

The theological justification for the Conquest of the New World was the evangelization of its inhabitants, and religious architecture and art were a key means of communicating this Catholic Christian message and implementing a Catholic Christian way of life within a settled community of Native Americans.[1]

This ideal was already old in the New World when Fray Junípero Serra founded the first mission. By their heroic dedication, the first dozen Franciscan "apostles" had converted the Indians of the Valley of Mexico and its environs by the hundreds of thousands, leading the friars to hope that the long-desired millennium might occur, might arrive in the new world among its innocent American Adams and Eves whom they had protected from the avarice that had tainted old-world Christianity. But by about 1570, the King of Spain had swung the pendulum away from the medicant missionaries and the Indians and toward the diocesan clergy and the settlers, and the friars soon took their evangelistic preaching, their art, and a simplified version of their mission architecture northward into "la otra México – the other Mexico City," as New Mexico was then often called. After the failures of Europe and Mexico, the friars may have chosen this northernmost frontier as the best place to give salvation history a third opportunity to turn out right; then by about 1770, when the settlers had come to dominate New Mexico, the friars may have turned to California as a fourth chance. [2]

Old-world Catholicism renewed itself by entering into a newly-discovered world and learning how to come to be at home there on the northern frontier of New Spain. In a classic 1917 essay, Borderlands historian Herbert Eugene Bolton differentiated the dynamic westward frontier of Anglo America from the often static northward frontier of Hispanic America; one important difference was the

[1] Enrique Florescano, *Myth, Memory, and Time in Mexico* (Austin: University of Texas Press, 1994), 77; Christopher C. Wilson, Mexican Devotional Retablos from the Peters Collection (Philadelphia: Saint Joseph's University Press, 1994), 18.

[2] On the Franciscans, see Robert, Ricard, *The Spiritual Conquest of Mexico* (Berkeley: University of California Press, 1966), 128-32; John Leddy Phelan, *The Millennial Kingdom of the Franciscans in the New World* (Berkeley: University of California Press, 1970); Florescano, 78. Joachim of Fiore's Millennial expectations predated the Franciscan movement, seriously infiltrated it during its early years, and remained as a quiet but powerful force for several centuries. On the shift of royal favor to the docile diocesans and away from the Franciscans, see Richard, 245; Phelan; John Frederick Schwaller, The Church and Clergy in Sixteenth-Century Mexico (Albuquerque; University of New Mexico Press, 1987) 4-5, 70-71.

lack of missionaries in the former and their presence in the latter. Spain spread her language, her law, her religion, and her religious culture over most of the western hemisphere, and five hundred years later most Americans "still speak the Spanish language, still worship at the altar set up by the Catholic kings, still live under laws essentially Spanish, and still possess a culture largely inherited from Spain."[3]

Once the settled Native Americans of the southern parts of New Spain were converted, there was vastly more to be done for the nomads of the north, and the missionaries had to do most of it. They had to convert the natives from wandering to sedentary as well as to convert them to Catholic Christianity. They had to lead them and, with the help of the presidio soldiers, protect them from their still-nomadic enemies. They had to train them at the primary-extraction and cottage-craft level and they had to civilize them to the extent that they became truly a part of the Madrid-centered Spanish Empire. And so, from the end of the sixteenth century, the mission was the active ingredient in Spain's frontier process, for if the Indians were to become both good Christians and good subjects of the King as well, they had to learn the basics of citified living; the missions were not only schools of Christianity, they were also frontier bastions to control the nomads and train the sedentary. The Spanish government estimated that each salary did as much to pacify the frontier as a dozen soldiers, and therefore Spain paid each missionary friar's annual salary out of the Ramo de Guerra – the War Fund. When the Pentagon pays up, you know it's for something politically essential.[4]

Spain's colonial policy was better than that of any other European nation, for it looked always to the natives' survival and to their gaining at least a limited citizenship and local self-government. For this, discipline was essential for learning and practicing the skills of domestic and village living, and each mission was a little civic cosmos – a little island of comfort and security in a sea of struggle. In the California missions, there were ten head of cattle, ten head of lesser animals, two horses, and four bushels of grain per capita for all the men, women and children who, before the mission came into their lives, made many a meal from a half-rotten jackrabbit left over from a successful surround a week earlier.[5] "Ubi panis, ibi patria – where there is food I find my homeland," as the old saying goes.

But there was much more than just food and shelter. It is hard for us to imagine what life was like with very few images. A mission with a gilded retablo above the altar and a pantheon of other statues and paintings fulfilled the Tridentine and Baroque penchants for powerful effects. How dazzling the mission must have been for tribal peoples just being 'reduced' from the nomadic to the settled condition. In the Indians' former world, images had been scarce, simple, and usually monochromatic, but the friars opened a new world to them, the heavenlike realm

[3] Herbert Eugene Bolton, "The Mission as a Frontier Institution in the Spanish American Colonies," *American Historical Review* 23 (1917-18), 42.

[4] Bolton, pp. 44, 47, 50-51

[5] 4 Bolton, pp. 52, 59-60.

of the splendid and dramatic estofado and encarnado statues from Guatemala Antigua and la Ciudad de México.

And the missions did even more than evangelize and civilize the Native Americans who dwelt there, they also imposed a Christian and European matrix of meaning. The focus of the Franciscans who brought Spanish Catholicism to eighteenth-century California was primarily on time and not on space. God did not mainly bestow upon us Judaeo-Christian Western-European Americans a sacred land in which to live, as He did to the Native Americans. He first and foremost sent us off on an adventure through history.

Dedicating the church of a town plaza or the chapel of some placita was the ordinary way of inserting space into sacred time, because the dedication inserted the church or chapel and the population that belonged to it into the liturgical calendar. In this manner the town or village and the land around it became part of the Christian cosmos. "A cada capillita se viene su fiestecita," the old dicho goes, "For each little chapel its little fiesta comes around." Thus indeed the big fiesta of the parish seat and the smaller fiestas of each of the many villages fall on different dates, the saints days scattered throughout the solar part of the liturgical calendar. Each feast day repeats itself annually on the same day of the same month. The Franciscan padres created a space-conception of immobile centers that would truly enable the holy persons who watched over them to take control of the lands they inhabited.[6] The chief means of incorporating hitherto profane space into the sacred cosmos of order and beauty was naming their mission churches and the settlements that surrounded them in honor of the saints of the liturgical calendar. No matter how wild the wilderness and how strange the place, the very act of naming it confers power over it and allows the community settling there to Hispanicize and Christianize it. By building a mission or a presidio chapel and naming it in honor of some holy personage, the padres conceived the pre-existing space in a new manner. They centered the surrounding landscape on the holy structure, inserted the whole pais into the liturgical calendar, the sacred time which sanctifies space, and thereby validated themselves and their neophytes as a community of Christians. The local fiesta was their annual celebration of this foundational triumph of cosmos over chaos, of sacred order and beauty over an alien wilderness.

The missions of California were focal points of sacred unity in a vast and beautiful landscape of diversity; they were valiant attempts at making Franciscan California a millennial Communion of Saints.

Thomas J. Steele, S.J.
Albuquerque, New Mexico
December 2000

[6] God is a good administrator, so he knows how to delegate authority. In a low-tech culture, saints are not primarily models of good example and ethical purity, they are primarily sources of aid; and they are powerful because holiness is identically power for life.

I am exceedingly grateful to my wife and best friend, Alisanne, for all of the encouragement and support she has given me through the years. I especially appreciate her very pragmatic approach as to what this book should be. I also extend thanks to her for all of the long drives which she cheerfully shared, crossing the desert from either Oklahoma or New Mexico in order to reach the Alta California missions.

To my daughter Virginia Ford, I give my heartfelt thanks for believing in this project and actually making this book a reality. I also thank my daughter Leah for all the aid she has given to me in the overall preparation of what has turned out to be a rather cumbersome manuscript.

I owe a particular debt of gratitude to my good friend Santero Filimón Aguilar of Bernalillo, New Mexico. Without his help, especially in accurately identifying the many santos and their attributes that I encountered in the Alta California missions, this endeavor would never have come to fruition.

Special acknowledgment is also due Father Thomas J. Steele, S.J., of Albuquerque, New Mexico, an authority on Hispanic religious art. His review of the manuscript, in spite of a demanding personal schedule and his willingness to contribute the preface are greatly appreciated.

LOCATION MAP OF SPANISH COLONIAL MISSIONS

WITH DATE OF ESTABLISHMENT AND SECULARIZATION
(city name in parenthes if differnt than mission name)

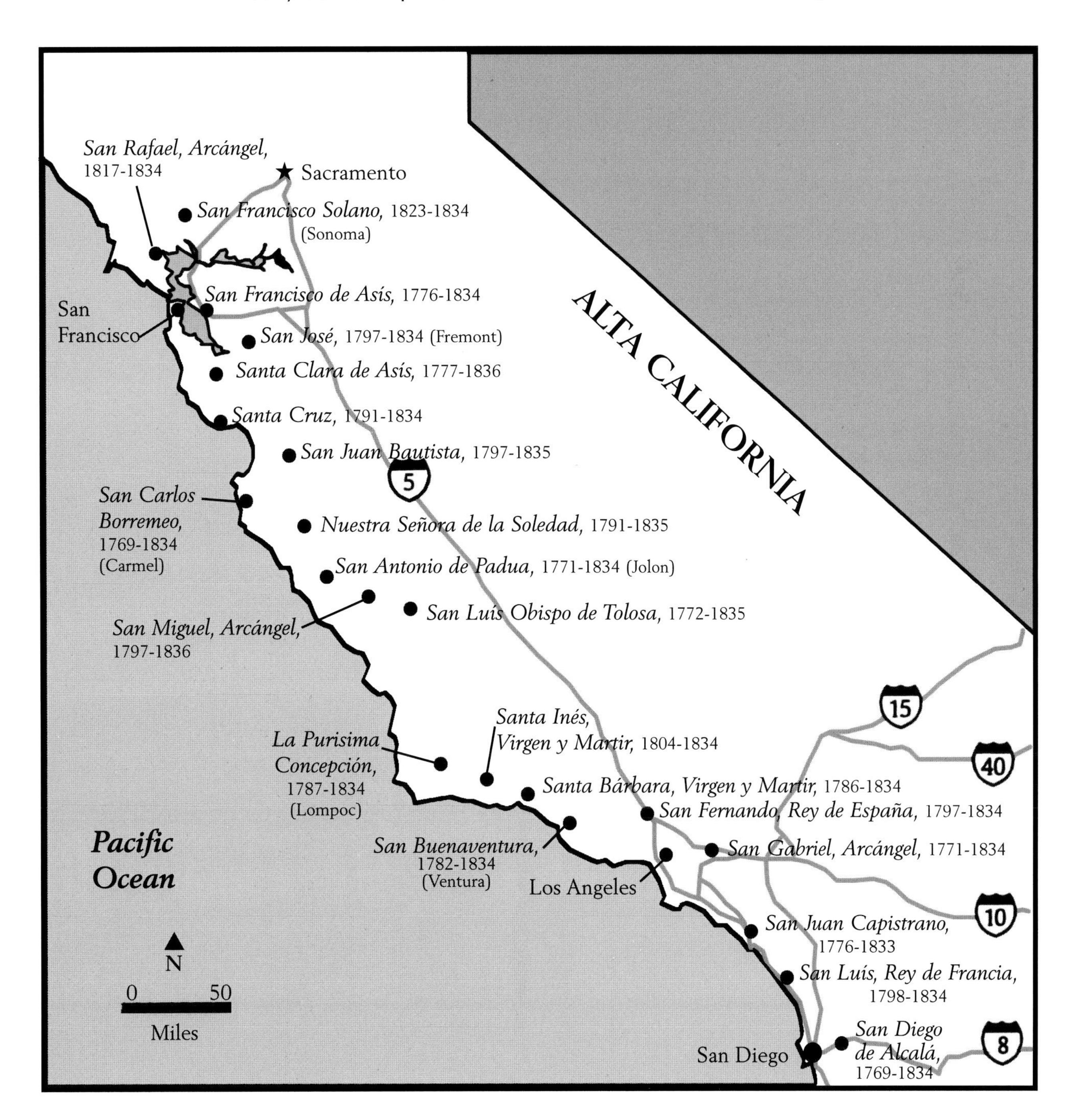

CHAPTER ONE

THE SPELL OF CALIFORNIA'S SPANISH COLONIAL MISSIONS

INTRODUCTION

A dramatic larger than life bronze sculptural rendering of Father Junipero Sera (1713-1784), first father-president and founder of the Alta California mission chain; statue is sited in front of city hall, Ventura, California.

WHY MISSIONS? The narrative of the Spanish colonial missions predates by two hundred years the primitive shelter erected at San Diego in 1769 by Father Junípero Serra, and his small band of soldiers and colonists under the leadership of Don Gaspár de Portolá. Spanish explorers had discovered the California coast when Juan Rodríguez Cabrillo arrived here in 1542, and pronounced the climate "delicioso." In 1602, Sebastian Vizcaíno sailed the coast and in an exaggerated description identified a bay he called Monterey as "the best port that could be desired." However, Spain had been content to develop what they had established in New Spain (Mexico) and to exploit its rich natural resources. In the interim they consolidated their hold on Baja California but looked upon unknown Alta California with mere curiosity. It was not until 1740-1765, when Russian explorers and fur traders explored the coast and eventually established outposts as far south of Alaska as the Farallon Islands near San Francisco, that Spain awakened to the imminent danger. This Russian encroachment forced the Spaniards under King Carlos III to re-examine the situation.

It should be remembered that during the 15th and 16th centuries Spain dominated the New World. By the late 15th century Spain had claimed title to half the known world, a claim recognized by Pope Alexander VI in 1493 with a papal edict that divided the world into two parts, one assigned to Spain and the other to Portugal, Spain's principal colonial rival.

Spain's colonies were administered under a clumsy overdeveloped bureaucratic system. Primary authority was vested in the King and his councilors in Spain. Partial delegation of power was given to viceroys, who were appointed one year at a time and who controlled civil, military, and religious affairs within the colonies. The establishment of the Alta California missions was under the auspices of the Viceroy of New Spain in Mexico City. Government transactions, conducted solely in writing, moved with glacial inertia. Actual colonial exploration and settlement was carried out under close cooperation of the military and the religious. In regions where the native inhabitants were known to be docile the clergy opened the frontier, generally with a minimal military escort for protection. This was the method employed in establishing the Alta California missions.

For the crown, the mission as a colonial enterprise was economical to both establish and maintain. In essence, the mission system allowed the Spanish to occupy and control the land. To prevent foreign incursion the system called for the missionaries to convert the native populations to Christianity. They would reduce the nomadic peoples to a sedentary state and "civilize" them through education both sacred and secular with the ultimate goal of making them loyal Christian citizens of the Empire. The overall government investment was small since each mission would only require two padres and a few soldiers for

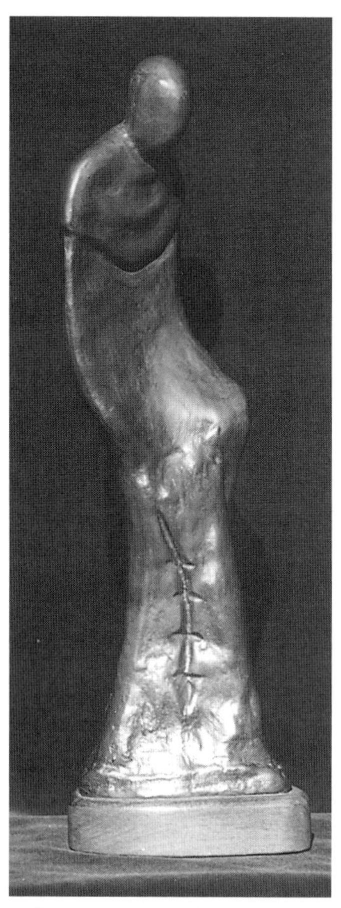

A bronze casting of Father Junipero Serra by the late Arizona artist Ted De Grazia; this more abstract 1968 redition is thirteen inches high and is numbered 85/200.

protection. Consequently, after only a few years of supply, the mission ought to become self-sufficient. After ten years of education and vocational training, mission holdings were to be turned over to the native Indians, since the padres owned no property. Most important, a factor not considered beforehand, was the effect the system would have on the native populations. The practitioners of the system brought to the region European diseases which decimated the multiple and varied Indian peoples indigenous to the Alta California coast. It introduced, and forced upon them, a Eurocentric culture that was alien to their traditions, culture that some would say was a thinly disguised form of slavery parading under a pious banner. Still, Spanish treatment of the native populations, though strongly criticized in terms of contemporary political morality, was little different from that practiced in other colonial empires of the time. In Alta California, it was a conflict of two cultures in collision, with the inevitable crushing of the weaker by the stronger.

DRAMATIS PERSONAE: The name of Fray Junípero Serra (1713-1764) is inextricably associated with the Alta California missions; he has even been referred to as the "First Californian." Born in Petra, on the Mediterranean island of Mallorca, Spain, in 1713, he had previously served the Franciscan order as brilliant teacher and philosopher, devout friar, and skilled administrator. As a young man he had hoped to do missionary work in the New World, but it was not until the spring of 1749 that he set out for New Spain (Mexico). On New Year's Day of 1750 he arrived at the College of San Fernando in Mexico City. From 1750-1758 he served in Querétaro in the rugged Mexican countryside of Sierra Gordo. Thereafter he spent ten years in various areas of central Mexico, developing his pastoral and missionary skills. With the expulsion of the Jesuits in 1767, Serra was appointed Superior and Father-President of the missions of Baja California, headquartered in Loreto. Serra had hardly begun this assignment when news reached him that he was to turn over the Baja to other hands. Under the direction of the King's personal agent in New Spain, Inspector-General José de Galvez had drawn up plans for an expedition to establish a chain of missions in Alta California. Military leadership of this endeavor was entrusted to a proven Catalonian soldier of noble rank, Don Gaspár de Portolá, who had recently been appointed governor of Baja California; Father Serra became head of the religious arm of the expedition. Serra welcomed this opportunity as something he had personally longed for all his life, the desire to bring the message of Christ's salvation to peoples who had never heard it.

Father Junipero Serra established the first mission of San Diego de Alcalá in 1769, followed by San Carlos de Borromeo (Carmel) in 1770, San Antonio de Padua in 1771, San Gabriel Arcángel in 1771, San Luís Obispo in 1772, San

Francisco de Asís (Dolores) in 1776, San Juan Capistrano in 1776, Santa Clara de Asís in 1777, and San Buenaventura in 1782. Serra presided over the Alta California mission system from his headquarters at Mission San Carlos de Borromeo, where he died on August 28, 1784. It is to be remembered that Father Serra was already fifty-five years of age when he was chosen as Father-President of the California missions; he was quite an old man for the times. In physical stature he was only five feet two inches in height, and he weighed slightly over one hundred pounds. However he was a man of boundless energy and determination, one who did not suffer fools readily—a distinct detriment in his dealings with a number of Spanish officials.

At Serra's death in 1784, Padre Francisco Palóu (1723-1789), a close colleague and fellow Mallorcan, became temporary Father-President of the mission system, serving in this position for a little over a year. Palóu was born in 1723 and had journeyed with Serra to the New World. In 1767 he was part of the Franciscan contingent assigned to assume charge of the Baja California missions. In 1773, Palóu found himself at Mission San Diego de Alcalá serving as superior pro tempore while Serra was away on one of his many journeys. In 1776, Palóu journeyed north and celebrated Mass on June 29th, formalizing the establishment of Mission San Francisco de Asís (Dolores), where he served for nine years as head missionary. Fray Francisco Palóu is perhaps best known as the author of the first California biography, "Relacion Historica de la Vida del Venerable Padre Fray Junípero Serra," written at Carmel and Dolores missions and published in Mexico City in 1787. Renowned California historian H. H. Bancroft regarded Palóu's magnum opus as the source book on early Alta California mission history.

Serra's actual successor as Father-President of the Alta California missions was Fray Fermín Francisco Lasuén. He was born in Victoria, Spain, in 1736. As a young man he joined the Franciscan order and volunteered for the New World missions, arriving in Mexico in 1759. He served in the Sierra Gordo region until 1767, at which time he began six years of missionary service in the Baja California missions. Father Lasuén spent time in the Alta California missions during Serra's presidency, serving at Missions San Gabriel, San Carlos, and San Diego. His tenure as Father-President of the Alta California missions lasted from 1785 until his death in 1803. Father Lasuén founded nine missions: Santa Barbara in 1786, La Purisima in 1787, Santa Cruz in 1791, Soledad in 1791, San José in 1797,San Juan Bautista in 1797, San Miguel in 1797, San Fernando in 1797 ,and San Luís Rey in 1798.

Father Fermín Lasuén was a distinguished successor to Junípero Serra. He doubled the number of missions and converts. He also brought about an economic transformation in mission agricultural and livestock husbandry. In addition, he introduced the now familiar mission style architecture of tile, stone,

Detail of the arched corridor at Mission San Antonio de Padua showing the uneven width of the burnt brick arches

and adobe. He was an extremely able administrator who had personally dealt successfully with missions beset with problems. As Father-President he carried forward Serra's great dream with diplomacy, tact, skill, and energy. Like Serra, he died in harness, at the age of sixty-seven. For a total of thirty-four years these two men controlled the destiny of the Alta California missions. In the remaining years, before secularization began in the 1830s the mission chain was administered by some very capable successors. Notable are Fray Estevan Tapis (1803-1812), who founded Mission Santa Inés in 1804, Fray Mariano Payeras (1815-1819), and Fray Narciso Durán who served three terms as Father-President (1825-1827, 1831-1838, and 1844-1846). Still, none of the succeeding Father-Presidents approached the stature of either Serra or Lasuén.

SECULARIZATION: Secularization of the Alta California missions–taking them from the care of religious orders and placing them in the care of diocesan,"secular" priests—spelled the death knell for the mission system. As a government policy the Spanish Cadiz Cortes had already considered doing so as early as 1813 (Jackson & Castillo, 1995, p. 88). Eventual secularization of the missions was one of the cornerstones of Franciscan mission administrative policy. This was brought to a head in the 1820s during the time of turbulent Mexican political struggles that followed Mexican Independence from Spain in 1821. The Alta Californian Franciscans had strongly objected to implementing this policy during the 1820s on the grounds that the Indians were not ready to conduct their own affairs. Perhaps more importantly, the civil authorities were not anxious to enforce secularization because they recognized that the missions, and their Indian labor force, comprised almost the entire economy of the colony and was, for all practical purposes, the sole source of food. Recognizing this, they foresaw the disastrous results that would occur with the dispersal of the mission enterprises and labor force. When secularization was finally ordered in 1833 some of the missions complied almost immediately, for others it went on for a few more years. Accordingly, the mission compound buildings were divided into religious and public segments, and the land turned over to the Indians. Untrained, incapable of utilizing their newly acquired land to advantage, and almost totally unaware of the significance of land acquisition, the Indians fell prey to unscrupulous land speculators, many of whom were politicians within the new republican government. It does not require much imagination to visualize the tragic effects secularization had on the lives of the mission Indians. Dependent on the regimentation of mission life for years, they were unable and probably unwilling to return to anything like their previous existence. Most remained on the land and transferred their labor to the new landowners. Many of the new "patrons" cared nothing for the general well-being of the Indians and treated them virtually as an indentured labor force. The padres who remained behind at some of the missions since the diocese was unable to provide replacements were able to offer only a slight measure of comfort and succor to their former charges. With mission discipline severed they could no longer help the native populations support themselves. Thus came an end to a system and a way of life that had a viable existence of a little more than sixty years and that brought with it profound changes both good and bad. It was a system that even today has left much doubt and concern in our minds.

Statue of Father Junípero Serra with his arms around a mission indian boy; this work was created by the sculptor Gutzon Borglum in 1914, and is sited adjacent to the bell wall at Mission San Juan Capistrano.

MISSION RUINS AND THE ARTISTS: Following secularization the mission fields, herds, orchards, and livestock rapidly disappeared into private hands. In a matter of only a few years little was left to demonstrate the prosperity and industry of the once thriving mission system. In the late 1840s, along with American occupation, the U. S. Federal Land Commission reviewed the mission's property titles and land grants, and some of the original lands and buildings were restored to the church by acts of Congress in the 1850s and 1860s. The Church found itself with real estate too vast for religious functions. Many of the mission buildings were leased to private parties, and commercial ventures occupied buildings where the padres once meditated. Cases in point were at Mission San Fernando Rey de España where a pig farm operated for a number of years and at Mission San Juan Capistrano where Father Serra's chapel was utilized for hay storage. The tile roofs were removed to pay debts, to be incorporated into new settler haciendas, and in later years mission tiles were used in the construction of railroad stations. Roofs collapsed, and once their protection was gone, the adobe just melted into the landscape. Without active parishes the missions fell into ruins. A number of decades passed before public-spirited citizens began to take serious interest in what was left of the missions. Above all, it was the artists of the day who discovered their romantic and picturesque decay and who initially came to their rescue. The mission ruins were recorded in oil paintings, etchings, and watercolors by a group of artists collectively known today as the "California Impressionists" (see Stern, Miller, Hallan-Gibson, & Neuerburg 1995). A fine collection of oil paintings done in the manner of the great English painter Turner were created by the artist Edwin Deakin (Mills & Cutter, 1966).

Following the artists came the photographers, with the result that a flood of stereopticon views of mission ruins appeared on the market. Both the art and the photographs attracted great attention, and so began a flood of tourists in the late 1890s and early 1900s. There were even special railroad excursions to the missions, accompanied by a plethora of guidebooks, all geared to the tourists. Along with this conspicuous interest, wealthy individuals organized groups to "Save the Missions." Foremost among these was the California Landmarks Club, an organization founded by Los Angeles newspaperman Charles Fletcher Lummis. The club raised monies to keep several southern California missions from complete devastation. In a number of instances these early restorations, though well intentioned, were badly executed, primarily because of lack of information on the original form of the mission buildings. As we will see in later chapters, restoration is a dicey business, and during the early days it proceeded along an uneven course.

THE "RAMONA" SYNDROME: In 1884, Helen Hunt Jackson's book *Ramona* was published. This book sold more copies than any novel written in America between Uncle Tom's Cabin and Gone with the Wind (Kennedy, 1993, p. 172). The California mission revival owes much to this seemingly harmless romantic novel. Jackson sought to use her novel as a weapon for social reform on behalf of the California Indians. She had previously tried history with her book *Century Of Dishonor* and social science with her detailed report to the U. S. Department of the Interior, but to no avail. She felt that perhaps she could catch both the government and the nation's interest and conscience with a sugar-coated romantic novel of Indian life set within the California Spanish Colonial mission system. The perfumed story overwhelmed the message, and resulted in mission revival instead of social reform. The California Mission Indians were left behind and the good padres romanticized so that everyone succumbed to whitewashed adobe and red tile roofs. California missions revival was well on its way!

It must be remembered that after the 1850s, settlers from the eastern states moved into Alta California in increasing numbers, and to them the mission ruins were compelling. They found them to be romantic. As newcomers, they needed a history in this new land, and they turned to the ruins. As they did so, they began to invent a history that offered them a measure of comfort and security in their new surroundings. For the historical record they selectively chose the evidence they wanted to believe. In this manner they created the myth of the missions with peaceful padres, buildings with whitewashed walls and red-tiled roofs, and happy docile Indians—a myth that is still perpetuated today among persons who are more interested in their own emotions than in the welfare of their fellow men and women.

RESTORATION MAKES ITS MARK: Those California missions that escaped the ravages of time fell prey to the "modernizer," those well-intentioned people who wanted to bring the shabby old adobe buildings into the modern

age. We will see how the "modernizer" set to restoring the missions in the following chapters. Suffice it to say that in many cases they were misguided and the overall results questionable at best. Still, in some missions, parish life has gone on under modernized roofs and stabilized adobe walls, unquestionably brought about by the enthusiasm unleashed by Helen Hunt Jackson's *Ramona*. Yet from a religious view some of the missions are extinct as places of worship. Where they do serve an ongoing function and are alive, the priests and people are continually faced with hard choices about how to balance the basic necessities of a devout worshipping congregation and the advantages of tourism. It is undeniable that many of the California Spanish Colonial missions are sanctuaries of great beauty, but one should be cautious in taking them at face value as evidence of history. Many are painstaking reconstructions utilizing original materials; others are handsome reproductions done with modern materials. The latter are what one might have expected the good padres to have constructed if they had come into California during the height of the mission craze that occurred in the 1920s and 1930s. During the last fifty years or so, restoration has proceeded on a more scientific and historically valid foundation. Archaeological research and consultation of old records have led to impressive and authentic results. The most outstanding reconstruction endeavor has been at Mission La Purisima Concepción. Here, faithful and accurate restoration has been accomplished by the National Park Service and the Civilian Conservation Corps during the 1930s. The overall intrinsic value of mission reconstruction varies from mission to mission. Some are overly commercialized and indifferently maintained, in spite of (or maybe because of) the hordes of tourists that storm the gates each day. Viewed principally as structures, they are very worthwhile tourist destinations. The Franciscan padres, with their attendant Indian labor, were basically untrained artisans, yet the buildings are compelling objects because of their honest and unpretentious design, their simple construction materials and methods. The Franciscan friars favored art as an aid to worship and a means to embellish the house of God. With their sparse resources and lack of formal art training, they did surprisingly well. Many of the mission churches reverberate with fantastic color, chosen to please the Indians and make for them a place where they could begin to absorb the rudiments of an alien religion. In an effort to recreate some of the grandeur

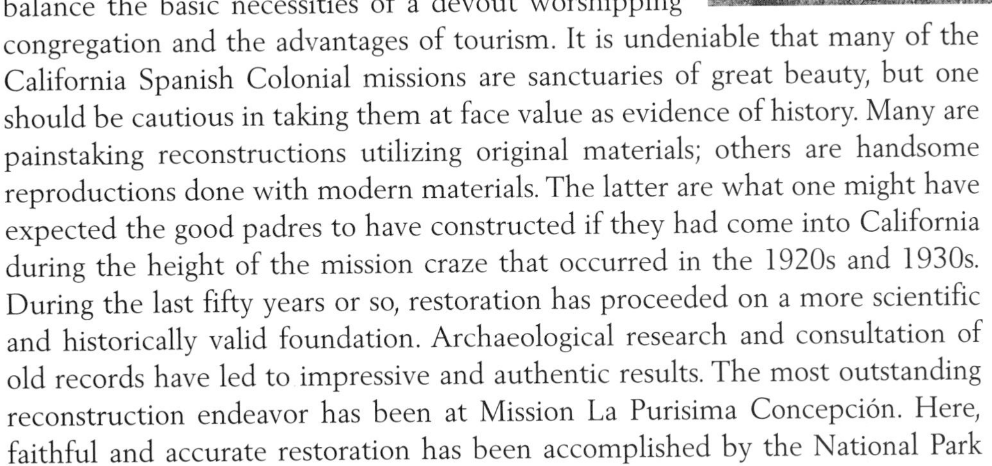

West end of the monasterey building at Mission La Purisima Concepción de Maria Santisima showing the prominent buttresses which added strength and support for earthquake protection

The residence/workshop building at Purisima has a number of recreated rooms illustrating a particular craft or function: this room served as a candle producing entity and has a rotating candle dipper.

of their homeland churches, the padres trained the Indian artisans to paint imitation marble on the church interiors and to incorporate painting perspective into altars, niches, alcoves, doorways, and corridors. The results are most charming, and they give the modern day tourist one additional compelling reason to visit these shrines dedicated to a time long past.

MISSIONS AND TOURISM: Stretching along the California coast from San Diego to Sonoma sit twenty-one Spanish colonial missions (see Fig. 1) that together attract more tourists than any other historical attraction in this tourist-minded state. Many of the missions are enclosed on all sides by urban sprawl. Others stand free and uncluttered in a setting that is close to their original siting. Nearly all are remnants of structures that were miniature self-contained worlds. For different reasons the California Franciscan missions exert a spell over those who come to view them. For many, the appeal is that of historical antiquity, for these are the oldest buildings along the California coast. For others, the main appeal lies in the accomplishments of a handful of dedicated and profoundly religious men who were able to create monuments to their faith. In the process of proselytizing the Indians they firmly believed they were bringing the Christian message to a Stone-Age people and introducing them to a better Eurocentric way of life. However, the history of these missions as institutions, sealed their successes and their failures. It is a fascinating story that even today kindles our imagination and genuine interest. Margolin (1989, p. 48) summarized it all quite realistically in a totally unvarnished manner saying, "Many of the missions have been restored often with a high level of scholarly involvement. Many of the architectural and artistic details are amazingly exact. The human details, however, are invariably omitted: the sight of men and women in irons, the sound of the whip, the misery of the Indians. Without acknowledging the pain and agony that were a major part of mission life, today's carefully restored missions do not portray history. Rather, in the manner of theme parks, they use the ornaments of history to create a soothing world of fantasy."

The literature on Alta California Spanish colonial missions is extensive, but little of it is easily available to the average tourist. Generally, what has appeared during the last twenty years has been a deluge of picture books. These are replete with glorious examples of the photographer's art, but sadly lack basic historical information such as the history and identification of outstanding religious objects within the mission churches and the fascinating historical narratives proper to each mission. I hope this present book will overcome those deficiencies.

CHAPTER TWO

TWO SPANISH COLONIAL MISSIONS SEPARATED BY 450 MILES:

SAN DIEGO DE ALCALÁ 1769
AND
SAN CARLOS BORROME0 DE CARMEL0 1770

The rather plain white-painted facade and companario of Mission San Diego de Alcalá: when restoration was undertaken a small portion of the facade was the only standing wall.

The top three bells are thought to be replicas; lower bell on left was recast in 1894 and weights 1200 pounds, whereas the bell on the right is dated 1802 and weighs 805 pounds.

MISSION SAN DIEGO DE ALCALÁ:

Synopsis: First Spanish colonial mission and presidio on the coast of Alta California; Mission San Diego founded by Father Junípero Serra on Presidio Hill on July 16, 1769; named for its patron Saint Didacus of Alcalá, Spain; original mission site moved six miles inland to present location in 1774; Indian attacks in 1769 and in 1775, when mission was burned to the ground; churches: 1769, 1774, 1776, 1780, 1813; earthquakes: 1803, 1812; secularized in 1834, after an active mission life of sixty-five years; sold in 1846; restored to Church in 1862; occupied by U. S. Cavalry 1847-1862, falling into ruins thereafter; some salvage restoration from early 1890s to 1907; additional restoration for 1915 Panama-California Exposition; major restoration completed in 1931; reinstated as a parish church in 1941; designated a Minor Mission Basilica in 1976.

Location: Mission San Diego de Alcalá is located five miles east of State Highway 5, off State Highway 8, at 10818 San Diego Mission Road, on the outskirts of the city of San Diego. Ruins of Presidio Real de San Diego are located at Presidio Park, San Diego, the present site of the Father Junípero Serra Museum.

San Diego de Alcalá, Saint Didacus of Alcalá, became its patron in 1602 when Captain Sebastian Vizcaíno discovered it on November twelfth. The name was subsequently applied to both the first Spanish colonial presidio and mission in Alta California by Father Junípero Serra on July 16, 1769.

Diego was born of humble parents near Seville, Spain, in the Andalusian village of San Nicolas del Puerto, circa 1400. He was attracted to the spiritual life very early, and he lived as a hermit before becoming a brother in the Franciscan order. He was a successful missionary in the Canary Islands, so much so that he was chosen as guardian of the Franciscan community on Fuerteventura from 1445 to 1449. He journeyed to Rome in 1450 to be present at the canonization of Saint Bernardine of Siena. In Rome, he resided in a monastery where he showed great skill in nurturing the sick and was credited with miraculous cures. Later on, he returned to Spain and worked in the infirmary of the University of Alcalá in Castille. He died there on November 12, 1463, and is buried under the high altar of the cathedral. Diego was canonized by the Franciscan Pope Sixtus V in 1588. He was especially devoted to the Cross and was very concerned with the care and feeding of the poor and the welfare of the less fortunate. Once, after being reprimanded for giving away monastery food he was asked to open his habit to reveal the bread he had taken, only to have it transformed into roses. Accordingly, images of the Cross, roses, and bread traditionally appear in most portrayals of him.

He was a popular subject in Spanish art of the seventeenth century, and there are paintings and sculptures of him by many of the renowned artists of the day. In Alta California, paintings and sculptures of him appear to have been limited only to the mission and presidio of San Diego. Both had bultos of him. An oil painting of Diego arrived at the mission in 1772 but was damaged during the Indian attack on the mission in 1775. By 1777, a large oil painting of him had arrived and hung for a time in the presidio chapel. A third, smaller painting was sent from New Spain in 1782. The first painting, by renowned Mexican artist José de Páez, has recently been restored and presently hangs in Mission San Diego, the second oil painting is currently at the Mission of San Luís Rey de Francia, and the third is on loan to the Serra Museum in San Diego.

The bay at San Diego had been known to the Spanish since 1542, when Juan Rodriguez Cabrillo discovered and mapped it, but was an ideal location to establish the first of eventual twenty-one missions along the coast of Alta California. A mission, coupled with a military garrison, a presidio, would formally establish Spain's claim to the land. However the enterprise was fraught with much difficulty. Inspector-General José de Gálvez, the Viceroy of New Spain, outlined the plans and appointed Captain Gaspár de Portolá to head both land and sea expeditions. Father Junípero Serra, designated to become Father-President of the missions, headed the religious arm of the expeditions. Two land forces were formed, one under the command of Captain Fernando de Rivera and the other under Portolá. Two packet ships, the San Carlos and the San Antonio, composed the sea expedition and set sail for San Diego on January 9, 1769. The Rivera party departed on the same day, followed a month later by the Portolá land party. The packet ship San Antonio dropped anchor in San Diego Bay on April 11, 1769, whereas the San Carlos, forced off course by storms, limped into port much later after losing many of her crew to scurvy. The overland Rivera party arrived on May 14th, with Portolá not arriving until June 29. Father Serra made his appearance two days later on July l, 1769.

On July 2nd, the Feast of the Visitation of Our Lady, Father Serra sang a Mass of Thanksgiving to her Most Holy Spouse, San José, patron of both the land and sea expeditions. This was Junípero Serra's first Alta California Mass, and it was celebrated at the site chosen for the military presidio on a hill two miles inland overlooking the bay near the San Diego River.

On July 15th, after a High Mass in honor of San José, Captain Portolá began his overland search for Monterey Bay to the north. His expedition comprised seventy-four men: Frs. Juan Crespí (1721-1782), and Francisco Gómez (1729-1784), Sergeant José Francisco Ortega as scout, Miguel Costanso as engineer, Captain Don Fernando de Rivera and Lieutenant Pedro Fages, soldiers, and Christian Indians from Baja California. Remaining behind on Presidio Hill were Frs. Junípero Serra, Fernando Parron (Ca. 1728-?), and Juan Vizcaíno (1728-?), Dr. Pedro Prat, soldiers, and Baja California Indians, forty persons in all.

Terra cotta statue of Father Junípero Serra kneeling in prayer at the side of a cross, and sited adjacent to the entrance of Mission San Diego de Alcalá.

After the Portolá expedition had left Fr. Serra turned his attention to constructing the mission. Having chosen a site on Presidio Hill, he and the others began erecting a few simple structures, the largest to serve as a temporary church. Then on the morning of July 16, 1769, Father Junípero Serra founded Mission San Diego de Alcalá for its patron Saint Didacus. Two soldiers raised the large wooden cross as Fr. Serra blessed it. He then sang a High Mass and preached a sermon. Later that afternoon, Serra inscribed the initial pages for the registers of baptisms, marriages, and burials.

Serra described the first few months as trying and quite unrewarding. When local Indians visited the mission, he gave them trinkets to win their confidence and good will. However, some of them began to steal anything that was not securely fastened down, and they often molested the sick soldiers and sailors. Becoming increasingly bold they mimicked the gunshots the soldiers fired to warn them off. The Indians were enamored with cloth, and one night they were caught trying to cut down the sails of the packet ship San Carlos. Indeed, Serra was faced with a communications problem. Within a month the Indians had tired of the Spanish presence and decided to assert themselves with a show of force. On the Feast of the Assumption, August 15th, Fr. Parrón and two soldiers went out to the San Carlos to say Mass. Meanwhile Frs. Serra and Vizcaíno were offering their Mass in the mission chapel back on Presidio Hill. Right after Mass, four soldiers headed for the San Carlos to accompany Fr. Parrón on his return. The Indians, noticing the mission was relatively unprotected, quickly assembled and attacked it. Serra and Vizcaíno remained in one of the huts praying there would be no casualties. On his knees, Serra fervently prayed to God to intervene, while a rain of Indian arrows descended all around him. Fortunately, Fr. Serra was not injured, but José María Vergerano, Serra's servant and faithful companion who accompanied him from Baja California, was hit by an arrow. It was a fatal wound, and he died in Serra's arms as he absolved him. Others on the Spanish side that were wounded included Fr. Vizcaíno, Chacón the blacksmith, and a Christian Indian. This initial battle for San Diego in which the Spanish routed the Indians appears to have turned the tide in the Spanish relationship with the Indians. From this point on, the Indians became more peaceful. It was at this time that a stockade of timbers was erected around the presidio/mission perimeter to prevent future surprise attacks. As the months went by Serra and his companions, isolated as they were, filled their time on the hilltop with prayer.

On January 24, 1770, their vigil came to an end when the seventy-four men of Portolá's expedition came into sight. During their six months expedition they had marched over nine hundred miles through uncharted territory. Portolá, Costanso, and Crespí each returned to San Diego with detailed diaries of their adventures and discoveries. They had camped at what would later become the city of Los Angeles, and they had discovered San Francisco Bay. Unfortunately, they had failed to identify Monterey and its bay.

With Portolá's return to Presidio Hill there were now more mouths to feed and food supplies were dangerously low. Unknown to this intrepid group, the supply packet ship San José that was to arrive from Baja California had been lost at sea. Portolá decided that the expedition had not come this far only to die of starvation. The San Diego outpost might have to be abandoned. He decided that unless relief arrived by March 19th, the Feast of San José, the expedition would return to New Spain. The idea of abandoning their toehold in Alta California was a severe blow to Serra; his entire nature rebelled at the idea of turning back. Discussing the matter with Fr. Crespí, he found that he too was of the same mind, and if the expedition were to be abandoned they would remain behind. As March 19th approached, all members of the expedition joined in a novena to San José. On the morning of the 19th, Serra celebrated High Mass and preached a sermon. After breakfast all began packing for their departure the next morning. Around three in the afternoon, a lookout spotted sails on the horizon. The packet ship San Antonio had at last been sighted. It seemed a miracle! The atmosphere in camp was completely transformed. All followed Serra into the temporary chapel where their voices broke forth in thanks to God. For Junípero Serra, this event was so significant that as long as he lived he always celebrated a High Mass on the nineteenth of every month of the year.

The original mission site on Presidio Hill was moved to its present location in 1774, when it was decided to distance the mission from the soldiers of the presidio. The Indians were increasingly harassed by the soldiers, and the women in particular were not safe. Father Luís Jayme (1740-1775), who in 1774 had succeeded Serra at Mission San Diego, petitioned the Viceroy to move the mission location six miles northeast of the presidio, and closer to an Indian village. The original site lacked good water, had poor soil, and did not have a sufficient labor supply all of which made it impossible to produce enough food to sustain everyone. Under the direction of Frs. Luís Jayme and Vicente Fuster (1742-1800), a church and subsidiary buildings were completed by December 1774, and by that time 60 Indians had been baptized.

In front of the altar rests the remains of five Franciscan padres who died in service at the mission; Padre Luís Jayme, the first to die at Mission San Diego was martyred during the indian attack on the mission in 1775

Meanwhile in October of 1775, a number of disciplinary problems had arisen in regards the Indians. Since the move from Presidio Hill the previous year, the crop harvest had been very small, and although many Indians had been baptized most could not live and be fed at the mission site. Instead, they lived in nearby rancherias, where their religious instruction was carried on by those better instructed among them. In reality, the Indians at Mission San Diego had been very difficult to bring under full mission control. Some of the more rebellious of the Indians went from one village to another enciting trouble. Late in that month a few Indians had been flogged for attending a native dance, and in the heat of the moment Fr. Vicente Fuster had unwisely threatened to set fire to their village. A number of the Indians ran away from what they regarded as uncompromising injustice. In the days that followed the padres were warned that an attack on the mission was imminent, but Fr. Jayme refused to believe it, instead admonishing those who brought him the news for their lies. Then in the early morning of November 5, 1775, some 600 or more Indians reached the mission undetected. Of this group, half continued on to the presidio. The Indians first surrounded the huts of the converted Indians and threatened them with death if they raised the alarm. Meanwhile other Indians crept into the church, removed the bultos of Nuestra Señora de la Purísima Concepción and San José, and handed them to women who spirited them off into the hills. Nothing was heard; the mission guards were all sound asleep! One of the attackers picked up a firebrand and ran about torching all the structures. Soon the flames and general pandemonium awakened everyone. It was a bloody attack on the unsuspecting mission by the Tipai and Ipai Indians, and many fatalities occurred. Padre Luís Jayme was killed, as was the blacksmith José Romero; a carpenter named Urcellino was wounded and died five days later. The Indians had seized Fr. Jayme, dragged him into an arroyo, stripped him of his clothing, beat him to death with clubs and rocks, and riddled his body with arrows. Those Indians that were supposed to attack the presidio turned back when they saw the flames of the burning mission, fearing that the presidio had been alerted. They then hastened back to join in the pillaging of the mission. The presidio had slept through it all!

Padre Luís Jayme became California's first martyr at the age of thirty-five. His remains lie beneath the sanctuary of the mission, and a large white painted concrete cross sited on the mission grounds marks the approximate location of his martyrdom. When Father Serra was informed of Jayme's death he wrote: "I would welcome such a fate with God's grace and favor. Thanks be to God, now indeed the land has been watered with martyred blood; certainly now the conversion of the San Diego Indians will be achieved" (Morgado, 1991, p. 45). From the gutted mission ruins some supplies were retrieved, along with other items. All the survivors retreated to the presidio where they remained for some time.

Eventually the Indians realized they could not successfully compete with Spanish arms, and they cooperated with the padres in rebuilding the mission church on the same charred grounds. This larger church, on the order of eighty feet in length by fourteen feet in width, with a thatched roof, was built in October 1776, as were other subsidiary buildings. By 1780 the mission church was enlarged, with adobe walls three feet thick. The roof was constructed of poles and tule reeds, and covered with a layer of mud to add some protection against fire. Reconstruction of the mission was completed by 1785, with many of the mission buildings repaired and further strengthened. By that time the mission had developed what was to be the customary quadrangle setting that gave a sense of protection to all that lived within it. In 1792, fired roof tiles replaced the grass roofing on most of the mission buildings, and by 1797 a series of aqueducts and an irrigation system had been completed. At that time the mission agricultural enterprise had 50,000 acres of cultivated land. Mission inventories list close to 32,000 head of livestock that year. The padres trained the Indian women in candle and soap making, sewing, weaving, and cooking. Most men worked the fields; others were trained as blacksmiths and leather tanners.

The mission church of San Diego de Alcalá, and its outbuildings, were severely damaged in an 1803 earthquake, and rebuilding was undertaken once again. The present mission church was begun in 1808 and was almost completed when it was damaged during the 1812 earthquake. Following that disaster, the padres incorporated unique buttresses into the mission church building to better withstand future earthquakes. Dedication of the new buildings took place on November 12, 1813. The timbers used in constructing the buildings were carried by the Indians from the Pala Mountains 60 miles away.

Mission San Diego de Alcalá achieved both spiritual and material growth until 1824. The highest number of mission Indians in residence was in 1829. However, continued problems with the Indians plagued the mission. Added to this were the intrusion of civilian settlers and the ongoing struggle over control of the vast mission properties both of which accelerated the decline of Mission San Diego. By the late 1820s and early 1830s, the influence of the padres and the mission system itself were in terminal decline. Beginning with José M. de Echeandia (1825-1831), the first official Mexican governor, the Mexican government introduced policies to bring about complete secularization of all the Alta California missions. In 1846, Mission San Diego was put in charge of a politico, Santiago Arguello, as a reward for his previous service to the government. The last Franciscan padre to serve the mission during this time was Fr. Vicente Oliva Pascual (1780-1848), who in late 1846 retired to Mission San Juan Capistrano. Following secularization and the resultant unsettled times, the mission fell into decline and its large land holdings passed into private hands. Then in 1847, the U. S. Army moved cavalry troops into the mission compound. The army remodeled the church building into a two-story barracks with the soldiers living on the upper floor and the horses stabled on the ground floor. The army remained here until 1862, and during that interval the mission compound suffered much structural damage. When the American traveler and artist Henry Miller visited the site in 1856 he noted (1997, p. 59) that

> *the mission buildings have lost their ancient appearance, having been renovated by the government and serve now as the quarters of United States troops. There are several buildings erected by the government and a tall flagstaff with the Star Spangled Banner waving from one. Being built on an elevation, it offers a fine view; below it are numerous olive trees, together with some palm and fruit trees*

Miller also included a drawing of the mission on page 58 of his account.

View of the small baptistry area in the mission church: the front is a replica of the one Father Serra was baptized as a child on the island of Mallorca; bulto above font is of Santa Ana and is thought to be of sixteenth century Spanish origin.

It was not until 1862 that the United States Government, by a proclamation signed by President Abraham Lincoln, formally restored some 22 acres to the Church, specifically for religious use. Before the Church was able to occupy the property much work had to be done to restore the property so that it could be utilized for religious services. All of the church materials and decorative

A polychrome bulto of San José, on a pedestal, is sited in a large square nicho within the sanctuary; note the Indian-style painted floral decorations around the upper portion of the nicho, and the decorated panel at the base.

ornaments had disappeared. It was during this period between the United States Army occupation and the restoration to the Church that many of the mission's adobe buildings simply fell into ruins.

On February 24, 1874, when H. L. Oak visited the mission accompanied by the renowned California historian H. H. Bancroft and his daughter Kate, he noted (Oak, 1981, p.24) that

> *the mission building faces the west and commands a fine view across and up and down the valley. It is not only badly ruined but has been repaired at different times for different purposes so that the original plan is somewhat hard to make out. The walls of the church are about five feet thick. The tower that formerly rose four stories ....has disappeared. A modern shingle roof covers the church. The whole building as now repaired is used for stables and for the manufacture of olive oil. The structure is of adobe with a few tiles used in forming the arches; some hand-sawed beams built into the walls. Some brick foundations of small buildings are to be seen about the main structure....some standing in spots six to ten feet high. A shed formerly extended along the front supported by fifteen pillars....has entirely disappeared the plaster still remains on the church.*

Oak also sketched a ground plan of the entire mission.

By the middle 1880's little more than the front wall of the mission church remained standing. It was during the tenure of Padre Anthony Ubach as parish priest that the first serious thought was given to restoring Mission San Diego. The padre started an Indian school in some of the rundown mission outbuildings and over a twenty-year period initiated a crusade to rebuild the mission church. He also made a concerted effort to retrieve some of the mission's original objects, and through his steadfast efforts he instilled a new interest in the restoration of the mission church. During this interval, the Sisters of Saint Joseph of Carondolet were given charge of the school, but after Fr. Ubach's death in 1907, mission restoration ceased, and the school fell into decline. The school was eventually moved to Banning, east of Los Angeles. Here it is known as Saint Boniface Indian School and is commonly referred to as the Boys' Town of the Desert.

Some restoration on Mission San Diego was carried forward and completed by a non-sectarian group during the time of the Panama-California Exposition of 1915. During the late 1920s serious restoration was planned and carried out, mainly accomplished through private donations for the overall reconstruction of the mission. Under the direction of Archbishop John J. Cantwell and J. Marshall Miller, supervisor of the restoration, the work was completed and the restored mission church rededicated in September 1931. The Apostolic Delegate to the United States presided at the ceremony. Over time much of the mission compound has now been rebuilt and restored. The restored mission church of San Diego de Alcalá measures 150 feet in length, 35 feet in width, and 29 feet in height. On February 2, 1941, San Diego de Alcalá was reinstated as a parish church in the Diocese of San Diego, and in 1976, Pope Paul VI designated the present mission church a Minor Basilica *(color page V)*.

Today, the mission church serves a multicultural congregation of over 800 families. Its location, hidden away against a hillside, forms a pleasant oasis in a valley overrun with condominiums, shopping malls, and a very large football stadium.

Interestingly, when the rebuilding and restoration of Mission San Diego were undertaken, no description of the original church interior could be found, yet the restoration team admired the plain facade that remained of the church and carried that idea of simplicity into the church interior. They were also influenced by subsequent information gathered from other Alta California mission restorations, all of which reinforced their desire to keep the overall design simple and the earth colors muted.

Indeed, the exterior facade of Mission San Diego is very plain a fact further emphasized by its being painted in a stark white color. Pilasters, pillars attached to the walks, bracket the arched entranceway, and with the exception of a narrow window above the entryway, they are the only other decorations on the facade. The other exterior architectural features, are two large buttress wings extending at angles from the facade, to give support to the front of the building. On the left side of the facade, behind one of the angular buttresses, is the very distinctive campanario, which was built as a single wall and is not attached to the church. It stands 45 feet in height, pierced with arches to hold 5 bells. Only the 2 larger bells on the lower level are original. One of those, the Mater Dolorosa, originally cast in New Spain in 1796, was recast in San Diego in 1894. An inscription on the other bell reads: "San Juan Nepomuceno Ave María Purisima 1802." Atop the campanario is a cross made from original mission church timber which was wire-brushed, fastened with handmade nails, and bound with rawhide.

View of the mission church reredos; since no records describing the original altar and reredos survived the restored reredos follows a rather simple line and is modeled on other old mission examples.

Behind the campanario is a well tended landscaped cemetery, the oldest cemetery in California, the resting-place of hundreds of mission Indians. Their presence is memorialized by several fired tile crosses and with contemporary statues of Saint Francis of Assisi and Saint Joseph.

Behind the church sacristy is a small museum dedicated to the martyred padre Luís Jayme. This museum, though worth a visit, is not as complete as some other mission museums, since some of its more interesting holdings are on display at the Father Serra Museum on Old Presidio Hill.

The interior of the mission church of San Diego de Alcalá reflects the original intent of the restorers and is marked by its overall basic simplicity. This has been further emphasized by the use of a plain square table that serves as an altar at the front of the church. Church records indicate that early sea captains visiting the port of San Diego furnished wooden planks from their ships to build the altar.

The reredos in the sanctuary is of relatively recent Mexican origin. It is narrow and vertical in shape, with two tiers. The larger, square bottom tier has an oval arched nicho with a tabernacle and an overlying crucifix. Above this, the second tier is narrower, with an oval arched nicho containing a polychrome bulto of the Holy Mother and Child. The reredos is capped by a glided, rayed polychrome relief carving of God the Father. On the left of the reredos, carved into the wall, is an oval nicho with a polychrome bulto of San José, and to the right of the reredos, a nicho with a dressed bulto of Our Blessed Mother and Child. Both nichos are framed with painted floral decorations. In the sanctuary, in larger square nichos cut into the sidewalls, stand large polychrome bultos of San José on the left side and Our Lord on the right side. Both of those nichos are also framed with lovely painted floral decorations incorporating the pilgrim's shell. Some of the polychrome bultos sited in the nichos are from the early mission period. Paintings of the Stations of the Cross hang on the white plastered walls of the mission church interior. These were brought from Spain by Father Ubach sometime in the late 1890's.

The ceiling of the mission church comprises whitewashed boards supported by frescoed timbers 34 feet in length. In the small Baptistry, on the left side as one enters the church, is the oldest bulto in Mission San Diego. It is of Santa Ana, and it sits on a pedestal overlooking the baptismal font. It is believed to be of 16th century Spanish origin. The actual baptismal font is a replica of the one in which Father Junípero Serra was baptized as a child on the Island of Mallorca.

The inner patio is part of the restored mission quadrangle, and in the center stands a flowing fountain and pool of Mexican granite. It is not original, but it is the focal point of one of the mission's more tranquil settings. Along the south wall of the quadrangle is an area where faculty and students of the history Department of the University of San Diego have undertaken archaeological investigations since 1966. They have uncovered the foundations of a number of rooms of the original mission compound, and these may in time be restored. These investigations have been the basis of a university course in historic site methods.

The rebuilt and restored Mission San Diego de Alcalá draws thousands of tourists every year. Each visitor comes in his or her own way, seeking to relive the early California mission experience and to marvel at the faith of those intrepid Franciscan padres who made it a reality.

Very friendly church volunteers staff a large, well-stocked gift shop at the mission entrance and strive to answer any questions a visitor may ask.

View of the Serra Museum at Mission Park atop Presidio Hill, San Diego; the museum was built in 1929 as a tribute to Father Junípero Serra and gift to the city by philanthropist G. W. Marston.

PRESIDIO SAN DIEGO DE ALCALÁ:

When Mission San Diego de Alcalá was moved 6 miles inland in 1774, Presidio Hill, the original founding site, remained a military establishment. This was an enclosed stockade area on a sloping hill overlooking the Pacific Ocean. For a time it served as the only source of military protection for the missions and settlements along the Alta California coast. It fell into ruin during the Mexican period from 1821-1846, and after American annexation in 1848, livestock grazed the abandoned site.

Richard F. Pourade in his 1961 book *Time of the Bells* presented a painting (p. 128-129), by the illustrator D. Wayne Millsap, showing the square-shaped enclosed San Diego presidio as it appeared in 1823. In the north stood the commandant house, to the east the chapel and cemetery, and on the south the guardhouse, gate, and the jail. Pourade also included a listing (p. 240) of the Spanish and Mexican commandants who served the presidio from 1769-1840. The presidio population probably never exceeded 175 men, women, and children. There is even some evidence that the presidio was enclosed only on two or three sides until at least 1792.

During the life of the presidio the structure suffered neglect from both the Spanish and Mexican governments. In fact, in 1826 a commission composed of Captain Pablo de la Portilla, Lieutenant Romualdo Pacheco, and Cadet Domingo Carrillo completed a survey of the presidio and found the buildings to be in a deplorable ruinous condition, with at least $40,000 needed to complete overall repairs. The centeral government ignored their findings. By 1830 the San Diego Presidio ceased to function as a viable military establishment.

The larger than life bronze sculpture and upclose details of Father Junípero Serra, sited below the Serra Museum on Presidio Hill, created by sculptor Arthur Putnam.

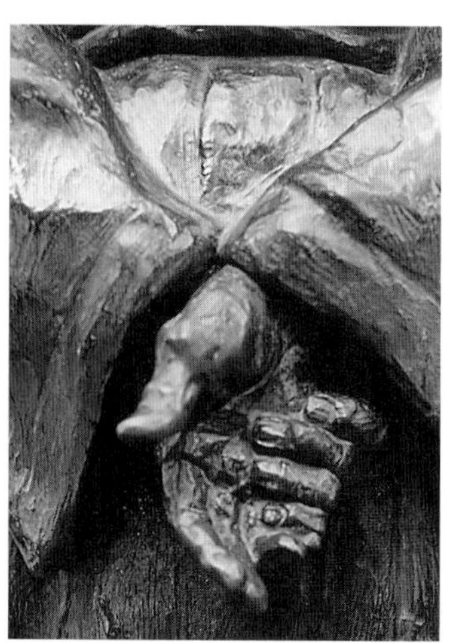

The American sailor Richard Henry Dana Jr., author of the renowned 1869 autobiography *Two Years Before the Mast*, arrived in San Diego on March 13, 1835. He and another sailor rented horses for a land outing and noted:

> *the first place we went to was the old ruinous presidio, which stands on a rising ground near the village which it overlooks. It is built in the form of an open square, like all the other presidios, and was in a ruinous state, with the exception of one side, in which the commandant lived with his family. There were only two guns, one of which was spiked and the other had no carriage. Twelve half-clothed and half-starved looking fellows composed the garrison; and they, it was said, had not a musket apiece.*

On February 24, 1874, historians H. L. Oak and H. H. Bancroft visited the old presidio site and reported (Oaks, 1981, p. 20):

> *the presidio was located on the hill on the bank of the San Diego River in the northern part of what is now Old Town....On the summit of the hill the ruins are still visible and seen by us, in the shape of irregular mounds of adobe overgrown with greenery. Here was all that was secular of the settlement of San Diego down to 1824, conducted under strict military discipline. In 1824, Captain Francisco Ruiz obtained permission to come down the hill and to settle at its foot on a lot now occupied by Judge Hayes' residence, and from that time the pueblo or town spread over the present limits of Old Town, and the hill was long used as a burial-place. The town was governed by the Military Commandante down to 1835; by an Axuntamiento from 1835-1839; by Jueces de Paz from 1839-1849: with an intermediate admixture of alcaldes, and prefects....The secular and ecclesiastic authorities seem to have been entirely independent of each other.*

Today, atop old Presidio Hill sits the Father Junípero Serra Museum built in 1929. The museum was funded by San Diego philanthropist George White Marston as a tribute to Junípero Serra and as a gift to the city of San Diego—William T. Johnson designed the building, which houses notable collections of period furniture, Indian artifacts, photographs, paintings, and various relics from both the original presidio and mission. The museum is operated by the San Diego Historical Society.

Below the museum is a park area with a large unique cross made of excavated floor tiles from the ruins of the original presidio *(color page B)*. The "Order of Panama Civic Club" commissioned this monument and the blessing and dedication of the cross occurred on September 27, 1913. It marks the approximate site of the first cross raised by Father Junípero Serra in Alta California, his first celebration of Holy Mass, and his first mission. The irregular mounds of earth that dot the landscape mark the unexcavated portions of the original presidio. Close to the large tile cross stands an imposing bronze statue of Father Junípero Serra, created by the blind sculptor Arthur Putnam.

ASISTENCIA SANTA YSABÉL:

In the hills almost sixty miles east of Mission San Diego de Alcalá, stands a small white stuccoed church, St. John the Baptist, on the site of a chapel (asistencia) founded by the padres in 1818. It was established to serve 250 Santa Ysabél Indians who found it a hardship to journey to Mission San Diego to attend religious services. Although padres from San Diego periodically visited the area, they thought that the Indians would greatly benefit from an asistencia. Accordingly the padres petitioned Governor Pablo Vicente de Sola to accede to their proposal to found an asistencia. The governor was unenthusiastic about their proposal, so the padres took matters into their own hands and erected an enramada (a brush shelter) in 1818. Fr. Fernando Martín (1770-1838) celebrated the first Mass on September 20, 1818, on a nearby site, and by 1822, Santa Ysabél had a chapel, cemetery, granary, and a number of houses, and 450 Santa Ysabél Indians dwelt at the asistencia. Sometime later, two bells hung on a simple timbered framework along the side. The bells were dated 1723 (the oldest mission bell in Alta California) and 1767; both were stolen in 1926 and have never been recovered.

View of the present-day St John the Baptist Catholic Church on the site of the original Asistencia Santa Ysabel; the church was dedicated in 1924 as a personal legacy of Father Edmond La Pointe.

After secularization in the 1830's, neighboring large landowners plundered the asistencia and its lands and allowed the chapel to disintegrate into ruins. The Santa Ysabél Indians carried on as well as they could, but priestly visits and religious services were infrequent. Local tradition holds that religious services have been held here under ramadas erected against one wall, after the chapel roof collapsed.

The present church, designed with dignity in a simple California mission style, was dedicated in 1924. It was built with monies from a personal legacy by Father Edmond La Pointe, a Canadian-born missionary priest who had served this area for twenty-nine years. He is buried alongside the building he endowed. The church is presently served by the Sons of the Sacred Heart, who celebrate the Feast of All Souls in the campo santo each November 2nd with an evening candlelight vigil.

A view from the mission entrance showing the facade of San Carlos Borromeo de Carmelo with it's Moorish-like architectural style.

MISSION SAN CARLOS BORROMEO DE CARMELO:

Synopsis: Second mission; founded by Father Junípero Serra at Monterey on June 3, 1770; named for Saint Charles Borromeo, a 16th century Italian Cardinal of the Church; original mission site moved from Monterey Presidio to Carmel in 1771; churches: 1770, 1771, 1773, 1778, 1793, and 1797; minor damage in 1812 earthquake; secularized in 1834 after an active mission life of sixty-four years, during most of which time it served as the headquarters for all the missions of Alta California; mission in ruins by 1836; in 1851 church roof collapsed; mission restored to Church in 1859; restorations: 1884, 1924, 1930-1980 and ongoing; reinstated as parish church in 1933; raised to status of Minor Basilica in 1960; visited by Pope John Paul II in 1987.

Location: Mission San Carlos Borromeo is located off California Highway 1 at Rio Road and Lasuen Drive, in the city of Carmel.

San Carlos Borromeo (Saint Charles Borromeo), was chosen as the patron of the second Alta California Spanish colonial missions on June 3, 1770, as a gesture to honor King Carlos III of Spain.

Charles Borromeo was born of the nobility, in Lombardy, northern Italy, in 1538. His mother was a Medici, sister of the future Pope Pius IV. Charles showed an inclination for the religious life as a youth. When his uncle became pope in 1559, the twenty-one-year-old was summoned to Rome and was given a cardinal's hat as a layman, since he was not ordained. He served in the Vatican Curia as Papal Secretary of State. Contrary to what one might expect of such a flagrant example of nepotism, Charles proved to be a brilliant administrator who lived an austere and humble life. He was responsible for putting into effect the reforms of the Council of Trent, which had reconvened in 1562. In 1560 he had been nominated as Archbishop of Milan, but he was not consecrated until after he was ordained a priest in 1563. He was an effective reformer and cleansed some of the religious orders of notable abuses. He was especially concerned for the sick and poor; he mobilized the forces of the Church to contain the terrible plague of 1576, visiting the sick himself. He was a member of the Third Order of St. Francis. After a life characterized by exemplary humility and piety, he died in 1584. He was canonized in 1610, and his feast day is November fourth.

Numerous paintings and sculptures of him were produced by Italian artists in the decades following his death. There is a colossal bronze statue of him overlooking Lake Maggiore near the Swiss border. In devotional art, he is generally portrayed in the robes of an archbishop or cardinal, wearing a mitre or a cardinal's hat, and holding a staff or crozier.

In Alta California, images of him were present only in Carmel and Monterey. There was once a bulto of him in a nicho in the Monterey Presidio Chapel, while two oil paintings now lost were reported at Mission Carmel. A large polychrome bulto of San Carlos was sent from Mexico in 1791. It presently crowns the reredos of the mission church of San Carlos Borromeo de Carmelo.

Once Mission San Diego de Alcalá was in order, and resupplied, Governor Gaspár de Portolá and Father Junípero Serra could look forward to fulfilling Inspector-General José de Gálvez's orders to locate the bay of Monterey and choose additional mission sites. The original intention was for Monterey to be the northernmost mission site, to stem further Russian encroachment along the Alta California coast. Plans were formulated for Portolá to undertake a second overland expedition, which would meet up with the packet ship San Antonio in Monterey. This sea expedition would carry Father Serra. Fr. Juan Crespí was to be the chaplain of Portolá's overland party to locate Monterey Bay. The San Antonio set sail the day after Easter with Captain Don Juan Perez in command, Serra, Dr. Pedro Prat, engineer Miguel Constanso, and its crew. The following morning, April 17th, Portolá began his march northward. The group included Lieutenant Pedro Fages, twelve Catalonian volunteers, seven leather jackets, two volunteers, five Baja California Indians, and Fr. Juan Crespí. Sergeant José Francisco Ortega was left in charge of Mission San Diego with eight soldiers, twelve Baja California Indians, and the two resident padres.

By retracing his route of the previous year, Portolá arrived in Monterey on Ascension Day, May 24, 1770. This time Portolá recognized Monterey Bay, in spite of Vizcaíno's exaggerated description. Portolá, Crespí, and a soldier walked south over the hills to Point Pinos, where the year before they had planted a large wooden cross which overlooked Monterey Bay. To their surprise, they found the cross still standing and surrounded by broken Indian arrows stuck into the ground, and the ground covered with feathers. Later, they learned that this was a sign signifying friendliness. They then hiked further south along the shoreline to Carmel Bay. Here they met a small group of Indians and exchanged gifts. A week after Portolá's arrival in Monterey, the packet ship San Antonio was sighted, and a little later the two parties were reunited. All explored the area, and it was jointly decided that June 3rd, Pentecost Sunday, would be the appropriate day to found Monterey Mission Presidio.

On Sunday morning, Portolá and his men greeted the ship's crew under a large oak tree close to the shoreline, believed to be the same one under which the Carmelites of the 1602 Vizcaíno expedition had offered the first Mass. The two groups came together at this spot with a clanging of bells suspended from the oak tree. Father Serra was vested, and when all were kneeling he intoned "Veni Creator Spiritus," blessed salt and water, and asked all the men to help raise the large wooden cross prepared beforehand. Serra then blessed it, chanting the prayers of benediction; the men then planted the cross in the ground and everyone venerated it. With shouts of "Long Live the Faith" and "Long Live the King," the site was dedicated to San Carlos Borromeo. Father Serra sang a High Mass and preached a sermon on the gospel of the day. At the conclusion of the Mass, Serra intoned the "Te Deum Laudamus." The officers then conducted the formal ceremony of taking possession in the name of the King. With the formal ceremonies completed, Portolá and his men returned to their camp at Carmel, while Serra and his group returned to the ship. On the following morning, June 4, 1770, work began at the sites for mission and presidio. The soldiers moved their camp from Carmel and assisted the sailors in unloading supplies from the San Antonio. Two structures were quickly erected, one for the presidio, the other for the mission chapel. Serra and Crespí lived on board the San Antonio until the chapel and suitable dwellings were available for them.

The packet ship San Antonio sailed from Monterey Bay on July 9, 1770; on board were Portolá and Constanso. Lieutenant Pedro Fages was left in charge of the presidio as Commandante along with forty men. Gaspár de Portolá returned to New Spain and passed out of Alta California history.

The new military commandante was quite different from the easygoing Portolá, and it was not long before he began to inject himself into mission affairs. Serra realized that a mission would be more apt to prosper at some distance from the presidio and its rowdy soldiers. From the very beginning, Fr. Serra did not believe a mission would prosper at Monterey since the essential ingredient, an Indian village, was lacking. In the summer of 1771, Fr. Serra formally moved the mission from the presidio at Monterey to a site five miles

Detail of Jo Mora's 1924 bronze and stone commemorative cenotaph showing Father Juan Crespí praying over a recumbent Father Junípero Serra.

south, in the valley of the Carmel River. Forty Baja California Indians, five sailors, and three soldiers began building the mission. The first buildings were jacal—made of logs stuck upright in the ground to form walls, then logs were laid across the top, and filled in with sticks and grasses. The church was a brush enramada erected alongside a large wooden cross. Around the initial buildings a pole fence (palisade) was erected. A series of churches followed until the present stone church was dedicated in September 1797.

Conditions at the mission were not to Fr. Serra's liking, especially the fact that necessary supplies arrived so irregularly and the relationships between the Indians and the military were in a continual state of deterioration. Moreover, relations between Serra and the military were often far from harmonious. Something needed to be done. Serra, now close to sixty years of age, decided that he should undertake the arduous journey to Mexico City to present his views to the Viceroy and appeal directly to him for an improvement in overall mission conditions in Alta California. The trip to Mexico City was most demanding for the old padre, and it was fraught with difficulties and sickness along the way. After several brief recuperations during the journey, Serra finally arrived in Mexico City and met with New Spain's Viceroy Antonio María Bucareli y Ursua. He was requested to present his appeal in writing for formal presentation at court. Junípero drafted a thirty-two point petition which clearly outlined Alta California's problems and needs. The viceroy was so impressed with the petition that he and the junta voted in favor of it. The results of Serra's "Bill of Rights" for Alta California, which was put into effect January 1, 1774, was to provide for expansion of the mission system. In addition the welfare of the Indians was placed exclusively under the control of the padres, there was a redefinition of presidio-mission relationships, a proposed increase in the flow of supplies to the colony, and encouragement of Mexican emigration into Alta California. This document, for which Father Serra was almost totally responsible, became Alta California's civil code until Spain ceded to Mexico in 1821.

Large oil painting, in the Carmel Mission Museum, which is a copy of the frontispiece engraving from Father Francisco Palóu's 1797 biograpy of Father Junipero Serra.

After an absence of almost two years, Serra returned to Mission Carmel on May 11, 1774. The mission compound had been expanded during his absence and now boasted a new church (jacalón) of log planks, eighty-four feet in length, and adorned with some religious paintings, in addition to other subsidiary buildings. Commandante Pedro Fages was replaced by Captain Fernando Rivera y Moncado, who eventually proved more difficult to Serra than Fages. In later years Rivera was assigned to Baja California and Felipe de Neve became governor of Alta California.

When Serra returned to Mission Carmel he found that food supplies had again run low and the mission narrowly averted famine. However, by harvest time a substantial crop of wheat, corn, and beans helped fend off disaster. The following year the harvest was even more plentiful.

During this time the capital of the colony was moved from Baja California to Monterey. This meant that Alta California was no longer under the jurisdiction of the friendly Viceroy Antonio Bucareli but to the newly created office of Commandant-General headed by Teodoro de Croix. The latter, uninterested in mission affairs, relied more on de Neve's judgment than on that of the padres. He regarded the colony as an outpost of Spanish Empire and was not personally interested in the welfare of the Indians, whom he distrusted. He was more inclined to remake the Alta California missions into well populated thriving communities (pueblos) comprised of citizens of Spanish blood. Towards accomplishing this goal, he began to force the padres out of the political and economic life of the colony and aggressively encouraged a policy of emigration from Mexico. Serra openly opposed this overall policy with the unfortunate consequence that it caused a continued breach in the relationships between the military and the religious. The result was a further delay in future mission expansion.

Serra continued his efforts at Mission Carmel baptizing a number of Indians, who now joined the four hundred Indians in residence at the mission. On January 1, 1782, Padre Juan Crespí, Serra's lifelong friend and colleague from Mallorca, died at age fifty. Serra too, was in failing health, but for the next two years he struggled on. Father Junípero Serra died at Mission Carmel on August 28, 1784. He had devoted fifty-four years of his life to the Franciscan order, of which the last fifteen years in Alta California had been for him the most difficult and surely the most challenging. Serra had baptized over six thousand Indians during his service in Alta California. Father Francisco Palóu, Serra's close friend and fellow Mallorcan, became temporary Father-President of the missions until he retired to Mexico City in 1785. His successor, Father Fermín Francisco Lasuén, became Father-President of the Alta California missions at age forty-nine and served in this capacity for almost twenty years. He died at Carmel on June 28, 1803, and was interred next to Father Serra in the sanctuary of the Carmel mission church. It was under Lasuén's administration that the Alta California missions reached their greatest spiritual and economic prosperity.

Detail of the upper portion of the facade of the mission church of San Carlos Borromeo; note the distinctive Moorish-like window above the entrance.

In September of 1786, Monterey Presidio and Mission Carmel had their first foreign visitors. French explorer and navigator Jean François de la Pérouse arrived in Monterey Bay on the evening of September 14th. This scientific expedition consisted of two vessels with numerous scientists and artists aboard. The expedition spent ten days within both the presidio and mission areas. On September 16th, the padres of Mission Carmel, Fermín Lasuén and Matías Noriega (1736-?), arrived at the presidio to invite the Frenchmen to visit Mission Carmel. Two days later, accompanied by the presidio commandante, they were formally received at Mission Carmel.

It is difficult for us today to comprehend just how isolated Alta California was in 1786. Monterey Presidio and Mission Carmel, a few miles south, were at that time just a cluster of very primitive buildings. They had only tenuous links with the rest of the world. They had to be refurbished with either irregularly scheduled supply ships from San Blas, Mexico, or along the thin north-south overland trail with the pretentious name "El Camino Real."

Father Lasuén received the Frenchmen at the mission chapel where he conducted a "Te Deum" in thanksgiving for the happy outcome of their voyage to date. In honor of this notable occasion the mission Indians were lined up outside the chapel for inspection, and had been given an extra ration of food that day. Pérouse was given a tour of the mission facilities, and was duly impressed both with the mission and with what the padres were attempting to accomplish spiritually in this isolated area of the Spanish Empire. His journal descriptions of conditions at Mission Carmel convey the first authentic look at mission life and its effect on the Indians. Margolin (1989, pp. 1-50), in his introduction and commentary on the Pérouse journals, gives perhaps the most balanced account and inclusive summary of just what it was like to be a Mission Indian at Carmel. La Pérouse's description of the Mission Indians is almost nightmarish. He describes them as anonymous, lifeless, and robbed of spirit, a people that seemed to be traumatized, exhibiting what we would today characterize as a psychotic level of depression—all in all, a rather devastating description of Indian life at Mission San Carlos Borromeo de Carmelo. At the time of Pérouse's visit there were seven hundred and forty Indians living in what he described as fifty wretched huts, within the mission compound. After a ten days visit, La Pérouse's vessels left Monterey Bay on September 24, 1786.

In 1792 and 1793, the English explorer George Vancouver visited Mission

Carmel. Both the La Pérouse and Vancouver reports were quite complimentary as to what the missionaries were attempting to accomplish, and their drawings and observations are among the earliest glimpses as to what mission life and conditions in Alta California were all about.

In 1791, master stonemason Manuel Estevan Ruiz was imported from Mexico City to design and supervise building stone churches at the presidio and Mission Carmel. It is interesting to note that Father Serra had planned a stone church for Mission Carmel in 1781, and had even ordered the quarrying of the local sandstone. There have even been suggestions that Serra might have sketched out a rough design of what he hoped the stone church would look like. Ruiz laid the cornerstone for the Mission Carmel church in 1793. He and his Indian laborers worked on the church for four years, and the stone building was dedicated in 1797. The Indians quarried a local sandstone, from the nearby Santa Lucia Mountains. Mission Carmel and the Monterey presidio church are unique in being built of stone, bypassing the typical mission adobe construction. Carmel Mission Church is a mixture of architectural elements: two mismatched bell towers, one with a Moorish-style dome; an unusual star-shaped Moorish-style window set into stones above the front door with stone arches, and a unique catenary-arched ceiling.

The high point of Mission Carmel was probably attained in 1794, when the Indian population reached nine hundred and twenty-seven and the yields from the mission agricultural enterprises were plentiful.

In November of 1818, the pirate Bouchard plundered the California coast. He sacked and torched Monterey and the presidio, destroying most of the town's supplies. Mission Carmel was evacuated but was unharmed. In 1821, a mortuary chapel for the Indians was added to the mission church. By 1823 the mission Indian population had dwindled to fewer than four hundred residents.

In 1833, Padre José Rael took charge of the mission, and secularization occurred in 1834. The mission lands were then taken over by the neighboring Hispanic settlers, and the remaining mission Indians dispersed. For all practical purposes mission life at Carmel was destroyed by 1836. At this time, Padre Rael moved his residence to Monterey and held only monthly services at Carmel. San Carlos was in ruins and continued to go through decades of neglect; the roof collapsed in 1851 and the structure remained roofless for the next thirty years. By 1856, when the traveler Henry Miller visited the mission site he reported (Miller, 1997, p. 19) his visit of May 22, 1856:

> *I went to the Carmel Valley, near the seashore at the mouth of the Carmel River where stands the remains of the Mission San Carlos. With the exception of a few adobe houses, the whole is a heap of ruins. The old church, which must have been a handsome one, is partly fallen in; however, the front with two strong belfries over it is in good condition. There are still remaining*

two cracked bells....The inside of the church has some fresco painting and inscriptions from the bible. Some saints, as large as life, cut in wood and painted, are still to be seen; they are riddled with bullets, having served as a target. The mission buildings form a large square.

Miller did a sketch of the mission and surrounding area.

On October 19, 1859, President James Buchanan restored the mission ruins to the Church. Then in 1870, Father Angelo D. Casanova, rector of the Monterey parish (1870-1893), arrived on the scene with the intention of restoring the mission church. He spearheaded a drive, which raised funds, and was able to remove the debris that had accumulated in the church interior, and he reroofed the church with shingles on a rather incongruous steep-pitched roof. He also located the graves of Fr. Serra and the other early Franciscan padres, all with the intention of rededicating the mission church on the centenary of Fr. Serra's death in 1884. In order to quell rumors that the remains of Father Serra had been stolen, on July 3, 1882 he organized a gathering of four hundred people to witness the removal of the redwood coffins containing the remains of the early padres. With identification ascertained, the graves were closed and marble slabs placed over them in the church sanctuary. Serra's remains were again disturbed in 1943, in connection with the proceedings leading to his canonization as a saint of the Church. In 1987, his remains were examined to verify that they are those of the Venerable Servant of God; the coffin was resealed and returned to the vault. Junípero Serra's beatification occurred in St. Peter's Square, Vatican City, on September 25, 1988, with Pope John Paul II officiating. This means that Father Junipero Serra can be called by the name Blessed and that his feast, on his birthday into heaven, can be celebrated in the place and manner established by canon law. Father Serra is presently undergoing consideration for canonization as a saint of the Church.

A small corner of the restored simple bedroom/cell used by Father Junípero Serra

After Father Casanova passed from the scene, all that was done in the way of restoration at Mission Carmel was simple maintenance in order to prevent the building from falling into further ruin. It should be noted that ever since the mission was restored to the Church in 1859, religious services were held continually on a monthly basis in the church sacristy, which somehow had managed to survive the general collapse of the building. Those masses were conducted by padres from the Monterey Presidio Church and from other nearby mission churches.

By the early 1920s, serious consideration was given to the overall mission

Painted Indian style wall decorations and prayer in our Lady of Belen Chapel; inscription reads: "O heart of Jesus always burning in splendor make my heart burn with divine love, angels and saints we praise the heart of Jesus.

restoration. Those desires however were hampered by the fact that no original plan of the mission had survived. Accordingly, extensive archaeological excavations of the surrounding bean fields had to be accomplished in order to find the foundations of the original mission quadrangle. These were begun in 1921, when only the mission church remained standing. By 1924, Father Ramon Maestres restored the first room. Here the California artist Joseph Jacinto Mora (Jo Mora) created, an elaborate memorial cenotaph of travertine and bronze on a twelve foot by eight foot base, which became the focal point for further mission restoration. The bronze sculpture portrays a recumbent Father Junípero Serra surrounded by three life-size bronze statues of grieving padres; standing at Serra's head is the statue of his lifelong friend and colleague, Fr. Juan Crespí.

Plans for the overall mission restoration continued but were only implemented in 1933 when the mission became a parish church. This coincided with the assignment of Father Michael D. O'Connell as pastor and the enlistment of lay curator Harry Downie to initiate mission restoration, a process that would involve fifty years of Downie's life. Kennedy (1993, p. 174-175) described Downie as a "magnificent character, a baronet by inheritance and a master cabinetmaker by trade. He was determined to make a vision of Ramona's California out of the mission's crumbling walls. Wearing a Franciscan habit, Downie raised money to restore as much of the original structure as possible and to locate many of the original furnishings as he could find." In the process he restored Mission Carmel into one of the most beautiful of all the Alta California missions. His was a labor of love and devotion, and at his death he was buried in the mission cemetery.

In 1960, Pope John XXIII designated Mission San Carlos Borromeo as a Minor Basilica because of the important role-played in the life of Father Junípero Serra. Then on September 17, 1987, the Holy Father, Pope John Paul II, after an outdoor Mass before a crowd of fifty thousand people, visited Mission Carmel and knelt and prayed before the high altar. He then walked a few steps to Father Serra's grave where he prayed and laid a wreath. After this he delivered a fifteen-minute address to an overflowing church audience. He then proceeded down the church aisle and into Our Lady of Bethlehem side chapel (the old mortuary chapel), where he paused to pray, as Junípero so often did, at the foot of the bulto of Our Lady of Belen, probably California's most historic statue *(color page P)*.

Detail of the top of the Carmel reredos with 1791 Mexican bulto of San Carlos Borromeo with carved Holy Spirit above.

Today, as the visitor enters the mission grounds, he or she will note that the church facade is Moorish in appearance and is made up of brown sandstone, with five-foot-thick walls at the base. Two dissimilar belltowers form the campanario and crown the facade. The larger of these holds nine bells, most of which are original; they are reached by an outside staircase. The 1880's shingle roof of Father Casanova was removed and replaced with a low-pitched tile roof by Harry Downie in 1936. The outside walls curve inward to form a vaulted ceiling thirty-three feet in height. The ceiling is composed of painted redwood planks. A Baptistry to the left of the church entrance still boasts its original stone baptismal font. Farther down the aisle and on the left side, is the old mortuary chapel built for the Indians in 1821. Sitting on the chapel altar is the restored Our Lady of Belen bulto. This early eighteenth century Mexican bulto originally belonged to Archbishop Francisco Antonio Lorenzona y Britron of Mexico City. The bulto was donated to the 1769 expedition to Alta California so that it might travel with the appellation of "La Conquistadora." It was present both at the founding of presidio-mission San Diego de Alcalá, and at the founding of presidio-mission San Carlos Borromeo at Monterey. Housed at Mission Carmel since 1771, it was cared for, after the mission's abandonment in 1845, by the last resident mission Indians and then by several generations of Monterey Hispanic families. It was returned to Mission Carmel in December 1945. Six gold-plated chandeliers hang from the mission church ceiling *(color page T)*. Halfway down the aisle, on the right side, is an alcove with an almost life-size dressed bulto of Jesús Nazareno. Further down the aisle, on the right sidewall, is the restored pulpit carved by Harry Downie in 1957.

Detail of polychrome bulto of Our Lady of the Immaculate Conception in one of the nichos on the mission church reredos.

Situated on the back wall of the sanctuary is a beautiful reredos. This too was hand carved by Harry Downie in 1956, using as his model the reredos of San Francisco's Mission Dolores. Several polychrome bultos stand within its nichos. Those include Our Lady of the Immaculate Conception, San Miguel Arcángel, San Antonio de Padua, and Santo Dominic. Above the tabernacle in a blue painted arched oval is a large crucifix with polychrome bultos of Mary and Joseph on either side. Crowning the top of the reredos is the 1791 polychrome bulto of San Carlos Borromeo; above it is a rayed, relief carving of a dove, representing the Holy Spirit *(color page E)*. Church records indicate that the original reredos was present in 1849, but it disappeared sometime later. The side walls of the church interior have framed oil paintings of the Stations of the Cross.

Outside and to the right of the basilica entrance is a cemetery containing the remains of 2,346 mission Indians, along with the remains of 14 Spaniards, all buried within the period from 1771-1833.

To the left of the basilica entrance is a courtyard shrine carved in stone. On it are the coats-of-arms of the brother orders of the Dominicans and Franciscans. The founders of the orders, St. Dominic and St. Francis, were close friends in life, and their two orders have always maintained close ties.

A charming bulto of San José enclosed within an ornate nicho present along the side wall of the Carmel Mission Church.

During the mission restoration, the usual workshop side of the quadrangle was not restored. Instead a contemporary elementary school has been built into the restored walls. The center of the mission quadrangle is marked by a graceful flowing fountain, and on the edge of the quadrangle is a large wooden cross.

During excavations of the quadrangle in 1939, Harry Downie found the remains of the original wooden cross Father Serra raised in 1771. Downie constructed a fifteen-foot high copy of the original cross, with its peculiar cap piece, and sited it where he found the fragments of the original cross. The northeast corner of the mission quadrangle has been studiously restored and contains an outstanding museum and a well supplied gift shop, in addition to a number of restored rooms where Fathers Serra and Crespí once lived, including Serra's bedroom-cell.

The Carmel Mission complex has been beautifully landscaped and is surrounded with colorful flower gardens. In one of those, to the right before you reach the church entrance, is a life-size bronze sculpture of a determined Fr. Serra holding a cross in one hand and a Bible in his other hand.

The Basilica of San Carlos Borromeo de Carmelo is a very popular tourist destination, for it casts a romantic spell over all that visit it. It is visited annually by over two hundred thousand people, many of whom regard Mission Carmel as the most beautiful of all the Alta California Spanish colonial missions.

Exterior view of the 1794 La Capilla Real, Royal Chapel Monterey Presidio, with a carved stone statue of our lady of Guadalupe in the nicho on the top of the facade

MONTEREY PRESIDIO CHAPEL:

Synopsis: Founded as a presidio-mission of San Carlos Borromeo on June 4, 1770, by Father Junípero Serra and Governor Gaspár de Portolá; first church was one room in a three-room jacal; mission moved by Serra to Carmel in 1771; new presidio church built in 1776; replaced by present stone building in 1794 and sited within the presidio walls; was principal Monterey church for many years and became parish church in 1840; known as San Carlos Church until 1967, when it became San Carlos Cathedral; this is California's oldest remaining original presidio chapel.

Location: La Capilla Real (Royal Chapel) the Monterey Presidio, is located in the city of Monterey at 550 Church Street, near Figueroa.

The first recorded Europeans to step ashore at what is Monterey were the explorer Sebastian Vizcaíno and his Carmelite chaplains, who offered Mass at the shoreline on December 17, 1602. Monterey was named for New Spain's Viceroy, Gaspár de Zuñiga Acevedo y Fonseca, Conde de Monterrey. One hundred and eighty-eight years later, on June 3, 1770, on Pentecost Sunday, the Feast of the Holy Spirit, Father Junípero Serra and Governor Gaspár de Portolá came ashore at the same

View of the altar in San Carlos Cathedral in Monterey; set into the wall and with central large crucifix with painted border of floral designs, and nichos with bultos of Our Lady of the Immaculate Conception and San Antonio de Padua; note painted coats-of-arms on wall above nichos.

site to confirm their rediscovery of Monterey Bay. Under an identified oak tree they enacted the founding of Presidio-Mission San Carlos Borromeo for Spain.

From June 4, 1770, to August 24, 1771, Father Serra lived at the Monterey Presidio where he and Fr. Juan Crespí served as the first mission padres. They resided within an enclosed stockade of pine logs and adobe. The first church was one room in a three-room jacal, with two other rooms serving as padre's quarters and storage areas. The mission Indians lived and worked outside of the presidio walls. After Serra moved the mission to Carmel in 1771 the presidio compound was expanded. The enlarged presidio consisted of a 1400-foot square, enclosed by adobe walls with a solid bank of one-story buildings around the perimeter. Yet in 1786 there were only eighteen soldiers on the presidio roster.

When Fr. Serra moved the mission to Carmel, the church at Monterey became the Presidio's Royal Chapel, "La Capilla Real." As Mission Carmel became more importantly religiously, the Royal Chapel became most important politically. This, because it was located in the provincial capital, within the quadrangle walls of the old presidio, and was the place of worship of the Alta California governors from Spain and Mexico. The presidio chapel was served by padres from Mission Carmel until 1840 when it became a parish church. It was still the principal church in Monterey for many years after the American annexation of 1848.

Detail of the 18th century richly dressed Mexican bulto of Our Lady of Solitude.

The present stone structure was erected in 1794, ten years after Ft. Serra's death. The building was designed and construction supervised by Mexico City's master stonemason Manuel Ruiz from 1792 until 1794. Ruiz was also the master stonemason in charge of building the mission church at Carmel. The stone detail of the entranceway at the presidio chapel, specifically the west transcept, is perhaps the most architecturally ornate among the Alta California mission churches. This is California's only remaining original presidio chapel, and the sandstone carving of Our Lady of Guadalupe; in the apex of the arched church facade, is California's oldest Indigenous sculpture. The building facade is quite an architectural triumph with its beautiful stonework, especially the carved pediment gables and the distinctive campanario.

Inside the present-day chapel stands one extraordinary piece of devotional art, the large eighteenth century Mexican bulto a vestir — a statue designed to be dressed — of Our Lady of Solitude. About forty years ago an anonymous donor gave this exquisite bulto, originally at Mission Soledad, to the Monterey Presidio Chapel; the Lady of Solitude wears heavy silver and gold brocade from head to toe, and she holds a lace handkerchief. Her face expresses the utmost sorrow, resignation, and serenity.

The church altar stands in an arched sanctuary, and a large and imposing crucifix stands above it, striking against a light blue background. Attractive floral designs decorate the arched alcove. On each side of the altar a smaller arched nicho holds a polychrome bulto, Our Lady of the Immaculate Conception on the left, with the Franciscan coat of arms painted on the wall above it, and San Antonio de Padua holding the Christ Child on the right, with the Royal Spanish coat of arms above it. In one corner of the church stands a contemporary dressed statue of San Carlos Borromeo.

The Cathedral of San Carlos presently serves a large multicultural congregation and remains the focal point of the city's religious community. Interestingly, in the garden behind the church is a preserved fragment of the oak tree under which Vizcaíno named Monterey Bay back in 1602 and under which Serra and Portolá later founded Presidio-Mission San Carlos Borromeo. It has been reported that until sometime during the 1930's, the paving in front of the church entrance was made up of whale vertebrae.

CHAPTER THREE

THREE MISSIONS SPREAD OUT FROM THE PORTS:

SAN ANTONIO DE PADUA 1771, SAN GABRIEL ARCÁNGEL 1771, AND SAN LUÍS OBISPO DE TOLOSA 1772

MISSION SAN ANTONIO DE PADUA:

View of the altar and reredos in the mission church of San Antonio de Padua with bulto of mission patron in center, flanked by bultos of San Buenaventura on the left and San Francisco on the right, with bulto of San Miguel Arcángel capping the reredos.

Synopsis: Third mission; founded by Fr. Junípero Serra on July 14, 1771; named for San Antonio of Lisbon, Portugal; moved to present site in 1773; adobe church completed in 1782; present building begun in 1810 and completed 1813; secularized in 1834 with an active life of sixty-three years; offered for sale in 1845, but there were no buyers; mission declined from 1882-1903; restorations: 1903-1907, and 1948-1949 and ongoing.

Location: Mission San Antonio de Padua can be reached by U. S. Highway 101, either twenty-three miles southwest of King City or twenty-seven miles northwest of Bradley.

The mission was named after San Antonio who was born in Lisbon, Portugal, in 1195. Son of a knight of the royal court he came to the spiritual life early on, first joining the Augustinian order, but later transferring to the Franciscans in 1221. In this year he journeyed to Italy where he was active in a chapter of the order of Assisi. He quickly demonstrated a remarkable ability at preaching and doing good works. Numerous miracles were attributed to him during his lifetime. He died in 1231 and was canonized the following year, one of the quickest canonizations in the history of the Church. He is a particular patron of the poor, and his help is usually called upon for finding lost possessions. His remains are in a basilica in Padua, Italy. In devotional art he is frequently shown with a book and a lily, and he is generally holding the Christ Child. Almost every California mission had one or more images of San Antonio, be it a bulto or an oil painting. After Christ and the Holy Mother, his image is the most popular in Hispanic California. A fine oil painting of San Antonio by the Mexican artist José de Páez was originally sent to Mission San Antonio in 1774; this painting now hangs in Mission San Miguel.

Mission San Antonio de Padua is located off the beaten path and lies in the midst of a military reservation. Although the mission has been restored, the traveler coming upon it today can sense the spaciousness and openness that characterized all the missions in their heyday.

Father Junípero Serra had just moved the Monterey Mission to Carmel, and while its building was in progress he set out with two padres, a few sailors, and some Indians to found Mission San Antonio in the foothills of the Santa Lucia

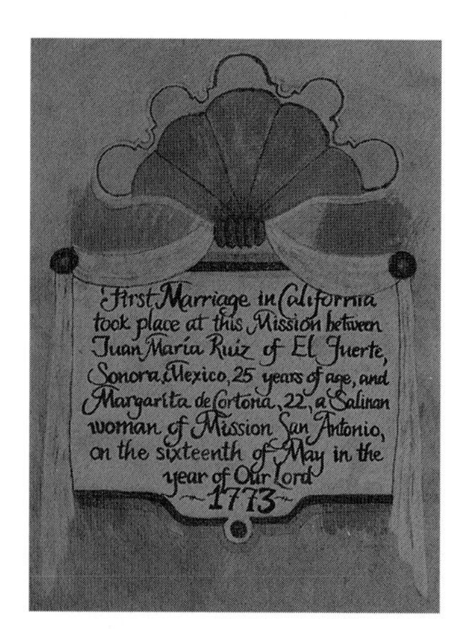

Frescoe painting in the church entrance commemorating the first marriage in California at Mission San Antonio de Padua in 1773

Mountains. This location had caught Governor Gaspár de Portolá's eye when he passed through here two years before. The Serra party reached the site that was well wooded with live oaks and other trees, which they called Los Robles. Here they camped near a stream, which Serra named Rio de San Antonio. Hardly had the small group settled-in, with only a bell hanging from a stout oak tree, when in a burst of unbridled enthusiasm Fr. Serra began to wildly ring the bell shouting for the Indians to come and hear the Christian message. Reminded by his colleagues there were no Indians in sight, Serra replied, "Let me give vent to my heart, which desires this bell to be heard all over the world."

Shortly thereafter Serra raised and blessed a cross and celebrated Mass in an enramada in honor of San Antonio de Padua. The date was July 14, 1771, and it was an auspicious beginning, for Fr. Serra caught sight of a lone Indian, doubtless attracted by the bell ringing. Serra approached him and presented him with a few small trinkets. This had the desired effect. Very shortly numerous Indians appeared to meet these strangers and receive gifts. In return the Indians brought gifts of food. The natives did not understand Serra's language, but they recognized his kindness and loving spirit. Serra remained at the newly founded mission for two weeks, after which he returned to Mission Carmel. He left two very competent padres in charge of further establishing the mission, Fr. Buenaventura Sitjar (1739-1808) and Fr. Miguel Pieras (1741-1795), both fellow Mallorcans. Fr. Sitjar served San Antonio Mission for thirty-seven years and was the architect of an extensive dam reservoir system which was largely responsible for the mission's agricultural successes. He also completed an Indian grammar and a four hundred-page vocabulary of the Mutsun language spoken by the local Indians. On the basis of those accomplishments he was able to prepare catechisms in their language, thus insuring that the Indians would understand the Christian message.

Detail of the altar highlighting the large bulto of mission patron San Antonio; note Indian-style painted decorations emphasizing stylized oak trees with acorns.

By the close of 1773 a small church and accessory buildings were completed. Among those Indians who came to the mission was an old woman called Agueda. She told the padres that in her father's time a man came to live among the Indians, who wore the same robes as the padres and taught the same things. She insisted that the robed person did not come on foot over the hills but by flying, she then expressed her desire to be baptized. When questioned by Fr. Pieras other Indians gave much the same account.

Fr. Francisco Palóu, serving at Mission Carmel at that time was keeping records of the mission settlements and Agueda's story was of particular interest. He proposed a theory that related to Sister María de Jesús de Ágreda (1602-1665), a nun of the Poor Clare order from Spain who was a mystic and allegedly had possessed the divine gifts of bilocation and spoke in tongues. Numerous southwest Indian and missionary accounts told of her micaculous evangelical visitations from Spain and of her preaching in native tongues which paved the way for later Christian conversions. Her life and her writings greatly influenced Serra and his fellow Franciscans, and copies of her book *Mistica Ciudad de Dios (Mystical City of God)*, published in 1670, were generally in California mission libraries at that time (Morgado, 1991, p.65).

In 1776, Lt. Col. Juan de Anza arrived at the Mission San Antonio with two hundred and forty immigrants from Sonora, Mexico, thus opening an overland road from Mexico into Alta California. This large party spent a few days at the mission recuperating from their journey, but their sheer numbers almost overwhelmed the mission's limited food supplies.

In 1794 Fr. Pieras, because of failing health, requested retirement to the College of San Fernando in Mexico City. Here he died in April of 1795 after serving Mission San Antonio for twenty-three years. Father Sitjar died at the mission in September of 1808 after serving it for thirty-seven years. The excellent leadership at the mission continued with the appointments of Frs. Juan Bautista Sancho (1772-1830) and Pedro Cabot (1777-1836), both of whom were also native Mallorcans. In 1810 trenches for the foundation of a new church were dug. By 1813 the church was completed. The dimensions were two hundred feet in length by forty feet in width, with walls six feet thick set on foundations of cobblestones ten feet deep. Windows and doorways were arched. Burnt brick was utilized in a decorative manner to form the outside colonnade. The church ceiling was of hand-hewn polished beams, ornamented with carvings.

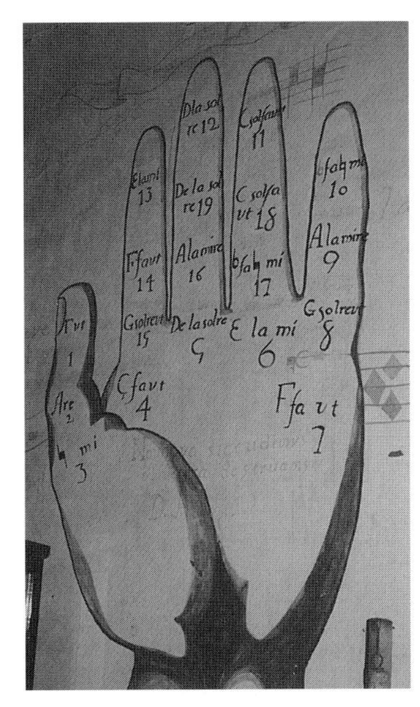

Museum display showing one of the devices used in teaching the mission Indians the basics of music.

Music was always integrated into mission life, and Fr. Juan Cabot trained and directed an excellent Indian choir and orchestra. He compiled a large book of church music beautifully rubricated in black and red on parchment pages. This book is on display in the mission museum.

In 1821 an arcade was built out from the portico of the church. With this addition the church presented a unique facade. It has three arched openings, the largest in the middle. On each side are square bell towers capped by brick cupolas. The central arch is higher and contains the large bell (osquila), which is original. Two smaller bells hang in the square bell towers. This charming facade is unlike that of any of the other Alta California missions.

By 1821, ten years had passed since financial and material support (memorias) had arrived from Mexico, and the missions found themselves as sole suppliers of food and materials for the entire colony. In that same year Mexico declared itself independent of Spain, and the situation for Alta California worsened, aggravated by contagious diseases, which decimated the mission Indian populations. In 1825 there were disastrous torrential rains which destroyed some of the mission buildings. In the same year the political situation further disintegrated with the appointment of José María Echeandia ("The Scourge of California") as governor of the colony. He was anti-religious and attempted to reduce the Church and its missions to servants of the politicians.

At the rear of the mission church is a small chapel dedicated to our Lady of Sorrows (Dolorosa); bulto is 40 inches in height and has real hair.

Detail of the large polychromed bulto of San Miguel Arcangel capping the reredos at Mission San Antonio de Padua.

Copper baptismal font sitting on a painted stone pedestal.

This untenable situation continued for the next five years, and in February 1830 Father Sancho died. The final death knell occurred when mission secularization was announced on January 6, 1831, and nine native Mexican padres were enlisted to replace the Franciscans. In 1833 Padre Cabot ceded the San Antonio Mission to Mexican padre Jesús María Mercado, and went into retirement at San Fernando College in Mexico City. By August 1834 secularization was complete. In November a new commissioner, Manuel Crespo, was appointed guardian of the mission and he turned guardianship over to his majordomo. Everything changed, and even Fr. Mercado was helpless to do anything about the situation. What followed was a period of rapid mission decline, and by 1842 mission rule had all but disappeared. In 1845 the mission was ordered to be sold, but there were no buyers; nothing much of value remained after the politicians appropriated the mission's furnishings, land, and livestock. On July 7, 1846, the United States Army took possession of the remaining mission holdings and did recognize the padres as the mission guardians. In 1851 padre Dorotheo Ambris became resident pastor of Mission San Antonio de Padua. His strenuous efforts gradually restored the mission to a semblance of its former life. The mission lands were officially returned to the Church in May 1862 in a patent signed by President Abraham Lincoln.

From 1851 to 1882 Fr. Ambris continued as resident pastor and was held in great esteem by the Indians. He was instrumental in re-instituting Patron's Day (June 13th) with a fiesta and a procession in which parishioners carried the original bulto of San Antonio. By 1880 Fr. Ambris had served the mission for nearly thirty years, and in February 1882 he took his journey into eternity. No resident priest replaced Fr. Ambris, but the mission was attended by padres on an irregular basis. The mission in dire need of loving care and repair continued to decline, and the church roof collapsed in 1900. In 1903 some spirited citizens from the San Francisco Bay area took the first important step leading to overall mission restoration. They organized as the California Landmarks League and choose as their initial project the restoration of San Antonio. Available funds were limited, but some tentative progress was made. However winter brought with it twenty-two inches of rain and caused the arch over the vestibule to collapse. Financial and volunteer aid from the Daughters of California Pioneers and the Native Sons of the Golden West made continuation of the work with the League possible in September 1906. Again, some substantial progress was made. Then on April 18, 1907, the great San Francisco Earthquake brought down the newly re-constructed and patched mission walls. The Landmarks League made one last heroic effort, and by August 1907 the rubble had been cleared away and minor restoration undertaken. However, from 1909 through 1921 with little maintenance the mission buildings continued to deteriorate and religious services were seldom held there.

In April 1921 local people formed the San Antonio Mission Restoration League but made very little progress. By 1926 only the chapel was left standing, flanked by the twelve remaining arches of the colonnade. In August 1928 the mission reverted to the Franciscans, and Patron's Day 1929 saw a celebration that included the return of the mission's artifacts and relics. The original bulto of San Antonio, cared for by the local Diaz family, was returned to the chapel.

A few years earlier, in 1925, newspaper magnate William Randolph Hearst had begun acquiring land surrounding the mission; by 1940 he owned 154,000 acres. Hearst built an elaborate Spanish style ranchhouse on a hill southeast of the mission and in 1939 Hearst donated twenty acres of land to the mission, increasing their holdings to fifty acres. In September 1940 the U. S. Government purchased the Hearst properties for the Hunter-Liggett Military Reservation, a subsidiary base of nearby Fort Ord.

By 1947 mission deterioration was almost complete. Happily, fate intervened, and in the summer of 1948 the Hearst Foundation initiated a $500,000 grant for California mission restoration, with $50,000 earmarked for the restoration of Mission San Antonio de Padua. In August 1948 the Franciscans began mission reconstruction. Fr. Augustine Hobrect took charge of this massive undertaking along with the renowned mission restorer Harry Downie. By spring 1949 the chapel was completely restored. In August 1949 Mission San Antonio acquired a resident Franciscan padre, the first since Fr. Ambris' death in 1882; he was Fr. Gregory Wooler. June 1950 marked the completion of restoration and the rededication of Mission San Antonio de Padua *(color page X)*.

The original bulto of San Antonio de Padua (39 inches high x 4 inches wide x 11 inches in depth); this bulto is presently in the baptistry chapel.

One can now walk down the aisle of the church and observe the painted walls with Indian decorations on the lower portion, and continue down the aisle where an arch painted with gold stars on a light blue background frames the sanctuary. Behind the altar is a painted reredos capped by a large polychrome bulto of the arcángel San Miguel, with wings extended. Below this, in the reredos center, is the bulto of the patron San Antonio. The reredos is flanked by two nichos. To the left, a bulto of San Buenaventura, whose feast day marked the mission's founding, and to the right the nicho contains a bulto of San Francisco. Two side altars are also present: on the right side is one dedicated to San José, and on the left side is one dedicated to Our Lady of the Immaculate Conception. Along the walls of the church are the fourteen Stations of the Cross, not original, they were painted by Carmel artist Micaela Martinez. In the rear of the church a small is chapel is dedicated to Dolorosa *(color page L)*, and adjacent to it stands a small Baptistry.

From 1950 to 1976 the mission served as a training center for the Franciscan Brothers. Restoration continues at the mission, and archaeological excavation is on going. The cemetery has been restored and is the resting-place for some 1200 Indians.

Mission San Antonio de Padua is one of the most faithfully restored of the Alta California Spanish Colonial missions. Most gratifying is the fact that the location has not been swallowed up in urban sprawl and surrounded by a busy city. Instead, it sits in the lovely peaceful Valle de los Robles just as it did over two hundred years ago.

Side view of the mission church of San Gabriel Arcángel; note the unique campanario and the distinctive buttresses capped with Moorish-style pediments.

North front of Mission San Gabriel with it's rather plain facade, and the relatively recent bronze statue of Father Junípero Serra.

MISSION SAN GABRIEL ARCÁNGEL:

Synopsis: Fourth mission: founded by Frs. Pedro Cambón (1738-?) and Angel Somera (C.1741-?) on September 8, 1771, at a site previously selected by Fr. Junípero Serra; moved to present site by Fr. Fermín Lasuén in 1775; present church begun in 1791 and completed in 1805; damaged by earthquakes in 1812, 1987, and 1994; secularized in 1834 with an active life of sixty-three years; mission property surrendered to creditors but restored to Church in 1859; in 1908 mission administration taken over by the Claretian Missionary Fathers.

Location: The mission complex is located in the city of San Gabriel at 537 West Mission Drive, about nine miles east of downtown Los Angeles.

San Gabriel Arcángel is the patron saint of this fourth Alta California Spanish colonial mission. The choice of the dedication had been made in 1770 by the Viceroy Carlos Francisco de Croix. The name Gabriel means strength of God. In the New Testament Gabriel announced the birth of Juan Bautista to Zacharias and the birth of Jesús to Mary. In early Christian times Gabriel is frequently represented as a winged figure holding a lily representing purity, bringing the message of the Incarnation of the Virgin Mary. 0il paintings of the Annunciation were at Missions San Gabriel, San Juan Capistrano, and San Fernando, but none have survived. Oil paintings of just the Arcángel Gabriel can be seen at Missions San Gabriel and San Miguel. Gabriel is principally God's messenger bringing enlightenment and announcing our good works to God.

After the arrival of ten additional Franciscans at Mission Carmel, Fr. Junípero Serra quickly moved to close the gap between Missions San Diego and Carmel. Before winter of 1771 Serra endeavored to have two new missions established: San Antonio de Padua, a day's journey south of Carmel, and San Gabriel, a convenient distance north of San Diego. Fr. Serra authorized Frs. Pedro Benito Cambón and Angel Fernandez de la Somera to establish the new mission on a site he had previously selected. The padres located the designated site near a river called Santa Ana, but named it Rio de los Temblores, because on the day they arrived several earthquake shocks were felt. Legend has it that as the padres were preparing to dedicate the mission site on September 8, 1771, a party of Indians threatened them. They were only pacified when one of the padres unrolled a small canvas with a painting of Our Lady of Sorrows. This ended their hostile intentions, and two of the Indian leaders took off their necklaces and placed them in front of the painting as gifts. This painting, in an elaborate wrought-iron frame can be seen today in the sanctuary to the left of the church altar. Morgado (1991, p. 78) notes that little is known of its provenance but that it is most likely seventeenth century Mexican. The canvas is twenty inches by twenty-four inches, and he states that it was stolen from the sanctuary in 1977. Later information (Weber, 1997, p. 141) reports that on January 5, 1990, the Federal Bureau of Investigation arrested one William March Witherell for the theft. When the FBI searched his home in San Gabriel they found hundreds of stolen rare books and religious objects, including the painting of Our Lady of Sorrows and two oil paintings that had long been missing from Mission San Fernando. All were returned to the appropriate missions in 1991.

The initial mission site was moved three times before settling in its present location in 1775. At the initial site the padres erected a large cross and celebrated Mass in a brushwood hut (enramada). The Indians willingly helped in the construction; however, later on when one of the soldiers forcibly seduced an Indian leader's wife and killed her husband to silence his objections, it was only quick conciliatory action by the padres that prevented a bloody Indian reprisal. Fr. Serra visited the mission seven times, the first two times at the original site. Progress continued, albeit slowly, since it took some time before the Indians came to trust both the padres and the soldiers. By 1775, both Frs. Cambón and Somera became too ill to continue their missionary endeavors and were replaced in February of that year by Frs. Antonio Cruzado (1724-1804) and Miguel Sánchez (1738-1803). This was the beginning of a thirty years' association and partnership at Mission San Gabriel. Interestingly, Fr. Cruzado, who grew up near Cordova, a city that had been transformed by the Moors between the eight and eleventh centuries, was responsible for the eventual

Original copper baptismal font on a decorated stone pedestal in the baptistry of Mission San Gabriel; copper bowl is a gift to the mission from King Carlos in the 1790's.

Moorish appearance of the church. In 1779 construction on a stone church began, but it was not until 1805 that this new church was completed. Cruzado and Sánchez, who had spent twenty-six years overseeing construction and administering to the Indians, both died in the year it was completed. Father José Mariá Zalvidea (1780-1846) was appointed to carry on the mission's work. For the next twenty years Zalvidea was the mission. He was a man of great physical strength, a born leader, and a religious zealot. It was under his dynamic administration that the asistencia at the Pueblo de los Angeles, "La Reina de los Ángeles de Porciúncula" (The Church of the Queen of the Angels) was completed in 1822.

In the great earthquake of 1812 the San Gabriel church was severely damaged and the belltower toppled. At that time the belltower was located at the north front corner of the church. Restoration from the earthquake damage was not completed until 1828, and the new campanario at the far end of the sidewall gave the mission a distinctive appearance. The campanario has six bells, two of which were cast by Paul Ruelas of Mexico City in 1795. Two others were cast at Medford, Massachusetts, by Major G. H. Hollbrook, who learned the craft from the American colonial patriot Paul Revere. The largest bell was cast in 1830, and the remaining one, which was part of the original set, disappeared from the mission in the 1870s but was returned in the 1930's.

Assignment as a missionary to San Gabriel was perhaps more demanding than at any other mission since the mission sat astride three well traveled routes. Accordingly it became a wayside stop for weary colonizing parties from Mexico and from the east. The mission was continually targeted by the military as a jumping-off location for northward expansion. In the early 1800s San Gabriel grew more wheat than any other mission. At one time it also had the largest winery in California, with grapes grown from cuttings brought from Europe by Fr. Junípero Serra.

Connell (1941, p. 37) stated:

> *that in 1826, H. G. Rogers, a fur trader accompanying the mountain man Jedediah Smith, visited the mission and reported that it consisted of four rows of buildings forming a square where there were all kinds of Indians at work....There were large vineyards and fruit orchards....There were upwards of one thousand people employed in the manufacture of blankets and other articles....The location is handsome....Streams of water running through.... Thousands of acres of rich fertile land.... Mission has upwards of thirty thousand cattle, and horses, sheep, and hogs in proportion.... They slaughter two to three thousand at a time; the mission lives on the profits.*

Mission San Gabriel was also noted for the soap and candles it supplied to the other missions.

The mission was secularized in November 1834. Fr. Tomas Eleuterio Estenega (1790-1847) who was then in charge of the mission, handed over the mission property to a politically appointed secular administrator. Mexican Governor Pío Pico then leased the mission and later sold it illegally. By 1840 there were fewer than a thousand head of cattle left, and when the padres came back in 1843 there remained very little of value. When secularization was completed mission properties and goods had shifted into the hands of California families identified with the military and civilian politicians, some of whom succeeded in having themselves appointed administrators of the mission lands, thus speeding up the overall plundering of mission properties.

In his account of a tour of the California missions and towns in 1856, the American traveler Henry Miller (Miller, 1997, p. 48-49) noted that

> *on 20th August I left Los Angeles for the Mission San Gabriel....I had my mule shod while I took a sketch of the mission (given on page 50; one of the earliest views of the mission) which forms at present a little village, the haunt of some notorious cattle thieves; murders are committed here frequently often as a result of the fandangos which are given almost every night, breaking up in a row and a stabbing or shooting affair....The mission church is well preserved, being built in a peculiar style different from the other churches. The other buildings, however, are dilapidated or totally in ruins.*

Detail of one of San Gabriel's original bells cast in Mexico City by Paul Ruelas in 1795; it's Latin inscription reads Ave Maria Purisima. S. Fran. co.

Actually, Mission San Gabriel was never abandoned as a place of religious worship, and the records show a continuity of pastors. The last Franciscan left in the early 1850's and was immediately replaced by clergy assigned by the bishop. In 1859 the mission property was given to two Americans to settle a debt, but in that same year, the U. S. Land Commission declared the transaction invalid and returned the property to the Church. The church proper was in comparatively good shape, but the mission outbuildings were in ruins. The mission served as the parish church of the city of San Gabriel from 1862 until 1908. At that point the Claretian Missionary Fathers took over the administration of the mission. They have done a very competent and massive job of restoring the church and the buildings of the mission quadrangle, in spite of devastation by earthquakes in 1987 and 1994.

Next to the church is a cemetery containing the remains of six thousand mission Indians, and with the graves of the many padres who have faithfully served the mission over the years. Behind the church is a relatively large museum containing an outstanding collection of church relics and artifacts. Perhaps most intriguing is a collection of paintings of the Stations of the Cross done by the Indians of Mission San Fernando. Professor Neuerburg did an intensive study of the paintings (1997, p. 329-382), and he concluded that they were too complex to be either original compositions by an Indian artist or

View of the altar and lower portion of the reredos in the mission church of San Gabriel with a large polychrome bulto of Our Lady of the Immaculate Conception in the center; to the left is a bulto of San Joachim, and on the right side a bulto of Santo Domingo.

copies of crude woodcuts in a prayer book or missal. Most probably they are based on a set of engravings ordered by Mission San Gabriel in 1771 and given to Mission San Fernando in 1798 when the older mission received a set of paintings from Mexico. The fourteen paintings were all painted on unprimed linen canvas, not sail cloth as has been asserted. Each is about 33 inches by 53 inches. The assertion that the colors were made from flowers and berries is sheer nonsense. The paints were powdered mineral colors, mostly from Mexico, mixed with linseed oil, also from Mexico. They were restored in 1954 by Donaldo Manuel and Corita H. de Manuel. A tradition of uncertain origin attributes the paintings to a San Fernando Mission Indian named Juan Antonio, but this has been seriously questioned. One can only guess at the date when they were painted, but it was probably in the 1820's, and more than one artist appears to have been involved, and those of varying talent. All would have had to have some instruction, perhaps from the priest who oversaw the project. This collection of paintings was exhibited at the 1893 Chicago "World's Columbia Exposition," then became part of the Los Angeles Chamber of Commerce, and were later given to Mission San Gabriel.

San Gabriel Mission church looks like a fortress. It has large buttresses along both sides that are designed to strengthen the walls and lessen earthquake damage *(color page A)*. The walls are four to seven feet in thickness. The roof has been of different materials, but for the last hundred years it has been shingled. The outside stairs lending to the choir were used until 1906, when inside stairs were built. The church is long and narrow— one hundred and fifty feet in length and twenty-seven feet in width; it is thirty feet in height.

The inside of the church is exceptionally well preserved. In 1886 the ceiling was wood paneled, covering up the old vigas in a Victorian manner, and painted with Indian designs in muted colors. As one proceeds down the aisle, on the right side is a small Baptistry. A small, hand-hammered copper bowl serves as a baptismal font, an original gift of the Spanish King in the 1790s. Above it is a beautiful painted frescoe of San Juan Boutista *(color page H)*. It is estimated that 25,000 persons, including 10,000 Indians, have been baptized in this room. Further along the aisle is the original rather undistinguished pulpit. At the front of the church stands the altar and reredos, both of which came from Mexico City sometime in the 1790's. The lovely reredos has six polychrome bultos that were brought from Spain. The center of the reredos is crowned with a bulto of the patron, San Gabriel. To his left is San Francisco, and to his right San Antonio. Below Gabriel is the Immaculate Conception, and to her left is San

Joachin, and to the right San Dominic. The altar and reredos were restored in 1993.

It is indeed remarkable that this mission, sited in such a bustling area and so close to downtown Los Angeles, has managed to preserve such a peaceful demeanor amid such urban chaos. Many of the other California missions have lost their tranquil setting being completely swallowed up in urban sprawl. This restored mission quadrangle, against all odds, has managed to preserve a great deal of the integrity of the early mission setting.

Early morning view of the front of the mission church of Our Lady of the Angels, located on Main Sreet in downtown Los Angeles.

ASISTENCIA IGLESIA DE NUESTRA SEÑORA DE LOS ANGELES, DE LA MISSION SAN GABRIEL, ARCÁNGEL

Located on Main Street in downtown Los Angeles, this asistencia to Mission San Gabriel was founded as a 1400 square feet chapel in 1784 to serve the local poblanos. The site chosen was at the first Spanish pueblo of Los Angeles, founded by Governor Don Felipe de Neve on September 4, 1781.

This first Spanish settlement in Alta California consisted of eleven families, comprising twenty-two adults and twenty-two children. The colonists had been recruited from Sinaloa and Sonora, New Spain. The goal was to establish a permanent settlement that would provide food for the settlers and the military. Of the adults listed in the 1781 census, eight were classified racially as mulattos, two as Spaniards, nine as Indians, one as mestizo, and two as Negroes. The oldest was sixty-seven years of age, and two of the children were just one year old.

The original chapel, constructed in 1784, continued in use until December 8, 1822, when the church was dedicated in honor of Our Lady of the Angels. The cornerstone for this building was laid on August 15, 1814, by Fray Luís Gil y Toboada (1773-1833). Mexican architect José Antonio Ramirez designed the building and supervised its construction.

The long time span from the laying of the cornerstone and the completion of the church in 1822 was caused in part by destruction of the original chapel due to flooding by Rio de la Porciuncula. Actual construction of the existing church did not begin until 1819. The lack of funds and actual engineering knowledge played a part in delaying the settlers' dream to have their own Los Angeles church. However, as the asistencia gradually developed, generous help from other established missions nourished the fledgling asistencia. From Missions San Miguel and San Luís Rey came 700 head of cattle; from La Purisima two mules and 200 cattle; a barrel of brandy from both Santa Barbara and San Fernando; 2 barrels of white wine from San Diego, and church furniture came from San Buenaventura. Mission San Gabriel donated two barrels of brandy, a bulto of San Vicente Ferrer, and two bells, both of which are still in use at Our Lady of the Angels Church. Funds were also provided by Missions San Luís Rey and San Gabriel, along with manpower toward construction of the church.

Outdoor devotional-area located on the right side wall of Our Lady of Angels Church, and dedicated to the Virgen de Guadalupe.

The Old Plaza Church has undergone a number of remodelings, restorations, and expansions over the years. In the 1840's it was extensively remodeled and the flat roof was replaced with a steeply pitched roof of wooden shakes. In 1861 a high gable was added to the facade along with a new campanario, and the church sanctuary was expanded into a cruciform shape. An increasing neighborhood population demanded additions to the church in 1912-1913. The most significant church restoration took place in 1965, when the 1913 earthquake damaged church was demolished and the present church built. The original padre's quarters has undergone various changes over the years. Presently, it forms an expanded rectory surrounding a large courtyard area comprising parish offices, padre's quarters, a social service office, and an assembly hall. Most of the changes have been motivated by the overall needs of the parishioners the Church so ably serves. Since 1908 the church has been operating under the auspices of the Claretian Missionary Fathers.

The exterior of the present church is architecturally quite simple. The building has been stuccoed and very attractively painted in a taupe color, highlighted with white trim. An oval arch trimmed in white delineates the front entranceway. It is squared-off with white painted pilasters. This is overlaid with a rectangular section pierced by two narrow windows. In the center of this space is a beautiful rectangular-shaped jeweled mosaic depicting The Annunciation. This is a 1981 reproduction of the image of Our Lady of the Angels in the Portiuncula Chapel at Assisi, Italy *(color page P)*. Above this section is a triangular gable, pierced in the center with an ocular window. The gable is capped with a square pediment crowned with a filigreed metal cross. The left side of the church facade is marked by an ocular window at the same level as the adjacent mosaic. This section is overlaid with a gracefully arched campanario with three bells and capped with a metal cross. Three buttresses divide the church proper from the campanario; these are stone capped with triangular pediments. The pediments run the entire length of the building at the roofline and impart a look reminiscent of the Moorish architecture of the mother mission of San Gabriel. On the right side of the facade is the entrance into the church courtyard. Adjacent to this entranceway is the El Camino Real mission bell originally placed by the California Women's League in 1906; the restored and refurbished bell was rededicated on May 22, 1998, by the Knights of Columbus Councils of southern California.

Original copper and zinc baptismal font still in current use in the baptistry of Our Lady of the Angels Church in downtown Los Angeles.

Inside the church a small Baptistry is located in the rear of the church on the left side. In the center of the red-tiled floor is a stone pedestal holding the original large circular baptismal font of hammered copper and zinc. In a corner of the room is a contemporary statue of San Juan Bautista. The baptismal font has been in constant use since 1822, and the present sacristan noted that from 35 to 50 baptisms still take place in this room each month.

Proceeding down the center aisle, one immediately notices the exquisitely gilded and ornately carved reredos. Instead of the usual reredos pierced with nichos to hold various santos, this reredos is composed of five large religious oil paintings ornately framed. Clockwise from the top these devotional paintings depict Nuestra Señora de los Angeles, Santo Domingo de Guzman, San Francisco de Asís, San José, and Santa Teresa de Avila.

In the center of the reredos, behind the altar and directly below the oil painting of Our Lady of the Angels, is a large square-shaped compartment which opens to display an imposing monstrance. Two side chapels are present on either side of the transept. On the left is a chapel dedicated to the Virgin of Guadalupe, and on the right one dedicated to Our Lady of Mount Carmel.

The arched overhead wooden ceiling is beautifully painted with a series of rectangular-shaped sections embellished with geometric and devotional design motifs.

Interestingly, the Stations of the Cross are located outside in the inner church courtyard. They are marked by relatively large simple wooden crosses each surrounded by flowering vines *(color page B)*.

Along an outside wall on the right side of the compound is a large public devotional area devoted to Nuestra Señora de La Guadalupe, made of ceramic tiles depicting the tilma image of Our Lady along with a kneeling Juan Diego.

Directly across from the church is old Olivera Street, which is presently undergoing a major restoration. Already completed are a large elevated gazebo and surrounding walkways, where on this location each April 22nd, since 1930, the blessing of the animals has taken place. Also within this area, two life-size contemporary bronze statues and various bronze plaques describe the early history of the area. One of the statues, closest to the church, is of a romanticized Governor Don Felipe de Neve founder of the Los Angeles Pueblo in 1781. This statue was created by artist Henry Lion and dedicated in 1931 by the Native Daughters of the Golden West. The bronze statue, on the opposite side, is of Spanish King Carlos III (1759-1788), created by Spanish sculptor F. Coullant-Valera in 1976, and dedicated by Spain's King Juan Carlos and Queen Sofia on September 30, 1987.

In an area completely surrounded by the artifacts of modern-day urbanization sprawl, the church of Our Lady of the Angels is an oasis for both parishioners and pilgrims. It is also a continually used sanctuary that provides a measure of comfort and solace to the many homeless people of the area, a reflection of one of the darker social problems of today's megacities.

View of the facade of Mission San Luís Obispo de Tolosa with a bronze statue of Father Junípero Serra and a large wooden cross adjacent to the mission church entrance.

MISSION SAN LUÍS OBISPO DE TOLOSA:

Synopsis: Fifth mission founded by Fr. Junípero Serra on September 1, 1772; site never relocated; named for San Luís, Bishop of Toulouse, France; present building with tile roof constructed 1792-94 after fires caused by Indian attacks in 1776, 1778, and 1782; vestibule added in 1820; mission secularized in 1835 after an active life of sixty-three years; building "modernized" with wooden siding and New England-style belfry in 1870's; earthquake damage in 1830, 1868, and in the 1880s when portico was removed; annex beyond side altar built in 1893; fire in 1920; buildings restored to original architecture in 1933.

Location: In the city of San Luís Obispo, on U. S. Highway 101, the mission is located at the corner of Monterey and Chorro Streets in the downtown area.

San Luís, Bishop of Toulouse, France was chosen as patron of the fifth Alta California Spanish Colonial missions. Luís was born in 1274 at Provence, southern France, the second son of Charles II of Anjou and King of Naples, and

Mary the daughter of King Stephen V of Hungary. He was also related to San Fernando, King of Spain. He and his two brothers were sent as hostages to Barcelona in exchange for their father, who had been defeated and captured in a naval battle. In captivity for seven years Luis he came under the influence of the Franciscans and resolved to join the order. He took the habit in Rome in 1296, and at the end of the year was consecrated as Bishop of Toulouse. He was much revered for his holiness, but died at the age of twenty-three. He was canonized in 1817 and was buried first in Marseilles but later moved to Valencia, Spain, where he now rests in the cathedral. Although a superb golden statue of him was created by the great Italian Renaissance sculptor Donatello in Florence, Italy, his image is rarely represented after the fifteenth century. In California, the only surviving images are a bulto which crowns the mission church reredos and an oil painting attributed to the Mexican artist José de Páez before 1794. The bulto came to the mission in 1791.

Unlike so many of the California Spanish Colonial missions, San Luís Obispo was not moved from the site originally chosen by Fr. Serra. His reasoning being that this mission would tie the two southern missions, San Diego and San Gabriel, with two northern missions, Carmel and San Antonio de Padua.

In 1772, when the four existing missions were in dire need of food and supplies, soldiers from Carmel and Monterey were dispatched to El Valle de Los Osos, a region that Gaspár de Portolá had found in 1769 to be heavily populated by bears. In three months' time the soldiers dried over four tons of bear jerky for both missions and presidios. Acting on the stories the soldiers brought back concerning this location, Fr. Serra decided to establish the fifth mission at a site in the Valley of the Bears. Accompanying Fr. Serra was Fr. José Cavaller (1740-1789), a recent missionary arrival from Spain. Serra selected the site, said Mass, and dedicated the mission to San Luís Obispo, a thirteenth-century Bishop of Toulouse, France.

Serra moved on to San Diego the next day, leaving Fr. Cavaller with five solders and two Indians to erect the first buildings. Fr. Serra visited this mission seven times during his tenure as Father-President of the Alta California missions.

The local Indians helped with both the building and supplying the small party with food. The Indians were most appreciative to have the valley cleared of the ferocious bears, which had caused them much grief over the years. Early building construction was with poles interlaced with tree branches and daubed with adobe. The roof was made of woven tule grass. On at least three separate occasions hostile Indians set the mission buildings afire with flaming arrows. As a consequence of those attacks baked red roof tiles were adopted to minimize any fire damage. By 1784 all of the missions had adopted red roof tiles and

View of the altar and reredos in the mission church of San Luís Obispo, with large polychrome bulto of patron in center, and in nichos on either side bultos of Our Lady of the Immaculate Conception and San Antonio.

would thus leave an indelible mark on California mission architecture. In due course the mission developed into a prosperous working institution and by 1783 was basically self-supporting. Fr. Cavaller utilized the services of an Indian boy as an interpreter, and through him was able to master the twelve to fifteen dialects of the various Chumash Indian groups. In spite of learning the Indian languages, church music was always sung in Spanish. The Indians at Mission San Luís Obispo, and in most of the other missions, loved music and developed into competent singers of harmony. Fr. Cavaller died in 1789 and is buried on the left side of the altar in the sanctuary. In the early 1790's master craftsmen were imported from Mexico to train the Indians in building permanent buildings. The present church was built by this infused labor force, and by 1794 the mission church completed under the guidance of Fr. Miguel Giribet (1756-1804), who had been appointed senior missionary in 1790. In 1798 Fr. Antonio Luís Martinez (1771-1832) was assigned to the mission and began thirty-four years of service.

Beginning in 1811 and continuing through 1820, an intensive building program proceeded, and by 1819 the typical mission quadrangle was completed. Arrival of three mission bells from Peru in 1820 was an auspicious occasion. Fr. Martinez, although loved and respected by the Indians, was an outspoken critic of the Mexican government's treatment of the missions. His criticisms grew, especially as political conditions in the colony worsened. In 1830 he was arrested by the government on trumped-up charges and banished to Spain. That same year an earthquake weakened the mission buildings, and thus began a forty years decline in the mission's fortunes. Secularization occurred in 1835 when formal possession of the buildings by the Mexican government took place. The last Franciscan at the mission, Fr. Ramón Abella, died in 1842, and by 1845 Governor Pio Pico sold the mission properties for $510.00! From this time on the mission sank into rapid decline.

The American traveler Henry Miller visited the mission site in 1856 and said, *after breakfast I took a ramble about the mission buildings, some of which are in ruins, though once remarkably strong, constructed of rock joined with a very hard cement....Of the once magnificent orchards there are only a great number of olive trees remaining, (Miller, 1997, pp. 29-30).*

Old oil panting of Our Lady of Refuge in an illuminated alcove off of the center aisle of the mission church of San Luís Obispo.

While at the site Miller did two drawings, a close-up view of the front of the mission and an overall view of the village showing the mission as the dominant architectural entity. In the late 1850's the mission lands were returned to the Church by the U. S. Land Commission. Until the 1870's the church facade remained essentially unchanged. The belfry-vestibule area had been damaged by two earthquakes, and a few years after the second earthquake in 1868, the roof tiles were removed to relieve stress on the building.

While preparing for the mission centenary in 1872 so-called "modernizers" moved in. The result was that Mission San Luís Obispo was transformed into a New England-style church. No longer did it look anything like the original mission of 1772. The original structure was encased in wooden clapboard siding, the bells removed from the belfry, and a New England type belfry erected. Inside the church, tongue-and-groove boards hid the viga ceiling, and wooden boards disguised the stone and mortar floor. In 1893, Fr. Valentin Aguilere enlarged the church with an annex to the right side of the altar. Ironically, a fire in the sacristy in 1920 exposed the true underpinnings of the building. The charred false wooden ceiling was removed revealing the original hand-hewn vigas. Later, in 1933, Father John Harnett removed the inappropriate outside clapboard siding and restored the building to its graceful Spanish style.

This present L-shaped mission is quite different from the usual long and narrow rectangles of most mission churches. The outside walls are made of several thickness of adobe, and then whitewashed. The center patio has beautifully tended rose gardens and grape arbors. The restored convento contains an outstanding museum and the almost inevitable gift shop. The front of the convento is set off by a distinctive colonnade of eleven rounded columns set on square pedestals that form an attractive corridor. In the church interior the upper walls are painted white, while colorful Indian design frescoes decorate the lower portion *(color page O)*. As one goes down the aisle there is an alcove on the right-hand side which contains a large illuminated oil painting of Nuestra Señora del Refugio (Our Lady of Refuge), which is perhaps the most outstanding piece of devotional art in the mission. Both the church interior and the reredos were restored in 1947. The wood on the reredos is painted to appear as marble, a common decorative technique employed in a number of missions. The gabled top of the reredos has a painting of the "all-seeing Eye of God". On a pedestal in the center of the reredos stands the original polychrome bulto of San Luís Obispo, patron of the mission. Bultos of the Immaculate Conception

Distinctive painted wood and bronze tabernacle sitting on the altar of the mission church of San Luís Obispo.

View of the convento and corridor at Mission San Luís Obispo, showing the rather distinctive rounded columns.

and San Antonio, both thought to have originally come from Spain, occupy nichos on either side of the altar. A handsome unique wood and bronze tabernacle sits on the altar. The annex to the right of the altar contains a contemporary small chapel and baptistry.

Mission San Luís Obispo de Tolosa is in the center of a busy city. The river and a well-landscaped park with tall eucalyptus trees enhance the setting of the mission. The park and mission together function as a site for many community activities.

CHAPTER FOUR

A PROSPEROUS MISSION TWICE FOUNDED:

SAN JUAN CAPISTRANO 1775 & 1776, AND MISSION GUARDIANS OF SAN FRANCISCO BAY: SAN FRANCISCO DE ASÍS 1776, AND SANTA CLARA DE ASÍS 1777

The ruins of Mission San Juan Capistrano showing the bell wall with it's four named bells: San Vicente, San Juan, San Antonio, and San Rafael, to the right is the statue of Father Junípero Serra with an Indian boy, and the walls of the old ruined stone church; note scaffolding denoting major ongoing rconstruction and restoration at the mission.

MISSION SAN JUAN CAPISTRANO:

Synopsis: Formally, the seventh mission founded by Fr. Junípero Serra on November 1, 1776; previously established by Fr. Fermín Lasuén October 30, 1775, but hurriedly abandoned because of an Indian uprising; named for a fourteenth century Italian theologian; large stone church begun in 1797 and completed in 1806; destroyed in the 1812 earthquake; secularized in 1833 after an active mission life of fifty-seven years; restored to the Church in the 1860s; major reconstruction and restoration in the 1920s and 1930s, and ongoing.

Location: Mission is located in the city of San Juan Capistrano off of U. S. Interstate Highway 5.

San Juan was chosen as the patron for the seventh Alta California Spanish Colonial mission by Viceroy Antonio Bucareli. Juan was born in the village of Capestrano in the mountainous Abruzzi region of central Italy in 1385. His father was a German baron and his mother was of the local nobility. He studied law at the University of Perugia, married a local woman in 1412, and was named governor of the city by the King of Naples. He was sent to mediate peace in a war, but ended up in prison. His wife died, and his other experiences led him to take holy orders as a Franciscan in 1416. He studied under Bernardine of Siena and became one of his closest followers. As a priest he was a powerful preacher whom the pope sent all over Europe. In 1455 he organized a crusade against the Turks and led a Christian army that defeated them at Belgrade in 1456. He died of fever shortly after this victory. He was beatified in 1690 and canonized in 1724—one of the few lawyers ever canonized. In devotional art he is generally shown in Franciscan habit wearing an armor breastplate. He usually carries a

Area within Father Serra's church dedicated to the Virgin of Guadalupe; painting illustrrates the popular Tilma representations of Juan Diego's spiritual experiences.

View of the painted wall dado with it's Indian-style frescoe decorations so common in the mission church of San Juan Capistarano.

banner with a cross and holds either a crucifix or a sword. Fr. Junípero Serra commissioned the Mexican artist José de Páez to do an oil painting of Juan in 1775, which now hangs in the new Capistrano parish church. An 1810 bulto of San Juan Capistrano is in a nicho on one of the side altars in Mission Dolores in San Francisco.

On October 30, 1775, Fr. Fermín Francisco Lasuén, accompanied by Fr. Gregorio Amurrió (1744-?) of Mission San Gabriel, brought bells and sundry items needed to establish a mission. On arriving at the chosen site, an enramada was hastily set up, near which the small party erected, blessed, and venerated a large cross. On an altar in the enramada Fr. Lasuén said Holy Mass. Work had barely commenced when word reached the group that there had been an Indian uprising at Mission San Diego de Alcalá. Stunned by this revealation the group quickly buried the bells and returned to Mission Carmel. A year later Fr. Junípero Serra, along with Frs. Pablo Mugártegui (1736-?) and Gregorio Amurrió returned to the site, dug up the bells, and repeated the founding ceremony on November 1, 1776. Fr. Serra occasionally offered Mass and presided at confirmations at the mission's first church. Today it is called Fr. Serra's Church and claims to be the only surviving church building where Serra celebrated Mass.

The mission prospered from the beginning. In due time a quadrangle, with kitchens, workshops, soldiers' barracks, and Indian and padre quarters was constructed. By 1796 Fr. Serra's Church was too small. Then in 1797 a great stone church was begun, the finest architectural building the Spaniards ever erected in California. Master stone mason Isidoro Aguilar was imported from Culiacan, Mexico, to supervise the overall construction and stone cutting. Teams of oxen hauled the sandstone for the building in carettas from a quarry six miles away. The stone church was nine years in building, and though unfortunately for Mission Capistrano, Isidoro Aguilar died three years before the work was completed. The lack of continued qualified supervision is reflected in the irregular wall measurements and a later catastrophic event. The overall church plan was very ambitious, and when the structure was completed was the most magnificent of all the Alta California mission churches. The building was cruciform in shape, one hundred and seventy feet in length. The width of the church varied from eighty feet across the transepts to thirty feet in the narrowest part of the building. The structure had a vaulted ceiling surmounted by seven domes. The church entrance was capped by a massive hundred-and-twenty-foot campanario with four bells that had been cast in Peru in 1796 and 1804. The completed church was dedicated with much pomp and ceremony on September 8, 1806.

At the conclusion of an early morning Mass, on December 8, 1812 (the Feast of the Immaculate Conception), a tremendous earthquake toppled the two-tiered campanario, killing forty praying Indians. The sanctuary was unscathed and many of the mission's furnishings escaped destruction. San Juan Capistrano recovered from the tragedy, but the padres did not have the resources to rebuild the church. Instead, they moved back into Fr. Serra's Church and did maintenance repairs. In 1813, the four bells that had been toppled from the campanario in the earthquake were hung in the wall adjacent to the church ruins. The largest bell is unique because it is inscribed with the names of the padres at the mission when the bell was cast. Since then, the bells have been rung by ropes attached to their clappers.

Mission San Juan Capistrano had carried on a thriving trade in hides and tallow which reached its peak before 1820. In 1818 the mission was sacked by the Argentinean pirate Bouchard and his men when his privateer put into Dana Point Harbor and the mission padres refused him supplies.

View along a typical arched corridor at Mission San Juan Capistrano.

After 1821 each mission was responsible for the care of the Indians and with supplying food and materials to the soldiers and the colonists, yet received no aid from the Mexican government: an unsatisfactory situation at best. After secularization in 1833 the mission's fortunes were dramatically altered. By 1834, when the Mexican government took control of the property, there were only some eight hundred Indians still in residence. At that point the mission came under the control of secular administrators (politicos) whose salaries were paid out of the Indians' hard labor. Under those poor conditions many of the Indians fled the mission compound. After secularization only Fr. José María Zalvidea remained to administer to the spiritual needs of a fast shrinking community. In 1840, the Mexican government sent William Hartnell to see to the upkeep of the mission property. In 1842 Fr. Zalvidea left the mission, and by 1845 the mission was a debt-ridden burden to the government. In December of that year, Pío Pico, the last Mexican governor of California disposed of the property by selling it to his brother-in-law John Forster for $710.00! By May 9, 1846, California was American. Forster lived in the mission for twenty years, in what is presently the gift shop. The Church was allowed to keep the Serra Church and a small room as a residence for the priest.

The American traveler Henry Miller visited the mission on September 21, 1856, and noted,

> *I had to ride along the seabeach, till I arrived at Mission San Juan Capistrano, the buildings of which are a few miles from the beach in a beautiful green valley which is well watered by a small stream....The principal feature of this mission is the ruins of a once magnificent church, built very solid of rock and cement, with arched roofs....Some of the mission buildings are in good condition, inhabited by the padre, and Mr. John Forster, an Englishman, a son-in-law (sic) of Pío Pico," (Miller, 1997, p. 61).*

Miller did a drawing of the mission ruins on this date (p. 62).

Detail of the original fine stonework in an arch and column within the ruins of the old stone church that collapsed in the 1812 earthquake; the fine masonry work is attributed to Mexican master stonemason Isodoro Aguilar.

The mission properties were restored to the Church in a patent signed by President Abraham Lincoln in 1864. The first attempt at mission restoration took place in the 1860's and was misguided in that it destroyed more than it restored. In 1874, H. L. Oak, accompanied by the renowned California historian H. H. Bancroft and his daughter Kate, spent a pleasant day visiting the mission ruins. Oak (1981, p. 45) recorded his impressions noting,

> *The church is built of rough stones and cement, the stones not being arranged in any order, but the walls, which are five or six feet thick, have the corners, arches, etc. built of cut stone, of a soft fine nature, neatly cut in simple ornamented lines and cornices....The ceiling on the interior was gracefully arched, the arch stones being carefully cut, and supporting probably the immense mass placed upon them.... The ceiling was plastered but has no signs of frescoing. The only trace of the altar at the back of the north wing are nine niches in the white wall....The belltower is said to have fallen in on the building at its destruction in 1812....From its top the ocean is said to have been visible. The walls of the tower are about seven or eight feet thick.*

Bancroft's journal of the same date notes that they met the American artist Lemuel Maynard Wiles (1826-1905) who was making oil paint studies of the mission. Wiles, a plein-air artist of the time, produced some of the first fine color studies of the California mission ruins. The mission ruins of San Juan Capistrano became a focal point for many artists from the 1870's onward. They did much to publicize the mission ruins and were instrumental in calling the public's attention to the need for restoration if the California Spanish Colonial missions were to survive. An excellent survey of the part played by California impressionist painters in mission restoration is given in Stern, Miller, Hallan-Gibson, and Neuerburg (1995).

Fr. José Mut, the last resident priest, served the mission from 1866 until 1886. By that time deterioration of the buildings was almost complete. In fact the only part of the quadrangle left standing was Fr. Serra's Church. Thankfully, the chapel roof was intact, only because the building had been used for hay and lumber storage, thus insuring that the adobe walls would not return back to the land. In 1895 fate intervened in the person of Charles Fletcher Lummis and "The Landmarks Club of Southern California." Lummis, the president of the club, convinced the group to make the restoration of San Juan Capistrano their first project. The group undertook basic restoration of the mission by placing supports on the few standing walls, reroofing the corridors, the church, and a few other outbuildings, thus saving the mission from utter ruination.

The mission was "discovered" by Hollywood in March 1910 when the famous motion picture director D. W. Griffith, along with his seventeen-year-old leading lady Mary Pickford, arrived to film "Two Brothers." In 1924 the Douglas Fairbanks film "The Mark of Zorro" was also filmed at the mission. Still later, other film directors used the mission as a picturesque background.

In that same year of 1910, a priest who would eventually be the lightning rod for serious reconstruction and restoration stepped off the train at Capistrano, slowly walked to the mission, and immediately grasped the bountiful challenges that would change his life focus. His name was Father St. John O'Sullivan. He was a young priest from Louisville, Kentucky, suffering from tuberculosis, who came to California with the hope of restoring only his health. Instead, he formulated a plan for what the mission could be with determined care and attention. He began to restore the mission with his own hands. In the beginning he lived in a tent in the inner patio because the buildings were infested with vermin. He rallied the townspeople and got them intimately involved by simply informing them that the mission was their legacy, one that should be passed on and cherished. His first major concern was Fr. Serra's Church. He cut new roof beams, traded new goods for some of the original tiles, nails, and adobes that had been appropriated from the original buildings, and hired Mexican workers to build the walls and to make materials in the old ways of mission days. To fund his dreams he enlisted the help and financial aid of some of the country's more prominent citizens. Soon, with good publicity, Mission San Juan Capistrano became an alluring tourist attraction. He even commissioned the renowned sculptor Gutzon Borglum (later of Mt. Rushmore fame) to create a bronze statue of Fr. Serra holding an Indian boy. Townspeople stood as models for the statue, which was dedicated on August 13, 1914. Today the imposing image of Serra with a young Indian boy stands adjacent to the bell wall.

On Easter Sunday, April 21, 1924, Mass was said in Fr. Serra's restored church for the first time in many decades. Father O'Sullivan, later Monsignor, who since 1910 had contributed so much time and effort to the reconstruction and restoration of San Juan Capistrano also recreated the lovely mission gardens, and the cemetery where he was buried after his death in April 1933. It is indeed remarkable that Father O'Sullivan arrived at the mission a tubercular patient hoping only to restore his health. Immediately he became inspired with a much larger quest to restore the mission to its former grandeur. In the process his tubercular condition went into remission allowing him God-given time to carry out his ultimate destiny.

The original high altar of Mission San Juan Capistrano had been destroyed, but Father O'Sullivan located a baroque reredos that lay in storage in Los Angeles. The reredos, intended for the new Los Angeles cathedral, had been sent to Los Angeles in 1906 from Barcelona, Spain, and had lain in storage until Archbishop John J. Cantwell sent the three hundred years old reredos to San

Overall view of the magnificent gilded three hundred year old Spanish reredos installed in the mission church in the early 1920's; top center bulto is of San Juan Capistrano, to the right San Miguel, and to the left San Pedro, below San Pedro is San Francisco, and to the right Santa Clara.

Juan Capistrano as a gift to the mission. The reredos and altar are twenty-two feet wide by eighteen feet in height. It was installed in the Serra Church during the 1922-24 period, although assembling it proved a formidable challenge as it arrived at the mission in three hundred and ninety-six pieces packed in ten large crates! When finally assembled it was found to be too large for the designated space, and it had to be trimmed down. A clerestory window bathes it in light, and anyone who observes it through the long church nave sees a truly memorable sight.

The altar and reredos are made of cherry wood and covered with gold leaf. They are adorned with fifty-two angels' faces, one for each Sunday of the year. The primary focus of the altar and reredos is the upper center bulto of San Juan Capistrano, the mission's patron. To the left is San Pedro, and to the right San Miguel Arcángel. Below San Pedro is San Francisco de Asís, and to the right is Santa Clara.

The Stations of the Cross lining the church walls are believed to be over three hundred years old. There are also bultos of Fr. Junípero Serra, Santa Teresa de Avila, and the Infant of Prague.A shrine dedicated to St. Peregrine, patron of cancer sufferers, is a more recent addition *(color page J)*. The church was redecorated in 1973-76 and again in 1993. The Indian fresco decorations on the ceiling and walls, done when the church was restored in the early 1920s, contrast remarkably with the elaborate sophistication of the gilded reredos. One of the mission's current parishioners, Tony Salas, who is originally from

Texas, fell in love with the mission after a long army career. He found that he possessed artistic talents and has been in charge of restoring the fading decorative paintings which adorn the church walls and ceiling, greatly enhancing the effect of this remarkable church *(color page D)*.

View of the enclosed inner patio at San Juan Capistrano showing the Four Evangelists Fountain and the beautifully landscaped inner quadrangle.

The restored mission quadrangle contains a small museum, the Indian kitchens and workrooms, and the obligatory gift shop. In the center of the beautifully landscaped patio gardens is the attractive Four Evangelists Fountain. All sides of the quadrangle have the familiar corridors with original columns supporting the ceilings. On the outside of the quadrangle is the cemetery where four thousand mission Indians are buried. Father O'Sullivan is also buried here adjacent to the large memorial cross. Every year on March 19th, St. Joseph's Day, the mission grounds are crowded with tourists who have come to witness the swallow's return to San Juan Capistrano on their migration north from their winter home in South America.

Restoration and care of the mission is an ongoing endeavor, and the padres who have followed Father John O'Sullivan have been repeatedly confronted with new challenges. In 1976, Father Paul Martin was assigned to the mission, and his most ambitious project has been the construction of a new church built to resemble, in part, the original old stone church. This church is now completed and serves as the parish church.

MISSION SAN FRANCISCO DE ASÍS:

Synopsis: The sixth California mission founded under the direction of Fr. Junípero Serra; formal founding, as recognized by the Church, occurred on October 9, 1776, with Fr. Francisco Palóu (1728-1789) officiating; named for founder of Franciscan order St. Francis of Assisi, Italy; mission more affectionately known as Dolores; present building begun in 1782 and completed in 1791; mission continually plagued by diseases and runaway Indians; secularized in 1834 with an active mission life of fifty-eight years; mission property restored to Church in 1858; survived 1906 and 1989 earthquakes; restored in 1917 and 1990-1994.

Location: Mission San Francisco de Asís is located in the bustling city of San Francisco on Dolores Street, between 16th and 17th Streets, three blocks south of Market Street.

View of the distinctive facade of the mission church of San Francisco de Asis

Saint Francis was named patron of the mission by Fr. Junípero Serra. Francis was born in 1182 at Assisi in the central Italian region of Umbria. As son of a wealthy merchant he led a frivolous carefree youth and planned a career in the army. A number of personal events changed the focus of his life, and he renounced his inheritance and commenced a life of poverty. His simple life attracted many disciples, and in due course he founded the order of the Friars Minor. Members of this order took vows of poverty, chastity, and obedience, with a special enphasis on poverty. The order was soon accorded papal recognition and approval. In 1223 Francis of Assisi began the custom of the Christmas crib. He was unique in his time because of his attitude towards the appreciation of nature and of all God's creatures. In 1224 he received the stigmata, the five wounds of Christ, regarded as a special sign of divine favor. He died in 1226 and was canonized in 1228. His remains are buried in a crypt of the basilica dedicated to him in his hometown of Assisi.

In devotional art, San Francisco is shown bearded, with his head tonsured, and wearing a brown robe with a rope belt. His image generally shows the stigmata, and he usually carries a cross or crucifix; a skull may also be one of his attributes. All of the California Spanish Colonial missions had either oil paintings or bultos of San Francisco. He is often paired with Santo Domingo whom he met in Rome. A number of original bultos and oil paintings of him still survive, although examples which show him to have received the stigmata are rare in the Alta California missions. An outstanding eighteen-century Mexican oil painting of San Francisco de Asís, by an unknown artist, hangs in the church of Mission San Fernando.

Before the actual founding of Mission San Francisco de Asís, Fr. Junípero Serra, in a conversation with the Visitor General of New Spain, José de Gálvez, remarked to him that no mission to date had been named for the founder of the Franciscan order. Gálvez tauntingly replied "If San Francisco wants a mission, let him show us his port and one will be built there for him," (Hall, 1990, p. 165). Later, San Francisco Bay was discovered by Sergeant José de Ortega, while scouting ahead of Governor Gaspár de Portolá's 1769 expedition to locate Monterey Bay. Discovery of San Francisco Bay had been elusive because of its narrow entrance. It had escaped the scrutiny of the few passing ships, and no overland explorer had come upon it. Thus its "discovery" by the Portolá expedition, searching for Monterey Bay, was indeed a surprise. Following earlier explorers' accounts, the expedition had not recognized Monterey Bay and bypassed it, eventually stumbling upon the much larger San Francisco Bay. It took subsequent expeditions before the Spanish recognized the extent of this magnificent port. When the Spanish authorities recognized it for its worth, the Viceroy ordered two missions to be established there, one with a presidio to protect this strategic location. To establish a viable settlement Lt. Col. Juan Bautista de Anza, a proven pathfinder, was placed in command of a substantial overland party. De Anza gathered over two hundred potential settlers from Mexico, and with their livestock and supplies they arrived at Monterey. Taking a small party he forged ahead to San Francisco where he selected sites for both a presidio and a mission. The chosen mission site was located on the bank of an arroyo he named Dolores because it was the Lenten feast day of Our Lady of Sorrows, the Friday before Good Friday. De Anza returned to mission headquarters at Carmel, pausing en-route to select the site of the second guardian mission of the San Francisco Bay area, Santa Clara de Asís. De Anza placed Lt. José Joaquin Moraga in command of the immigrants and headed home to Mexico. Moraga organized the De Anza colonists, and when the party arrived at the designated sites, a large group established a camp at the presidio location and a smaller group moved on to the Dolores site. Fr. Francisco Palóu, Serra's trusted friend and assistant, along with Lt. Moraga and his party, said the first onsite Mass on June 29th. About six weeks later the supply packet ship San Carlos docked at the port with materials for both presidio and mission. The site of the original mission church was less than a half mile from where it is located today. The first church building was a fifty-foot-long log and adobe structure roofed with tule grass. During the period 1776-1788 four churches were built, each taken down because it had been built on good agricultural land. At this point good farmland was more important to the mission padre and his Indian converts than a church! As it was, the overall mission food supply had to be brought from mission lands nineteen miles away. In 1785, Fr. Palóu began work on the foundations for the fifth and present church, but he left for assignment in Mexico City before the church was completed. Fr. Junípero Serra visited the mission four times. Fr. Palóu's replacements, Frs. Martín de Landata (1760-1809) and Antonio Dantí (1760-?) initiated an ambitious building program, and by December 1791 the church was completed and dedicated. The typical mission quadrangle was later completed in 1798. Frs. Landata and Dantí, although excellent administrators and builders, were regarded as overly strict disciplinarians. Their actions resulted in over two hundred instances of Indian runaways. The Spanish governor, Diego de Borica, insisted the padres stop the harsh punishments inflicted on the Indians and that they improve conditions for their charges. Some changes ultimately came about, and the Indians slowly returned to the mission. Fear and hunger were not the only problems faced by the Indians. More immediate were the diseases, especially measles, that the settlers introduced. In addition the damp and rainy climate resulted in much respiratory illness amongst the mission Indians. It should be noted that the Indians of the San Francisco area were perhaps the least gifted of all the coastal natives, even though the mission system offered them food and protection from their enemies. As Christian converts they left much to be desired. At Mission Dolores, Indian desertions threatened the very existence of the mission. The mission never reached a degree of agricultural prosperity attained by other missions, and epidemics took a tremendous toll. So

On the left side wall of the mission church is this elaborate niche with a large polychromed bulto of San Francisco de Asís with the stigmata.

common was illness among the Indians that the padres established a hospital on a site north of the mission. In 1817 this would become the site of Asistencia San Rafael. Indeed, the name Dolores seemed appropriate for this sorrowful mission.

In 1826, the English navy Captain Frederick William Beechey, as part of the British polar expedition searching for the Northwest Passage, spent 52 days anchored in San Francisco Bay. Here, with permission from the presidio commandante, Ignacio Martinez, he made a detailed marine survey of San Francisco Bay. He and his crew also spent time ashore visiting the presidio and Missions San Francisco de Asís and San José. His lengthy observations, including the status of the mission Indians, is very similar to what the French explorer Count Pérouse and the English explorer George Vancouver had reported some thirty years previously. Beechey's comprehensive report on the Mexican government's lack of interest in these northernmost outposts of the Spanish empire and the rather miserable conditions of the mission Indians leaves no doubt as to his overall unfavorable personal views. A good summary and commentary on Beechey's report are given in Paddison (1999, p. 167-198).

San Francisco de Asís was one of the first missions to be secularized in 1834. In 1845, the last Mexican governor, Pío Pico, declared that all of the runaway Indians must return to the mission or it would be put up for sale. Ironically, none of the Indians returned, and even sadder, no one showed any interest in purchasing the mission property when it was put up for sale. It then remained a property of the Mexican government until 1846 when California became American. At that point a few American priests arrived at the mission and began construction of a new church adjacent to the mission, to accommodate the burgeoning San Francisco population. This was at the height of the California Gold Rush, which totally changed the face of San Francisco. The mission was also directly affected when Gold Rush squatters, accompanied by saloons and gambling halls, were located on former mission property. In due course, the rapidly expanding city practically surrounded the mission. The American traveler Henry Miller in 1856 noted,

> *The mission nearest to San Francisco is the Mission San Francisco de Asís, now called Dolores, which is connected with the above city by a wooden plank road, constructed by a company which levies toll. This road would have been almost impossible to vehicles on account of the deep sand. Of the mission buildings remain only the Church and a building connected with it built of adobe or sunburnt bricks. The building was formerly inhabited by the missionaries but is converted into public houses where the inhabitants of San Francisco are in habit of resorting, (Miller, 1997, p. 3).*

Miller's travel account also included a drawing of the mission buildings given on page 2.

The mission property was restored to the Church by President James Buchanan in 1858. In 1866 wooden clapboard siding encased the mission exterior in an attempt to preserve the adobe walls. By 1876 the city had absorbed much of the mission area, and the mission property compressed to accommodate nearby street extensions. The mission church became too small and a large Victorian style church was built adjacent to the mission to serve the growing population. It was dedicated in 1876, on the centenary of the mission's founding.

The mission church survived unscathed in the Great San Francisco Earthquake of 1906 and the resultant disastrous fire, which stopped just short of the mission. The 1876 church did not fare as well. It was ruined and had to be dismantled soon after the earthquake. A wooden church built on back of the mission served the parish until a stone mission style building was completed and dedicated on Christmas 1918. This building was remodeled in 1926 for the sesquicentennial of the mission's founding, imparting to the structure an architectural style greatly influenced by building designs used at the San Diego Exposition of 1915.

View from the San Francisco Mission garden showing the rather ornate belltowers of the adjacent massive Dolores Basilica Church.

In 1917 the mission church was carefully restored under the direction of Monsignor John Sullivan in cooperation with local historic preservation groups. The wooden clapboard siding was removed, the beams strengthened with steel, and steel trestles utilized to further support the heavy tile roof. During the period 1990-1994 the mission underwent a complete restoration to repair the damage caused by the 1989 earthquake.

Mission San Francisco de Asís is situated in the midst of one of the busiest of American cities. It is the oldest building in San Francisco and is situated in the shadow of its sister church, the adjacent massive Mission Dolores Basilica Church. The church was designated a basilica by Pope Pius XII in 1952.

Although small in comparison, the mission church presents a picture of tranquil serenity. It has maintained this facade through both peaceful and turbulent times, absorbing the shocks of epidemics and secularization, the trauma of the Gold Rush, and destructive earthquakes. The mission church and adjoining cemetery are all that remain of the original mission complex. The outside of the church has been faithfully maintained and conveys its original appearance. The adobe walls, four feet thick, are plastered white. The facade itself is quite distinctive with its short, rounded columns sitting on square pedestals decorating the entrance. There is a wooden railing right above the entranceway, and above that, in narrow rectangular niches, are the three original bells that were cast in Mexico within five years of 1791. The bells are dedicated to San Francisco, San José, and San Martín. In 1868 the American writer Bret Harte composed a poem commemorating these bells. The red tile roof has a pronounced overhang giving to the building its very different overall appearance. This distinctive mission church is one hundred and fourteen feet in

View of the striking baroque altar and reredos of the mission church of San Francisco de Asis with bulto of San Miguel Arcángel (top center); note the Indian design painted chevron decorations of the ceiling beams.

length and twenty-two feet in width. The outside of the mission church contrasts markedly with it's colorful interior. Most eye dazzling is the mission church ceiling covered with original chevron designs painted by the Indians with natural pigments. This chevron pattern, in colors of red, gray, white, and gold, on beams and ceiling, makes for an immediate spectacular overall impression. When one can begin to concentrate on the church interior, the richly gilded Baroque altar and reredos at the front of the church are truly climactical. Neuerburg (1989, p. 51) states that these fixtures were imported from Mexico in 1796. The polychrome bultos in this sumptuous reredos comprise San Miguel Arcángel (top center), to his right Santa Clara de Asís, and to his left San Joachim; (below left) Our Lady of the Immaculate Conception, and on the right side Santa Ana. On either side of the top of the reredos, stand two smaller bultos of San Francisco de Asís in different poses. The bultos probably all came from Mexico in the early nineteenth century. However some historians have expressed the opinion that the bultos were carved from California redwood. If this is indeed true, there is the possibility that they were crafted in Alta California by the Indians, padres, or artists imported from Mexico *(color page G)*.

As one walks up the aisle from the entrance, there is on the left an elaborate Baroque niche with a large bulto of San Francisco de Asís showing the stigmata. Further along, on the same side is a small arched alcove that serves as a baptistry. In the arch is a lovely colorful Indian relief painting showing a padre administering baptism to an Indian family. Before one reaches the high altar and reredos, he comes to two large altars on either side of the church. Each is very elaborate with gold gilding, Ionic columns, and three nichos with large bultos of various santos.

This elaborate side altar is on the right hand wall and contains three large polychrome bultos of San Francisco, San Antonio de Padua, and San Francisco Solano.

Most recently (May 2000) it is reported that the so-called powderpost beetle has invaded the mission church. Specifically, it has infested the bultos on both the side altars and the reredos. Scaffolding was erected and the contaminated areas fumigated.Unfortunately, the church lacks the monetary resources to pay for yet another complete restoration, since one was done only a few years ago. This is a working class parish, and with a probable cost of up to one million dollars to repair the damages, the chances of the parish itself responding to this need are indeed small.

Dominating the right sidewall of the church is a large painting on canvas stretched over a substantial wood screen. It is a frontispiece that is placed in front of the high altar on Holy Thursday. It is probably Mexican and carries a panoply of religious images combining stories from both the Old and New Testaments. This is a unique decorative item not found in any of the other Alta California missions. The interior of this mission church and its devotional art are much more sophisticated than other Alta California Spanish Colonial missions.

Adjacent to the mission church is a beautifully landscaped cemetery. Situated under a fir tree is a stone statue of an idealized Father Junípero Serra, by the blind sculptor Arthur Putnam. Burials took place from the founding days until the 1890s. Along with the remains of five thousand Mission Indians are those of Lt. José Joaquin Moraga, one of the participants at the mission founding, the first Mexican governor of Alta California, Luís Arguello, in addition to prominent San Francisco pioneers, rogues, and multinational immigrants, all of whom played an important role in the history of San Francisco. The mass grave of the mission Indians is called the Grotto of Our Lady of Lourdes Shrine.

Inside the basilica church adjacent to the mission, the stained glass window below the choir loft shows the image of San Francisco de Asís. The lower stained glass windows that light the side aisles picture all twenty-one missions and their patrons, along with two in honor of Frs. Serra and Palóu, making for a remarkable encapsulated display of the history of the California missions.

It is indeed ironic that in over two hundred years the mission neighborhood populations, that were originally Spanish/Mexican/Indian, changed to Anglo-American, then to American/multicultural immigrants, and now back to an American/Hispanic/Mexican mixed population. The mission neighborhood population has come full circle.

Stone statue sited in the mission cemetery of a somewhat idealized Father Junípero Serra, created by the blind sculptor Arthur Putnam.

PRESIDIO DE SAN FRANCISCO:

At the beginning of 1775 the Spanish Crown had decided to establish a permanent outpost by the Bay of San Francisco.It was during this time that Commander Juan Manuel Ayala of the packet ship San Carlos anchored in the bay and spent two months exploring it and mapping its configuration.In October 1775 Lieutenant Colonel Juan Bautista de Anza began his overland journey from Sonora, New Spain, to the San Francisco Peninsula.The expedition along with two hundred and fifty soldiers, colonists, and their livestock reached the provincial capital of Monterey in March 1776.De Anza then led an overland party from Monterey to San Francisco Bay to establish both a presidio and a mission.On March 28, 1776 the group erected a cross to mark the site for the presidio location and officially claimed the land for the Crown.Fray Pedro Font (1738-1781), the Franciscan diarist of the expedition left a most lucid description of the presidio location.He perceptively described the location as one "that if it could be well settled like Europe, there would not be anything more beautiful in all the world, for it has the best advantages for founding in it a most beautiful city, with all the conveniences desired, by land as well as sea, with a harbor so remarkable and so spacious."This was to be Spain's third presidio following San Diego and Monterey.Its purpose to maintain the very long frontier line for which Spain, and later Mexico, provided very limited material and financial support.

On September 17, 1776, the first presidio building was completed.This was the first structure erected in the Bay Area and predates the mission by three weeks.

The early years of the presidio were characterized by both natural disasters and administrative incompetency.The winter of 1778 was marked by heavy storms which damaged a major portion of the presidio walls and a warehouse.In 1779 a fire destroyed the hospital and the officers' quarters.By 1780 few of the original presidio buildings were standing.

As Langelier & Rosen (1992, p. 27) noted

> *With many problems, the grand vision for the Presidio of San Francisco waned as the decade of the 1780s came to an end.Its defects as a barren site with harsh climate and remote location from the rest of New Spain weighed heavily against the garrison's success....After more than a dozen years of precarious existence San Francisco Presidio stood as an impotent sign of defense rather than a bastion of empire.*

Although the presidio was indeed strategically located as a guardian of the Spanish presence in Alta California, Spanish officials did not respond to repeated requests for material and financial assistance.The Commandante in 1790, Hermengildo Sal, documented the presidio's poor construction and rundown condition.His continuous complaints for presidio reinforcement only caught the attention of Spanish authorities after foreign ships began to appear outside of San Francisco Bay.In 1792, the English explorer George Vancouver's ship "Discovery" sailed into San Francisco Bay.The presidio fired its lone cannon in salute, and sent a boat out to escort Vancouver ashore.Here he was entertained by the officers of the Presidio.His description of the decrepit conditions at the presidio gave the British valuable information concerning the very weak state of the San Francisco Bay defenses.Later, when hostility between England and Spain heightened, Commandante Sal finally received the resources he had requested for a number of years.The presidio was then renovated and additional weaponry installed.During the 1790s the Crown renewed efforts to improve conditions at the presidio, thus saving it from collapse.In 1800, the presidio maintained a complement of thirteen infantry and five gunners.The Commandante complained he did not have enough soldiers to operate the guns and simultaneously guard the Indian labor force.

Stained glass window in the Basilica Church honoring Father Junípero Serra.

During the early years of the nineteenth century all of the Alta California presidios were in very poor condition.Starr (1973, p. 5) noted that in 1816 when the San Francisco Presidio cannon was fired to welcome Spanish Governor Pable Vincente de Sola it exploded and injured two of the gunners.Shortly thereafter the presidio attempted to answer a seven gun salute offered by a French ship in San Francisco Bay, this time two cannon burst apart. In still another instance, before replying to a ship's salute, the presidio commander had to be rowed out to the ship to borrow the necessary gunpowder!

By this time Russian fur traders and American and British merchants signaled the end of the San Francisco Bay's relative geographic isolation.In 1821 Mexico declared its independence from Spain, and in April 1822 the governor and the government officials took the Oath of Allegiance to the new Mexican government.Despite this change the presidio continued to suffer from neglect.Almost complete neglect and resultant discontentment characterized the years of Mexican authority (1822-1846).

It should be noted that all of the Alta California presidios had chapels to meet the religious needs of the soldiers, settlers, and Indians.The chapel at the San Francisco Presidio appears to have been unremarkable, in no way comparable to the Monterey Presidio chapel.In fact, the English explorer Beechey in 1826 noted that the presidio chapel and the Commandante's quarters were the only buildings that were distinguished by being whitewashed.The commander's quarters were situated at one corner of the presidio quadrangle, and formed one end of a row; on the other end was located the chapel.The opposite side of the presidio was broken down and contained little more than rubbish on which animals constantly scavenged.The remaining two sides of the presidio quadrangle contained storehouses, workshops, and a jail, all of them quite wretchedly built, though with burnt brick and roofed with tiles.

In 1830, the Commandante of the San Francisco Presidio, Mariano Guadalupe Vallejo, reported on the decrepit state of the buildings and requested additional soldiers.The central government paid no attention to his request.By 1833 secularization of the mission lands had begun, and the presidio's sister installation, Mission Dolores, was amongst the first to be secularized.In 1834 heavy winter storms caused further deterioration of the presidio.At this point General Vallejo recommended to the government that what could be salvaged from the presidio should be sold to provide back pay for the remaining presidio soldiers.In 1835, the presidio was no longer a fortified garrison, and although all but deserted it operated in name only as a so-called military post.

In 1841, the Frenchman Duflot de Mofras reported that the presidio had fallen into decay, was entirely dismantled, and was inhabited by one officer and five soldiers with their families.Alta California during the years of Mexican rule reflected the serious political instability that characterized Mexico itself.On July 9, 1846, the U. S. Army took possession and the Stars and Stripes flew over the remnants of the presidio.From 1846-1906 the presidio was turned into a U. S. Army Post.

In the Great 1906 San Francisco Earthquake the army post suffered relatively little damage, since it was anchored in stable bedrock.However, two of the three remaining original presidio buildings were too damaged to repair, leaving only the officers' quarters as the only standing adobe from the Spanish/Mexican period.On September 30, 1994, the U. S. Army Presidio Garrison was deactivated after 218 years as a military installation.Shortly thereafter the presidio became a part of the U. S. National Park System.

Detail of the church facade at Mission Santa Clara de Asís showing stuccoed architectural decorations and bulto of the mission patroness in the center.

MISSION SANTA CLARA DE ASÍS:

Synopsis: Eight mission; founded on January 12, 1777, by Frs. José Murguía (1715-1784) and Tomás de la Peña (1743-1806) under the direction of Father Junípero Serra; named for Santa Clara de Asís, a thirteenth century Italian nun who founded the order of the Poor Clares; early churches: 1777, 1779, 1781, 1784, and 1822; earthquake damage between 1812-1822; secularization in 1836, after an active mission life of fifty-nine years; remodeled in 1839, 1841, 1855, 1860, 1885; turned over to the Jesuits in 1851 to establish a school, which in time became the University of Santa Clara; fires: 1909, 1913, and 1926 when church was destroyed; rebuilt and restored in 1928 and into the 1930's.

Location: The mission church of Santa Clara de Asís is located on the campus of Santa Clara University, 500 El Camino Real, in the city of Santa Clara.

Santa Clara de Asís (St. Claire of Assisi) had been chosen as the patron of the eighth California mission by Viceroy Antonio Bucareli. She was born in Assisi in the Umbrian region of central Italy in 1194 of noble parents. From early childhood she showed a pious inclination, and later she refused to marry a wealthy suitor chosen by her father. A Lenten sermon given by Francis in 1212 so impressed her that she left home and took the Franciscan habit from Francis at the

Porciuncula. Francis placed her in a Benedictine convent, but later she founded her own order the Poor Clares, closely modeled on the order Francis established. She insisted on absolute poverty, and as a cloistered order, her nuns were dependent on the charity of the mendicant Franciscan Fathers. In 1215 she moved to the convent of San Damiano where she served as the abbess for forty years. The order flourished and other convents were established. Her prayers helped liberate the city of Assisi from the Muslims in 1240. She died in 1253 and was canonized in 1255. She was buried in a church built for her in Assisi, where her remains were discovered and identified only in 1850.

In devotional art she is generally shown in a brown Franciscan habit with a shoulder length black veil. In early portrayals she carries a scepter-like cross, a lily, or a book. Later representations show her with a monstrance and the staff of an abbess. Mission Santa Clara de Asís originally had a number of representations of her, oil paintings and bultos, but most have not survived, especially since the fire of 1926. The Mission Santa Bárbara Church has a large painting of three Franciscan women saints, with Santa Clara in the center.

A view from the south looking at serene tranquil setting within the mission grounds of Santa Clara de Asis.

The site for Mission Santa Clara de Asís was originally chosen by Juan Bautista de Anza on his return from San Francisco enroute to Mission Carmel in 1776. This site is forty-five miles southeast of Mission Dolores, close to a stream de Anza named Rio de Nuestra Señora de Guadalupe. Although Father Junípero Serra was not actually present at the mission founding, he directed Frs. José Murguía and Tomás de la Peña to establish a mission in the fertile lowlands of the River of Our Lady of Guadalupe. The padres constructed an enramada and on January 12, 1777 officiated at the founding services. Fr. Serra visited this first mission structure two times during 1777. In January 1779 the mission church was moved one-half mile south to higher ground to avoid flooding. Serra visited this site four times. On October 24, 1781 he blessed the cornerstone for a new more permanent adobe church that was to be built on the third site,a mile south of the second site. On May 15, 1784, Serra returned to dedicate the church. The dedication ceremony was for him a mixture of joy and sadness, because Fr. Murguía its principal builder had died suddenly on May 14th. He had been a close friend and colleague of Father Serra when years before both had toiled in the Sierra Gorda region of Mexico. Serra officiated at the dedication on May 15-16 and departed on May 24th. This was one of Serra's final acts before he died in August. This church was utilized until damages sustained in the 1812 earthquake forced abandonment of the site and relocation a short distance to the southwest where the present mission church stands. The original founding cross, blessed by Serra on November 19, 1781 was also moved, and years later a portion of the cross was encased in a protective redwood sheath and sited in front of the present church. The church cornerstone was also blessed on that date, as is recorded in the mission's "Libro

Detail of the carved bulto of Santa Clara de Asis sited along a side wall of the mission church.

Standing in front of the mission church at Santa Clara de Asís is a portion of the original founding cross that was blessed by Father Junípero Serra; carved into the crossbar is a passage from Matthew XXIV, 13: "He that shall persevere to the end shall be saved."

de Bautismos." The cornerstone was accidentally unearthed on June 8, 1911, by a workman digging for a gas main. In a cavity in the cornerstone a crucifix, religious medals, and several coins of the period were discovered. The cornerstone and its enclosed artifacts is on display in the de Saisset Museum on the campus of the University of Santa Clara (Morgado, 1991).

The original mission had been in existence for less than six months when Lt. José Joaquin Moraga arrived with a group of de Anza colonists who had been waiting at Mission San Gabriel. Moraga had been ordered to establish a new pueblo close to the mission, and this he accomplished without delay. Moraga's pueblo is now known as the city of San José. The padres were not too happy about the pueblo's close proximity, knowing the negative effect it would have on their efforts to Christianize the Indians, and they expected what would be a long series of disputes over land boundaries. As it turned out it was not until 1801 that an official survey was made and the boundaries between pueblo and mission fixed.

Two padres of outstanding ability and stature served the early Santa Clara Mission. Father Magín de Catalá (1761-1830) who arrived at the mission in 1794, was a sincere and pious missionary much loved and respected by the Indians. In latter life he suffered much from severe rheumatism. Legend has it that they called him "The Prophet" because of his ability to foretell future events. He and Fr. José Viader (1765-?), who arrived shortly after Catalá, were to be colleagues for thirty-three years. By contrast, Fr. Viader was a large man of great physical strength, with a warm heart to match. They were a fine working team and through their dedicated efforts the mission prospered. After only three years the mission had its largest wheat crop, the leading staple crop at Santa Clara through the years. As the mission continued to prosper there was however an uneasy relationship with the nearby pueblo of San José. Fr. Catalá partially remedied the situation by joining the two communities with a four-mile Alameda. Hundreds of Indians planted rows of black willow trees that acted as a border on the two-way road, that offered easy access to and from the mission.

The old adobe church had been so weakened by sporadic earthquakes from 1812 to 1822 that it was no longer safe, so a new church building was begun on the present site. This church was to be one hundred feet in length, forty-four feet in width, and twenty-five feet high. The adobe walls were four feet thick at the base, narrowing to two feet at the roofline. There was an attached adobe campanario. The forty-foot long ceiling beams, mainly of redwood, came from the Santa Cruz Mountains fifteen miles away. The church interior was painted with bright colors and designs by the Indians, who utilized natural pigments which served as a binder mixed with the juice of the maguey cactus. Later, around 1835, a Mexican artist, Agustin Davila, was imported to paint the sanctuary ceiling. He created a wonderful scene of heavenly beauty above the altar.

In 1830 Fr. Catalá passed to his reward after serving Santa Clara Mission for thirty-three years. Fr. Viader was forced to leave the mission in 1833 when Mexico became independent of Spain and ruled that all Spanish priests were to be replaced with Mexican priests.

Mission Santa Clara was one of the last missions to be secularized in 1836. The Mexican priests stood by helplessly as Mexican politicos trafficked in mission properties, often illegally. This left the Indians with two choices: leaving the mission and going back to their native state or becoming indentured peons to new masters. Since no money to run the mission was forthcoming from the Mexican government, it was only a matter of time before the buildings began to fall into decline. In 1839 heavy rains weakened the campanario which was replaced with a wooden one. After the American occupation of 1846 the mission properties were partly returned to the Church. In 1850, California became a state. That same year Jesuit priests arrived to take over jurisdiction of the mission. Father John Nobili was placed in charge of the mission and immediately began work to establish a Jesuit school on the mission site. He first had to move out the squatters who occupied the crumbling buildings. Then he had to retrieve the land around the mission that had been appropriated, sometimes illegally, by Mexican politicos and settlers. When this was accomplished he still had to repair the buildings so they could serve as classrooms. Somehow, with God's help, he succeeded in a space of only four years. The school eventually grew into Santa Clara University.

View of the restored neoclassical reredos at the mission church of Santa Clara de Asís with polychrome bulto of San Miguel (top center), below which is one of the patroness Santa Clara, and on the left Our Lady of the Immaculate Conception, and San José on the right.

In the 1860s the mission church was restored. The church was encased in redwood siding to protect the adobe walls. A second campanario was built on the right side, to match the other campanario. This addition altered the overall mission appearance. Due primarily to the fact that it now served as a college campus, the mission buildings were kept in repair. Undoubtedly this factor prevented Mission Santa Clara from sinking into ruin and decay, as did so many of the other Alta California missions during this time period. In the early twentieth century fire was the mission's greatest enemy. Two fires in 1909 did

Detail of the bulto of San Juan Bautista in a niche on the mission church facade of Santa Clara de Asis.

some damage to the church, but the great fire of 1926 destroyed most of the mission church. The fire broke out in the church campanario. Of the four bells, two of which were given to the mission by King Carlos IV of Spain in 1777, one bell was melted down and another cracked. One of the original bells survived and now hangs in the restored campanario. A replacement bell was sent by King Alphonse XIII of Spain in 1929 and also hangs in the campanario.

The 1822 church had a red tile roof; the tiles were removed in 1862 when the roof began to sag and leak water. At that point a wood shingled roof was put on and the old red tiles put into storage. When the church was rebuilt in 1928, after the disastrous 1926 fire, about twelve thousand of the original red roof tiles were put back on the church. Rebuilding and restoration of the mission church began in 1928 and continued into the 1930s.

The present facade of Mission Santa Clara Church is of stucco over concrete. In the past various designs and pictures of santos in nichos were painted on the 1822 church façade, probably by the Mexican artist Agustin Davila around 1835. A likeness of this early church facade was done as an oil painting by the contemporary artist Roger Arno and used as the cover illustration of Norman Neuerburg's 1989 book *The Decoration of the California Missions.*

After restoration, the present church facade consists of rather neo-classical false pillars (pilasters) and niches with bultos. In the center, above the entranceway, stands the bulto of the mission's patroness, Santa Clara de Asís. To the left is a bulto of San Juan Bautista, and to the right is San Francisco de Asís. Boulé (1988, p. 11) states that the bultos came from Germany in 1931 and are carved from pear wood. Above Santa Clara is an empty niche capped by a triangle with radiating rays symbolizing the Holy Trinity, and within, the all-seeing Eye of God.

The interior of the mission church is spacious and is decorated in a late Victorian style, not in the old mission style one might have expected. Many of the mission's original treasures were destroyed in the 1926 fire, but what few artifacts were salvaged have been put to good use. Each of the church sidewalls has three inset altars. The first side altar, to the right as you enter the church, is the original Baptistry in which over a thousand Indians were baptized. The side altar closest to the sanctuary is small, but hanging above it is the salvaged bulto of Christ crucified said to be over two hundred years old. This bulto was a particular favorite of the early mission padre Father Catalá, and he is buried at the feet of this life-size bulto. Beyond this is a rather imposing richly ornamented pulpit.

On the left sidewall of the church and close to the sanctuary stands a small attractive and very popular side altar dedicated to La Virgen de Guadalupe. On the wall above the altar is a large ornately framed painting of the Virgin of

Guadalupe, above which is a smaller ornately framed depiction of Our Lady of Refuge, held by two gilded angels. Sitting on opposite sides of the altar are two small bultos of San Joachim and Santa Ana.

Behind a railing is the high altar and reredos, both of which are reproductions of the originals created under the guidance of California mission restorer Harry Downie during the 1930s. The reredos is done in the neoclassical style with a polychrome bulto of San Miguel Arcángel (top center). Below Miguel, in the center, is a large bulto of Santa Clara de Asís, patroness of the mission. On the left is a smaller bulto of Our Lady of the Immaculate Conception, and on the right one of San José. On the wall on either side of the reredos are more recently painted religious murals. The sanctuary ceiling has painted on it a faithful reproduction of the original ceiling painting done by the Mexican artist Davila around 1835, which was destroyed in the 1926 fire. It depicts a scene of the heavenly court complete with angels, clouds, and the Holy Trinity *(color page I)*.

The lawns, arbors, and gardens that surround the back and sides of Mission Santa Clara de Asís are beautifully landscaped, imparting much tranquility and serenity to the overall mission complex, where there is not a gift shop in sight! There is an enclosed Mission Rose Garden, on the right side of the church, which was a cemetery for the early mission from 1820-1846.

View of a side wall chapel in the mission church of Santa Clara dedicated to the Virgin of Guadalupe.

This is the first Alta California mission to honor a woman saint. Although located on a busy college campus it retains all the qualities of a peaceful oasis in the midst of a modern American city. Fr. Catalá's four mile Alameda continues to instill hope and encouragement to the travelers and pilgrims that make the journey from city to mission.

CHAPTER FIVE

THE SANTA BÁRBARA CHANNEL MISSIONS:

SAN BUENAVENTURA 1782, SANTA BÁRBARA 1786, AND LA PURISIMA CONCEPCIÓN 1787

View of Mission San Buenaventura, the ninth California mission and the last founded by Father Junípero Serra on March 30, 1782.

MISSION SAN BUENAVENTURA:

Synopsis: Ninth mission; founded by Fr. Junípero Serra on March 31, 1782 (his last mission); named after San Buenaventura, a thirteenth century Italian Franciscan cardinal and renowned philosopher and theologian; first church destroyed by fire in 1791; present church begun in 1792 and completed in 1809; earthquake damage in 1812 and 1857; secularized in 1834 after an active mission life of fifty-two years; mission rented out in 1845 and sold illegally in 1846; restored to the Church in 1862; church "modernized" in 1893; restorations: 1956-1957, 1976.

Location: The mission of San Buenaventura is located on Main Street in the city of Ventura, east off of U. S. Highway 101.

Inspector-General Don José de Gálvez had selected San Buenaventura as the patron of the ninth Alta California mission. San Buenaventura had originally been designated as the patron for the third mission, but founding was delayed due to disputes with the military.

Buenaventura was born Giovanni de Fidanza in the village of Bagnorea near Viterbo, north of Rome, Italy in 1221. Legend has it that the name Buenaventura was given to him when he was four years old, after he was healed of an illness by Francis who exclaimed "0! Buona Ventura!" (Good fortune). As a young man he exhibited scholarly learning and eventually took his degree at the Sorbonne in Paris, at the same time as the Dominican Thomas of Aquinas. Buenaventura entered the Franciscan order in 1238 and later was elected

Detail of the bulto of San Buenaventura; altar and reredos were bought from New Spain (Mexico) in 1809.

minister general of the order. He did much to reform the Franciscan order. In 1265 he refused the archbishopric of York and instead became Cardinal Bishop of Albano in 1273 so that he might aid Pope Gregory X in organizing a council for the reunion of the Eastern and Western churches. He was effective in reconciling many of the inherent differences but died in 1274 before the council disbanded. He was noted as an outstanding philosopher and theologian, one of the finest minds of his century, and he was a prolific writer. He was buried in Lyons, France, site of the council, but his remains were desecrated by the Huguenots sometime later. He was canonized in 1482 and declared a Doctor of the Church by Pope Sixtus V in 1588.

In devotional art, he is generally shown wearing the Franciscan habit, sometimes with a surplice and a cardinal's cloak. He can be bareheaded or wearing a bishop's mitre, a cardinal's hat, or the biretta of a Doctor of Philosophy. He frequently appears with a book and a pen and occasionally holds a model of a church.

Mission San Buenaventura contains two bultos of its patron, one of which still sits in the church reredos, and an oil painting of him by the eighteenth century Mexican artist José de Páez, which is now in the mission museum. This painting was one of a few rolled-up canvases Fr. Serra found in Monterey aboard the supply packet ship San Antonio in 1770. Additional bultos of him are present at missions Carmel, San Antonio, San Gabriel, and San José. Others, now lost, were at La Purisima and San Luís Rey. An additional eighteenth century Mexican oil painting of him is presently at Mission San Miguel.

On Easter Sunday morning March 31, 1782, Fr. Junípero Serra raised the Cross at "la playa de la canal de Santa Bárbara" (the beach of the Santa Bárbara Channel). Assisted by Fr. Pedro Benito Cambón (1738-?), Serra celebrated a High Mass, preached a fervent sermon on the Resurrection, and dedicated the mission to San Buenaventura. Founding of this mission had been postponed for a number of years for one reason or another, generally because of troubles at other missions, which tended to require the services of the military, in addition to ongoing friction between Serra and the military governor. The mission was sited near a large Chumash Indian village, which Fr. Juan Crespí, an associate of Fr. Serra, named "La Asuncion de Nuestra Señora." The Chumash Indians were friendly, receptive to Christianity, industrious, artistic, and were noted for their well-crafted large canoes and beautiful basketry. The first mission church burned down in 1791, and the present church was begun in 1792. Additions to the outbuildings eventually formed a quadrangle enclosing a plaza. The church was situated on the southwest corner of the quadrangle, and a cemetery on the west side of the church is now the site of an elementary school. 01d photographs show that the mission quadrangle was still intact as late as 1875.

The church was completed and dedicated on September 9, 1809. Hand-hewn pine and oak ceiling vigas came from the mountain range north of the mission and were carried to the site by the Indians. Unfortunately, the mission church was only in use for three years before it was brought down in the Great Earthquake of 1812. The damage was severe, but repairs were completed within a year, including reinforcement of the church with the addition of huge buttresses. The campanario had also collapsed in the earthquake, and the mission complex was uninhabited for three months when padres and Indians moved into the hills. This was perhaps the only time the mission was without people.

View from the mission courtyard, with flowing fountain, looking towards the side entrance of the church; note the Moorish-style decorations over doorway.

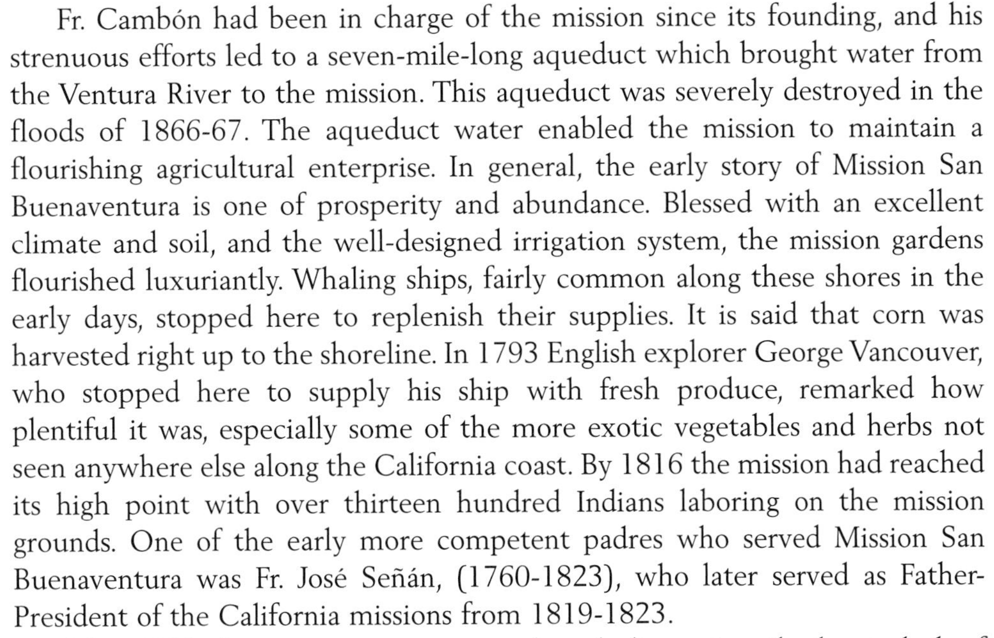

Fr. Cambón had been in charge of the mission since its founding, and his strenuous efforts led to a seven-mile-long aqueduct which brought water from the Ventura River to the mission. This aqueduct was severely destroyed in the floods of 1866-67. The aqueduct water enabled the mission to maintain a flourishing agricultural enterprise. In general, the early story of Mission San Buenaventura is one of prosperity and abundance. Blessed with an excellent climate and soil, and the well-designed irrigation system, the mission gardens flourished luxuriantly. Whaling ships, fairly common along these shores in the early days, stopped here to replenish their supplies. It is said that corn was harvested right up to the shoreline. In 1793 English explorer George Vancouver, who stopped here to supply his ship with fresh produce, remarked how plentiful it was, especially some of the more exotic vegetables and herbs not seen anywhere else along the California coast. By 1816 the mission had reached its high point with over thirteen hundred Indians laboring on the mission grounds. One of the early more competent padres who served Mission San Buenaventura was Fr. José Señán, (1760-1823), who later served as Father-President of the California missions from 1819-1823.

After 1820 the mission went into a slow decline primarily due to lack of support from the Mexican government. The mission was forced to both feed and supply the settlers and the military, an undesirable situation at best. Finally, in 1834 the Laws of Secularization divested the padres of any administrative control over the mission lands. Initially, it was a relatively easy transition due to the administrative efforts of the first secular administrator, Rafael Gonzáles, whose honesty and efficiently were traits not commonly seen during the secularization of the missions. In 1845 the mission was rented out to Don José Arnaz and Narciso Botello and illegally sold by the last Mexican Governor Pío Pico, who kept the money for his own use. After California became a state in 1851, Bishop Joseph Sadoc Alemany petitioned the U. S. Government to return the mission lands. This request was granted in a proclamation signed by President Abraham Lincoln on May 23, 1862.

On July 8, 1856, the American traveler Henry Miller arrived at the

Side altar in the mission church of San Buenaventura dedicated to Christ's Crucifixion; bulto of Cristo Crucificado is over four hundred years old, other bultos include San Antonio de Padua, Nuestra Senora de la Soledad , and San Blas.

mission and stated,

> *I arrived at last without accident at a spot where I left the sea beach, striking into a fine green country, being well watered, where I saw in the distance the belfry of the San Buenaventura Mission....I resolved to pass the night here.... I left in the morning, pursuing my road towards the mission....and where I arrived after crossing the San Buenaventura River. I found it to be quite a village of about seventy or eighty houses, inhabited principally by natives and Mexicans. The church is in tolerable good preservation, in which a French priest officiates. The mission orchard is still in fine condition, planted with several hundred large pear trees, loaded with fruit. Parts of the mission lands are claimed by some wealthy rancheros....After breakfast I took a sketch of the mission (Miller, 1997, p.40-42).*

In 1857 an earthquake destroyed the original tile roof and some of the mission outbuildings. When the debris had been cleared away the church was re-roofed with shingles. During March 6-8, 1874, the mission was visited by H. L. Oak with the California historian H. H. Bancroft. Oak (1981) reported that on March 7th.

> *In the morning after an hour spent in an examination of the mission, we had an interview with Sr. José de Arnaz, a Spaniard who came here in 1841....The mission buildings were in good condition when Sr. Arnaz came, and only began to be neglected after the padres lost their power. For a time Sr. Arnaz rented the mission property at $1200 per year....directing the Indians in their work and paying them in food and clothing as the padres had been accustomed to do....In November 24, 1845, Governor Pío Pico sold the mission at public auction for $7000....The mission buildings are in comparatively good condition, both church and most of the court buildings being still occupied, although the former has had a new shingled roof and some other repairs (Oak, 1981, p. 57-62).*

Oak included a sketch of the mission and a plan view of the mission complex.

The greatest danger to befall the mission during this time was the assignment of Fr. Cyprian Rubio. In the parlance of the day he was a "modernizer." When Fr. Rubio was in charge of the mission (1878-1895), the city of Ventura experienced a railroad boom and he undertook to "modernize" the old mission to match the spirit of the times. He undertook to modernize the church interior, and when he was finished there was nothing left from the old mission church period. He covered both the floor and ceiling with wood paneling, and he tore out a hand-carved pulpit hanging on the sidewall. He lengthened the widows to give more light, then proceeded to fill them with dark stained glass. He covered the original Indian decorations with mediocre modern decorations. All in all he thoroughly "Victorianized" the church interior. Fr. Rubio was also involved in the "modernization" of Missions San Luís Obispo and San Juan Bautista.

Side altar in the mission church of San Buenaventura dedicated to Nuestra Señora de Guadalupe; bultos include San Dominic, Santa Gertrudis, San Isidro, and San José.

Sometime later, the west sacristy was removed to provide for an elementary school, which was not built until 1921. During the pastorate of Fr. Patrick Grogan the roof of the church was again tiled and the present rectory and convent built. A major restoration of the mission took place in 1956-57, under the supervision of Fr. Aubrey J. O'Reilly. At this time the windows were reconstructed to their original size and the ceiling and floor uncovered. A parishioner commissioned a bell with an automatic angelus device and donated it to the mission. It presently hangs in the campanario above the four older hand operated bells. The entire church roof was replaced in 1976, and in December the church was solemnly consecrated by Timothy Cardinal Manning. In 1982 the Mission commemorated its bicentennial.

Mission San Buenaventura is located on Main Street in downtown Ventura. The city has surrounded the Mission with a plaza, fountains, and well-kept lawns, all of this done to help the mission complex blend into the city itself. Even though the mission is in the center of a modern city it is still a delightful and tranquil setting for traveler and pilgrim.

The mission church is large and built of adobe and stone with walls up to six feet thick. The church exterior is painted a light cream color with a maroon-colored trim outlining the eaves and campanario and a triangular gable above the entranceway. This perhaps symbolizes the Holy Trinity. At the apex of the triangle is a nicho with a bulto of San Buenaventura. In the middle of the gable is a clerestory window. The double front doors are carved with the "River of Life" design motif common in many California missions. The east wall of the church has a Moorish-style doorway. The attached three-tiered campanario is on the right side of the church and contains five bells. On the upper level is the most recent bell cast in Paris in 1956. Four older bells hang below it. Two date from 1781, one from 1815, and the fourth from 1825.

In the mission church proper, original hand carved vigas hold up the restored heavy tile roof. Four wooden chandeliers made by Harry Downie, the renowned restorer of California missions, hang from the ceiling. He also hand-crafted the front and side doors as true copies of the originals.

As one enters the church, the small Father Junípero Serra baptismal chapel stands on the left side. A hand-hammered copper bowl from early mission days serves as the font even today. On both sidewalls hang the fourteen Stations of the Cross from 1809. There are two side altars: on the left is the Shrine of the Crucifixion, which contains a four-hundred-year-old bulto of Cristo Crucificado; on the right side is the Shrine of Nuestra Señora de Guadalupe. Beyond those are the high altar and its reredos, both of which came to the mission from Mexico when the church was dedicated in 1809. They are carved of wood and done in a neoclassical style. The reredos has four fluted Corinthian columns faux painted to resemble marble. It is capped by a gable with a painting of the Holy Spirit. In the large center nicho is a bulto of the mission patron San Buenaventura. Two ornate niches on either side contains smaller bultos of Our Lady of the Immaculate Conception (left side), and San José (right side).

The church floor has been restored to the original tile laid by the mission Indians, where three early mission padres are buried beneath the floor and close to the altar. East of the church is a meticulously landscaped garden, in the center of which is a 1976 Mexican tile fountain. The original garden fountain built by the Indians was decorated with a sculptured bear's head (Boulé, 1988, p. 12). The rectory is across the back of the garden, and on the east side is an excellent museum built in 1929. The original church doors are displayed in the museum, as are two wooden "bells". The wooden "bells" are carved out of two-foot blocks of wood and were used during Holy Week when the metal bells are silent. The garden also has a stone grotto called Our Lady of the Apocalypse Shrine.

Unlike some California Spanish Colonial missions, which had to be rebuilt and restored from ruins, San Buenaventura only had to have the so called modernizing additions removed in order for the viewer and pilgrim to enjoy the original beauty of this early mission church.

MISSION SANTA BÁRBARA, VIRGEN Y MARTIR:

Synopsis: Tenth mission; founded on December 4, 1786, by Fr. Fermín Francisco Lasuén, his first mission after succeeding Father Junípero Serra as Father-President of the Alta California missions; named after Santa Bárbara a legendary martyred church figure; early churches: 1787, 1789, 1793; present church begun in 1815 and completed in 1820; earthquake damage: 1812, 1857, 1925; secularized in 1834 with an active mission life of forty-eight years; restored to Church in 1865; restorations: 1832, 1925-27, 1950-53.

Location: The mission is located in the city of Santa Barbara off of U. S. Highway 101, at the end of Laguna Street.

Santa Bárbara was chosen as the patroness of the tenth Alta California missions by the Viceroy of New Spain, Martín de Mayorga on December 7, 1780. The saint's name had been given to the channel by the Carmelite friars

Front view of Mission Santa Bárbara, the tenth Alta California Mission founded in 1786 by Fr. Fermín Francisco Lasuén, and the only mission with two belltowers.

who accompanied the explorer Vizcaíno in 1602. Later this name was extended to the presidio, mission, city, and county. According to tradition, Bárbara was the daughter of the pagan Dioscorus in Nicomedia, during the time of the Roman Emperor Maximinus (235-238 A.D.). Her father kept her shut up in a tower until she would agree to marry the suitor he chose. Instead, she secretly converted to Christianity and refused her father's suitor. While her father was away on a voyage he left instructions for a bath structure to be built and attached to the tower. During the building she had three openings installed in the tower symbolizing the Holy Trinity. Upon her father's return he discovered her conversion and decided to execute her himself. After carrying out the execution he was struck dead by lightning. The earliest version of this legend dates from the tenth century, although Bárbara's popularity dates from the seventh century. She was very popular during the Middle Ages and became the patron saint of fireworks makers, architects, stone masons, gravediggers, and artillerymen. She was also the protectoress from lightning, fire, sudden death, and impenitence. After the Second Vatican Council she was removed from the Calendar of Saints because her existence was considered highly dubious.

In devotional art she is generally portrayed holding the palm of martyrdom; she often wears a skirt with three tiers, and a tower with three windows stands in the background. She often wears the crown of a princess; she may also carry a monstrance. The Royal Presidio Chapel of Santa Bárbara had a bulto of her and had requested an oil painting. The oil painting, which now hangs in the

A decorated nicho in the Santa Bárbara Mission church with a statue of Saint Anthony.

restored presidio chapel, is attributed to the Mexican artist José de Alcibar and is dated 1785. The bulto of Santa Bárbara on the mission reredos came from Mexico in 1793, but its silver monstrance came from Mexico after 1834. A stone sculpture modeled on this bulto was carved by a Chumash Indian and placed in a nicho in the gable of the church facade in 1820.

After the founding of Mission San Buenaventura, Governor Felipe de Neve, along with Father Junípero Serra, Captain José Francisco Ortega, fifty soldiers and their families, and a few Indians, marched to Santa Bárbara to found the presidio. During a week's stay at Santa Bárbara, Governor Neve chose the presidio site. Father Serra officiated at the dedication ceremonies on April 21, 1782, of California's third military installation. He sang a Low Mass ending with an alabado rather than a High Mass with a "Te Deum" because he was the only priest present. The chapel was founded on the edge of a grove of oaks apart from the beach and the Indian village, not very far from the lagoon. When the religious ceremonies were concluded Governor Neve planted the Spanish royal standard alongside the founding Holy Cross. Father Serra was under the impression he was founding presidio-mission Santa Bárbara, but Governor Neve was opposed to any mission expansion at this time because he felt it gave too much economic power to the padres. He was thus able to block further mission expansion while he was in office. The Santa Bárbara Mission enterprise was delayed until after Fr. Serra's death, and moved to a different site. Serra visited the presidio chapel three times before his death in August of 1784. Governor Neve was succeeded by Pedro Fages in 1783, and during the summer of the following year he notified Serra that he could officially establish Mission Santa Bárbara. Serra's death intervened and it fell to his successor, Fr. Fermín Francisco Lasuén, to found Mission Santa Bárbara. He raised the Cross, blessed it, and dedicated the mission on December 4, 1786. Governor Fages was not present at the dedication ceremony, so another ceremony took place with the governor in attendance on December 16, 1786, when Lasuén said Mass and preached a sermon. The new Father-President of the missions appointed Frs. Antonio Paterna (1721-1793), and Cristóbal Oramas (Ca. 1759-?) as the mission's padres. The former an experienced missionary and a colleague of Father Serra. Oramas was a newly arrived priest from San Fernando College in Mexico City.

The Mission chapel during this early period was a simple enramada. A series of chapels followed, each grander than its predecessor. The first church, begun after the spring rains of 1787, was forty-four feet in length by fourteen feet in width. Shortly thereafter accessory buildings were added including a kitchen, granary, and housing for the padres and Indians, in addition to the sacristy, and the roof was covered with tiles. In 1789, construction began on a new adobe church with tile roof. When completed it measured one hundred and eight feet in length by seventeen feet in width. This church had the first true altar and tabernacle made of wood. In 1790 Governor Fages requested from Mexico a cadre of masons, artisans, and teachers to aid the padres in building permanent structures. In 1793 a third adobe church was begun. This was more elaborate, with six side chapels, and was completed in 1794 under the supervision of Fr. Estevan Tapis (Ca. 1756-1825). This structure was one hundred and twenty-four feet in length and twenty-five feet in width, with an adjoining sacristy twenty-six feet by fourteen feet. The church was dedicated on March 19, 1794. Continued construction on mission outbuildings formed a completed quadrangle by 1795, then somewhat later a second quadrangle, adjoining the first, was begun. On December 21, 1812 a disastrous, widespread earthquake damaged the mission extensively and the padres decided the church had to be completely rebuilt. They petitioned the government for permission to build a new church, and approval came through in 1815. Construction on the new church began almost immediately, but it was not completed until 1820. This church measured one hundred and sixty-one feet in length and twenty-seven feet in width, with a height of forty-two feet. A single three-tiered campanario—echoing Santa Barbara's skirt— rose to a height of eighty-seven feet; a second campanario was added during the period 1831-33. Father Antonio Ripoll(1785-?), with the assistance of master stonemason José Antonio Ramirez supervised construction of this church. Frs. Ripoll and Francisco Suñer (1764-1831) completed the church and dedicated it on September 10, 1820. The building is of dressed stone and mortar. The walls of solid sandstone are almost six feet thick and are strengthened by stone buttresses. The oldest tower (campanario) is the south tower, nearest the monastery. The massive buttress south of the tower was probably constructed after the earthquake of 1857. The second tower was erected in 1831 but collapsed shortly after because of faulty construction. The fallen tower was rebuilt in 1832 and blessed on January 15, 1833. The square towers hold six bells, which came from Peru and Mexico. The domed towers are surmounted by a smaller replicated tier with dome and a crowning cross. An unusual feature are the chamfered corners on the first two tiers of the towers, which reflect the light like the facets of cut crystal. The classical detail of the church facade was taken from the mission library copy of *The Six Books of Architecture* by the architect Vitruvius Polion, of the Roman Augustan period. This book was a standard architectural reference for centuries, and Fr. Ripoll used a drawing of a Greco-Roman temple as the model for Mission Santa Bárbara's facade. The facade is ornamented by six slender engaged columns with Greek Ionic capitals. In the center niche of the triangular pediment surmounting the columns is a stone sculpture of Santa Bárbara which was carved from native stone and was originally painted. The apex and angles of the pediment were also adorned with painted sculptures representing Faith,

Chumash Indian carved sandstone sculpture of "Charity" (50 inches tall) that originally stood on the pediment of the mission facade, but was toppled in the 1925 earthquake and is now in the mission museum.

Hope, and Charity. A stepped pediment of stone surmounted with a cross rises above and behind the facade gable.

A well-engineered irrigation system, including reservoir and dam, was built in 1807. The lovely Moorish-style fountain and adjoining lavanderia in front of the mission was built in 1808. The mission's front arcade of round Roman arches was finished in 1811. Originally it consisted of sixteen arches but was later expanded to eighteen arches.

The principal economic enterprises at Mission Santa Bárbara were agriculture and stock raising, and the main crops were wheat, corn, barley, beans, and chick peas. Grain production peaked in 1821 when almost 13,000 bushels were produced. Mission livestock herds reached their peak in 1814 when they comprised 17,000 animals. The largest number of Indians living and laboring at the mission occurred in 1803 when there were close to eighteen hundred. It has been estimated that the padres taught the mission Indians some fifty different trades.

In the spring of 1824 a Chumash Indian uprising against the increasing violence of the soldiers occurred at Missions Santa Inés, Purisima, and Santa Bárbara and spread to other missions. At Santa Bárbara, the uprising took place on February 22nd, when the Chumash Indians broke into the armory and overcame the mission guard; in the ensuing struggle two soldiers were wounded. Spanish reprisals were severe, so much so that those Indians not immediately caught fled the area. The Indians stayed away from Santa Bárbara for six months until the Father-President, Fr. Vicente Francisco Sarría (1767-1835), obtained for them a general pardon.

By the mid-1820s it was becoming increasingly clear that the mission system was breaking down. In part European diseases made the death rate in the Indian population exceed the birth rate. In fact, by 1828 all of the indigenous Indian villages in the Santa Barbara area ceased to exist. Most importantly, the mission system itself was doomed by the spectre of secularization, which was fueled by the republican ideals of an independent Mexico, in addition to the desires of the settlers to encroach on mission lands, in part encouraged by the military and enterprising but rather fraudulent land speculators.

In 1826, Governor José Maria de Echeandia took it upon himself to issue an edict requiring partial secularization of the missions and the so-called emancipation of the Indians. In the same year the Mexican Exclusion Act came into being. This law expelled or banished all Spaniards from Alta California, including most of the missionaries serving there. Both laws were not only impractical they were unenforceable and inoperative considering the overall situation in Alta California. By 1833-34 the Mexican government passed secularization legislation that made compliance mandatory within four months.

The current governor, José Figueroa, had no choice but to enforce the law. Within the next two years secular lay administrators were appointed to oversee the temporal affairs of the missions. The majority of those "administrators" were politicos, and incompetence and greed ruled the day. By 1843, a succeeding governor, Manuel Micheltorena, restored the missions to the padres. However by that time much of the mission's wealth and properties had disappeared. In 1845, Governor Pío Pico, the last Mexican governor authorized the missions to be either sold at public auctions or put up for rental. Mission Santa Bárbara was leased to the highest bidder that year, and it came into the possession of Nicholas A. Den and Daniel Hill. For almost nine years they paid whatever debts the mission had accrued plus a yearly rent of $1200.00. They also agreed to provide for the padres and for the mission church to continue religious services.

Arched colonnade corridor along the front of Mission Santa Bárbara.

One of the outstanding padres at Mission Santa Bárbara during those tumultuous times was Fr. Narciso Durán (1776-1846). In 1833, as then Father-President of the California missions, he transferred his headquarters from Mission San José to Santa Bárbara. In so doing, he brought all the documents relating to the founding and establishment of the mission chain, thus insuring that Mission Santa Bárbara became an official repository for California mission documents. This status continues today, and as a result Santa Bárbara has become one of the state's best archival repositories. Fr. Durán was also the friar at Santa Bárbara most gifted in music. In a ten-year period he formed and trained an accomplished band of Indian musicians, who were a great asset during church services and celebrations.

California's first Catholic bishop, Fr. Francisco Garcia, was also in residence at Mission Santa Bárbara from 1841 to 1846. He opened the first theological seminary at Mission Santa Inés in 1844 and planned other learning institutions for Santa Bárbara. Those plans were frustrated when Mexican President Santa Anna confiscated the Pious Fund on which the Alta California missions were greatly dependent. The presence of both Fr. Durán and Bishop Garcia simultaneously at Mission Santa Bárbara probably saved the mission from expropriation. However, both these resolute persons died within a month of one another in 1846. As a result of their efforts Santa Bárbara became the only California mission that has been in the continuous care of the Franciscans since its founding.

At this time a few of the Santa Bárbara padres chose to establish an Apostolic College as a missionary center for California. The school was not to be at the mission, but in quarters in the pueblo of Santa Bárbara. The college, Our Lady of Sorrows, opened on July 23, 1854, and accepted its first novices. The new bishop of Monterey, Tadeo Amat, chose Mission Santa Bárbara as his headquarters. He subsequently asked the college Franciscans to return to the mission, and they did so in 1856. Here they continued their Apostolic College activities until 1885. However the institution did not prosper, primarily due to

View of the Moorish-style fountain in front of Mission Santa Bárbara dating from 1808; note the Roman arch corridor of the monasterey in the background.

a lack of candidates and insufficient resources. During the period 1868-77 the Franciscans operated a boys' school at the mission (high school and junior college), but it also failed to mature as a permanent institution.

Necessary funds for mission repairs and upkeep were a continual problem at this time. From 1871 to 1874, Fr. José María Romo successfully labored to keep the mission properties in good repair and the institution functioning. Unfortunately, the impoverished mission did not fare very well in educational endeavors, and at the time serious thought was given to disbanding. In the end it was decided to join with another American Franciscan province in order to give new life and purpose to the mission. After consultations with Rome, is was decided to make the mission a house of the nearest Franciscan province, which was in St. Louis, Missouri, so in 1885 the Mission became part of the province of the Sacred Heart. New friars were sent to Mission Santa Bárbara and activity expanded until 1896 when the Franciscan houses were joined into a western division of the eastern province. In 1915 the western Franciscans became an independent province, and a year later Santa Bárbara's Province was installed at Mission Santa Bárbara.

In an earlier educational venture, Fr. Peter Wallischeck came to Mission Santa Bárbara in 1896 to found a Junior Franciscan Seminary. Beginning in September 1896 and continuing until 1901. At that time a new seminary, St. Anthony's, was completed; it is still functioning today in a modified form.

On the morning of June 29, 1925, an earthquake shook the Santa Barbara area, and the mission was not spared. The most severe damage occurred in the two bell towers and the church facade. One of the bell towers was toppled and the church facade was so weakened that it had to be pulled down and restored. Father Augustine Hobrecht, mission superior, was in charge of the restoration. The entire front of the mission church was reconstructed as it was before, and both the walls and roof further strengthened. The church interior was also redone including a new reredos, new altars, and an interior painting that adhered to the old painted church decorations. The financial cost ran close to $400,000, half of which was raised through public subscription. On December 3, 1927, Los Angeles Bishop John J. Cantwell solemnly consecrated the newly restored church. Then, some twenty-three years after the restoration, it was found that the bell towers and the church facade would again have to be torn down and rebuilt with even sturdier materials. Apparently a chemical reaction between various materials and the cement caused fissures and cracks to appear throughout the facade, making the building unsafe. The facade was dismantled in 1950 and was completely restored by August 1953 at a cost of over $300,000. As a result of this latest restoration, the mission church facade and bell towers are more strongly tied in with steel reinforced foundations. Payment of more than half of this financial burden was a gift from the Fleischmann

Foundation. The newly rebuilt facade was dedicated on December 4, 1953, by James Francis Cardinal McIntyre.

In 1956 the building of two quadrangles was initiated, one to replace the quadrangle of mission days and the new area to serve as the quarters for the theological seminary. Father Noel Moholy directed the construction, and the addition was dedicated on April 21, 1958. The entire construction costs were paid for by the Max Fleischmann Foundation. The newest addition to Mission Santa Barbara is the archival library, completed in 1969, which preserves and protects the mission's vast archival resources.

Mission Santa Bárbara has a unique, diverse, and compelling collection of devotional art, a portion of which is well displayed in the mission museum. Most of the sculptures and paintings in the mission collections have been meticulously described and documented by Baer (1955).

A unique sculptural piece of devotional art in Mission Santa Bárbara is the "Crucifixion Group" (36 inches high x 60 inches wide) showing the crucified Christ with the two Marys and Saint John.

As one enters the mission church, his or her eyes are quickly drawn to the altar and reredos at the front of the church. The original 1806 reredos was very distinctive in that it was a painted canvas which served as the altar backdrop. This was brought from Mexico, and since 1806 has been restored several times, most recently during the 1925-27 restoration. The painting style is neoclassical and is dominated by four columns with Ionic capitals that are faux-painted to resemble marble *(color page Q)*. As it presently appears, the prominent center position is occupied by a life-size polychrome wooden crucifix of Mexican origin, probably dating from the eighteenth century. This is set against the reredos background of gilded radiating rays of light. Directly below this is a life-size bulto of the mission patroness Santa Bárbara *(color page F)*. This piece is described on a Mexican invoice dated February 1793, and is one of the oldest pieces belonging to the mission. To the left of the patroness is a bulto of Our Lady of the Immaculate Conception (48 inches tall), and to the right is San José (also 48 inches tall). Both bultos were brought to the church by Fr. Estevan Tapis from Mexico in 1795. Immediately below the Immaculate Conception is a smaller bulto of San Francisco (30 inches tall). Baer (1955, p. 65-66) says, "It is one of the finest and most sensitively beautiful figures in any of the missions. The almost classical simplicity, suggests a possible late seventeenth century Spanish or Mexican origin." On the lower right-hand corner of the reredos is a charming bulto of Santo Domingo (30 inches tall) which was sent from Mexico in 1806.

The fourteen Stations of the Cross are painted in oil on canvas, each measuring 15 1/4" H X 24 1/2" W. They were sent to the mission from Mexico as a group in 1797.

Of the many oil paintings in the mission collections, two are of particular note. They are the largest canvases in any of the Alta California missions. One is "Assumption and Coronation of the Virgin," (168" high by 103" wide). Baer (1955, p.77) states, "This is a good example of the religious painting of the

Altar of the baptistry chapel at Mission Santa Bárbara, on which is placed the first mission tabernacle (1789) of which the decorative designs are the instruments of Christ's passion.

eighteenth century in Mexico. It is quite possibly a work from the Mexican studio of Miguel Cabrera (1695-1768). It was brought to the mission in 1798." The other painting, "The Crucifixion" (168" high by 126" wide) is probably of the same age but is not attributed to a particular artist.

At the rear of the Church, on the right side, is a small elaborately decorated baptistry chapel that houses the first mission altar and tabernacle (40" high by 42" wide). This is of particular interest since the carving and decoration of the tabernacle is the work of a Chumash Indian and presents a rather naive interpretation of church symbols.

Towards the front of the Church, on the right side, is the exit to the mission cemetery. On the wall that faces the burial ground, and above the Moorish-looking archway, is a carved stone skull and crossbones; below it, two human skulls and thigh bones are embedded in the masonry. The cemetery contains the remains of some four thousand mission Indians and some of Santa Barbara's pioneers.

Although Mission Santa Barbara has undergone rebuilding and restoration, it stands today as "Queen of the Missions," serene in a natural setting of an amphitheater bounded by an attractive coastline and the Santa Ynéz Mountains. The mission never suffered the destruction that occurred at other California missions after secularization because the Franciscan fathers guided it peacefully from a mission for the Indians to a parish church that now serves as a spiritual refuge for a multicultural urban population. It is the only California Spanish Colonial Mission that has remained continually under the aegis of the Franciscans from its founding to the present day.

EL PRESIDIO CHAPEL OF SANTA BÁRBARA:

View of the presently reconstructed and restored presidio compound with mission chapel in the center; to the left of the chapel were the padre's quarters, which now serves as a small museum.

Synopsis: Founded on April 21, 1782, four years prior to the founding of Mission Santa Bárbara, as the last in a chain of four presidios along the Alta California coast; site blessed by Father Junípero Serra on St. Joseph's Day 1782; visited by English explorer Captain George Vancouver in 1793; damaged by earthquakes: 1806, 1812, 1925; in ruins by the 1840's; town street cut through original site of presidio in the 1850's; restoration of area by City of Santa Bárbara initiated in 1960: formation in 1963 of the Santa Bárbara Trust for Historic Preservation with restoration of presidio compound as the primary objective; Trust presently operates restored presidio compound under an agreement with the California Department of Parks and Recreation; presidio chapel rededicated December 12, 1985.

Location: The presidio compound, including the chapel, is located in the City of Santa Bárbara at 123 East Cañon Perdido Street.

Santa Bárbara began as a military garrison in 1782. The last of the four royal presidios to be built in Alta California by Spain. Earlier presidios were built at San Diego, Monterey, and Yerba Buena (San Francisco).

In 1782, the governor of the province, Felipe de Neve, gave orders for the establishment of the last presidio along the Santa Bárbara Channel coast. In mid-April of 1782, Governor Neve and the Father-President of the Alta California missions, Fr. Junípero Serra, left the newly established mission of San Buenaventura and journeyed to a previously chosen site at a large Chumash Indian village called Siujtu. Here the governor and his entourage explored the area and decided on the location for the presidio within view of the ocean. They pitched camp and gathered timber, both for the large Cross that would be erected, and for the enramada in which the founding ceremony would take place. On the following day, April 21, 1782, the third Sunday after Easter, Fr. Serra blessed the site of the future presidio and set up and venerated the Cross. He then celebrated Holy Mass, which was attended by the governor, soldiers, and a group of Chumash Indians. Upon completion of the religious ceremonies, Governor Neve planted the Spanish royal standard alongside the Cross, thus officially founding the Presidio of Santa Bárbara, Virgin and Martyr. Since he was the only priest, Serra conducted a Low Mass, and instead of the customary "Te Deum Laudamus," he chanted an alabado.

During the following days trees were cut down to build the presidio chapel, padre's quarters, soldiers' barracks, and storehouses. Erection of a stout wooden stockade a thousand feet square was erected under the supervision of Lt. José Francisco de Ortega, the discoverer of San Francisco Bay, who now became the first Commandante of Santa Bárbara Presidio.

It had been Fr. Serra's intention to establish Mission Santa Bárbara as soon as workmen had completed the presidio. However, he was overruled by the governor, who declared a mission must wait until a permanent stone presidio had been completed. Fr. Serra, cognizant of the governor's authority, returned to Mission Carmel, where he died before Mission Santa Bárbara became a reality.

Lt. Ortega, after two years as Commandante, was assigned elsewhere and his successor was Lt. Felipe de Goycoechea. He undertook the task of erecting permanent adobe, stone, and tile-roofed buildings. Wooden beams for the construction were shipped in from Monterey, and twelve Mission San Gabriel Indians were imported in May of 1786 to manufacture both the adobe bricks and the roof tiles.

On the Feast Day of Our Lady of Guadalupe, December 12, 1797, the presidio chapel was blessed. Its dimensions were listed as fifty-four feet in length by eighteen feet in width. The presidio chapel was a place of worship for presidial families until July 1854, when the College of Our Lady of Sorrows was established.

View of the painted wall decorations adjacent to the side doorway of the chapel; note holy water stoup utilizing an abalone shell as the water receptacle.

Inside the presidio walls was a Plaza del Armas, or parade ground, three hundred and thirty feet square. The chapel occupied the center of the north wall. Thirty-six leather-jacket soldiers (so called because they wore leather jackets made of seven layers of deerskin that could stop an arrow), and nine Indians comprised the garrison roster. Interestingly, many of their surnames are still found in the Santa Bárbara city directory and telephone book, as descendants of the original Spanish and/or Indian presidio soldiers.

In the beginning the garrison population, which included wives and children, numbered about one hundred and fifty individuals. However, as each soldier retired he built an adobe home on donated land close to the presidio walls. These homes became the nucleus of the present city of Santa Bárbara.

The December 12, 1812, earthquake badly damaged the presidio and practically destroyed the mission. Unlike the mission, which was restored over time, the presidio was never completely restored, and had fallen into ruins when the Americans occupied the town in 1846.

In 1911, a Buddhist Church was built on the original presidio chapel site, but was razed in 1967. At that time excavations under the old dirt floor of the chapel uncovered skeletons in brick-lined vaults, probably the remains of the early settlers.

In 1960, the City of Santa Bárbara recognized the importance of preserving its Spanish colonial heritage. They created the El Pueblo Viejo Historic District, with the presidio at the center. Identified historic buildings in the area were protected by city ordinance, and new building construction in the district had to conform to the old Hispanic tradition. By 1963, the non-profit Santa Bárbara Trust for Historic Preservation was formed with restoration of the presidio as its primary goal. The Trust acquired an old historic adobe known as El Cuartel, restored it, and donated it to the State. Several other properties were also acquired, including the Canedo adobe home, and the area of the original site of the presidio chapel. Archaeological excavations were initiated within the presidio compound in the mid-1960s, and much has been accomplished since then.

The recreation of the late 18th century Spanish Royal Presidio Chapel began in 1980 and took five years to complete. It was rededicated on December 12, 1985, one hundred and eighty-eight years to the day from when the chapel was blessed for sacred services on the feast day of Our Lady of Guadalupe.

A watercolor painted by the American artist James Madison Alden in 1855 provided the basis for the exterior design of the chapel, while archaeological studies provided the foundation dimensions. An inventory of 1850 furnished information as to the chapel furnishings, but there are no known descriptions of the interior decorations. The late Dr. Norman Neuerburg, renowned art historian and California mission restorer, did much research on this aspect of the chapel reconstruction and restoration. He was able to apply his extensive knowledge and expertise of Alta California Spanish colonial buildings to this endeavor. In addition, as an artist himself, he was able to supervise and participate in the actual artistic design and embellishment of the chapel interior.

Today, as the visitor enters the restored chapel he or she is immediately impressed with the colorfully painted interior. The red dado along the bottom of the wall is a reproduction of one found in the Monterey Presidio Chapel. The floral/geometric design above it represents a cloth valance design found in the same chapel. The painted masonry design around the chapel side door was suggested by painted decorations around a doorway at Mission Purisima Concepción in San Antonio, Texas.

Interior view af the recreated Santa Bárbara Presidio chapel showing richly decorated walls, beamed ceiling, altar and painted reredos.

A carved altar railing, faux-painted to resemble marble, separates the sanctuary from the nave. The chapel altar and painted reredos is neoclassical in design. It is distinguished by four arched nichos carved into the wall. The central nicho is framed by an antique gilded wooden carving that once belonged to the De la Guerra family of Santa Bárbara. A 17th century Spanish polychrome bulto of the Madonna and Child occupies this prominent space. To the left of the Madonna is an 18th century bulto of St. Francis, and in the nicho on the right side is a 19th century bulto of St. Anthony. Directly above the central nicho on the bottom row is a nicho with an 18th century bulto of the Virgin Mary. On either side are two empty nichos *(color page R)*.

On each side of the altar and reredos, the wall is painted with designs that rise above a real and faux-painted doorway. Above these, painted draperies frame spaces for a pair of oval mirrors similar to those given to the chapel by English explorer Captain George Vancouver in 1793.

The sidewalls of the sanctuary area are painted with rich, colorful renderings of silk brocades of the type that covered church walls during special festivals. The painted vine design on the ceiling vigas comes from two Arizona missions, San Javier del Bac and Tumacacori, while the acanthus design painted on the corbels is derived from a design in the mission church of San Juan Capistrano. The velvet altar frontal is Spanish and dates from 1578. The fourteen Stations of the Cross line the sidewalls of the chapel and are copies of Spanish engravings. Interspersed with those are various 18th century religious oil paintings. Exceptional amongst those is a painting of San Juan Bautista, circa 1740, by Fr. Miguel de Herrera.

In the center of a courtyard adjacent to the presidio chapel is a bronze sculpture mounted on a stone pedestal of Spain's King Carlos. This gift to the city of Santa Bárbara from it's sister city in Spain had previously had been sited at another location in downtown Santa Bárbara.

Future plans call for additional reconstruction of buildings of the original presidio compound, and those buildings will house museum exhibits portraying life as it was during the Spanish colonial period. The park also has a successful living-history program which recreates the traditional Hispanic Christmas Shepherd's Play (Una Pastorela) and also celebrates the birthday of Santa Bárbara with a fiesta in April. Other living-history events are also on the park agenda.

Overall view at Mission La Purisima showing the colonade workshop bulding and detached padre residence or monasterey building.

MISSION LA PURISIMA CONCEPCIÓN DE MARÍA SANTISIMA:

Synopsis: Eleventh mission; founded on December 8, 1787 by Father Fermín Francisco Lasuén; named for the Immaculate Conception of the Most Holy Mary; churches: 1788, 1803, 1818; earthquake in 1812; fires: 1818; Indian uprising in 1824; secularized in 1834 after an active mission life of forty-seven years; sold in 1845; smallpox epidemics: 1844, 1853; partial return of mission lands to Church in 1874; property acquired by Santa Bárbara County in 1933-34; restoration by Federal Government (C.C.C.), State and local agencies 1934-1941; restored mission complex dedicated December 7, 1941.

Distinctive attached campanario at Mission Purisima as viewed from behind the Campo Santo wall and showing the church roofline.

Location: Mission Purisima is located four miles northeast of the city of Lompoc and fourteen miles west of Buellton, via State Highway 246.

The Virgin Mary under the appellation of La Purisima de María Santisima was chosen as the patroness of the eleventh California Spanish Colonial mission.

The Immaculate Conception signifies that Mary was conceived without the blemish of original sin, since she was destined to give earthly birth to the second person of the Holy Trinity in the form of Jesus. A pious legend of the Middle Ages contended that Mary was conceived when Joachim met his wife Ana at the Jerusalem Golden Gate and planted a kiss on her cheek, but this pleasant fantasy has never been countenanced by the Church. A strong theological argument for the Immaculate Conception was sought for centuries, and support was especially strong in Spain among the Franciscans, Mary under the title of Immaculate Conception was chosen as their special patroness, and she held that position in the California missions. The dogma of the Immaculate Conception was officially proclaimed by Pope Pius IX in 1854.

An iconographic representation of the Immaculate Conception does not seem to have been established until sometime during the sixteenth century. Prior to that the embrace of Joachim and Ana stood as the symbol for it. The iconographic type reached its fullest development in Spain, when Juan de Juanes's paintings from 1578 were displayed in the Jesuit church in Valencia. Her pose, standing with hands in prayer, generally dressed in white with a blue cloak, with the crescent moon at her feet became the standard iconography.

Because of her stature as the patroness of California the Immaculate Conception, whether bulto, painting, or print, would have been found in each of the Alta California missions. A number of outstanding bultos have survived in the missions, most often on the church reredos, such as found today at Missions San Luís Rey, San Juan Capistrano, San Gabriel, San Buenaventura, Santa Bárbara, Purisima, San Luís Obispo, San Carlos Borromeo, and San Francisco.

December 8, 1787, was chosen for the mission dedication, since it was the feast day of the Immaculate Conception. On that day at a site close to the base of the eastern hills of the Lompoc Valley, Fr. Lasuén performed the customary religious rites in the presence of California Governor Pedro Fages and others. Father Lasuén blessed a cross, planted it in the ground, and venerated it, then he said Holy Mass and preached a sermon, and finally the founding party recited the Litany of the Saints. On the following day Lasuén again said Mass, and returned to Mission Santa Bárbara in the company of the governor. Father Lasuén returned to the founding site the following April with the necessary supplies to establish the mission. Lasuén was accompanied by the two padres he had assigned to Purisima: Frs. Vicente Fuster (1742-1800) and Francisco José de Arroíta (1762?-1821). Fr. Fuster, originally from Aragon, Spain, had been Fr. Luís Jayme's companion at the time he was martyred at Mission San Diego in

View of the mission church altar at La Purisima showing the decorative painted wall, and three nichos cut into the wall, the center arched nicho with a large polychrome bulto of Our Lady of the Immaculate Conception, and in the smaller nicho on the left a bulto of San José, and on the right a bulto of San Antonio de Padua.

1775. He was serving at Mission San Juan Capistrano when assigned to Purisima. Fr. Arroíta was a native of Cantabria, Spain, who had been assigned to California in 1786. His first post was Mission San Luís Obispo, then in the spring of 1787 he received his appointment to Purisima. Accompanying the establishing party was a squad of soldiers and servants under the command of Sergeant Pablo Antonio Cota.

Since the indigenous Chumash Indians were friendly and amenable to Christian conversion, they readily helped with the mission construction. Purisima got off to a good beginning, and the padres performed their tasks with ability and zeal. The first crude buildings were probably enramadas, which as time progressed were replaced with adobe and stone buildings. In September Sergeant Cora was replaced by José M. Ortega, and by the end of the year fifteen soldiers were present at the mission, all detached from the Santa Bárbara Presidio. Fr. Fuster was relieved of pastoral duties in the summer of 1789 and replaced by Fr. Cristóbal 0ramas (Ca. 1754-?), then serving at Mission Santa Bárbara. He served at Purisima for three years and in 1792 retired to Mission San Gabriel. A year later, because of failing health, he returned to the College of San Fernando in Mexico City.

During 1790-91, Father-President Lasuén made three visits to Purisima, and during the next few years a number of outbuildings were added to the mission establishment. Mission Purisima had established a very good agricultural base and by 1799 attained its largest harvest and numbers of livestock. Mission Purisima was noted for its exceptional cattle and sheep. With a large supply of wool on hand the mission hired weaver Antonio Enriquez to teach the Indians the craft of weaving. By this time plans had been formulated for a new church at Purisima; the foundations were already laid by 1798, and by February 1803 this new church was completed.

The year 1804 was a landmark in the history of Purisima as late in the year Fr. Mariano Payeras (1769-1823), was assigned to the mission. He replaced Fr. José Antonio Calzada (1760-1814), who had succeeded Fr. Oramas in 1792 and who had long been in failing health. Mariano Payeras, like Father Junípero Serra, was a native of Mallorca, born on that Mediterranean Island in 1769. He received the Franciscan habit in 1784. He later volunteered for missionary work in the New World and in January of 1793 left for New Spain. He entered the College of San Fernando in Mexico City and remained there until 1796, when he was called to Alta California, arriving in Monterey in June. He served for a short time at Mission Carmel under the guidance of Fr. Lasuén and then was assigned to Mission Soledad, where he remained until 1803. He was then moved to San Diego and at the age thirty-four was assigned to La Purisima.

Carved and decorated pulpit with sounding board along the right side wall of the mission church of La Purisima; note painted wall dado topped by a linear strip of stenciled designs.

By the end of 1804 Mission Purisima had over fifteen hundred Indians in residence. As an agricultural enterprise it was fast becoming an outstanding venture. In his journal the very perceptive Payeras expressed concern over the four to one ratio of deaths to births, and the appalling number of Indian stillborn infants. However, this situation seemed never to be resolved. During his early days at Purisima, Fr. Payeras translated prayers, catechisms, and other religious items into the Chumash language, but unfortunately those have not survived.

Further building projects continued at Purisima, and by 1810 the monastery building had been renovated, including a tile roof. Payeras supervised the building of a well-designed aqueduct system for the mission. During this period master stonemason José Antonio Ramirez was hired to oversee and help in the construction work. In the same year two roads were opened in the mountains to improve communications between Purisima and Missions Santa Inés and San Luís Obispo. The year 1812 gave promise of success until the Great Earthquake of December occurred. Slight earth shocks were felt on December eight, but little damage was done. Then on the morning of the twenty-first came shocks so violent that it was difficult to stand erect. For ten days the ground trembled, and when the quake was over Purisima was a heap of ruins, luckily no one was killed. To make matters worse, torrential rains followed and converted the adobe ruins into a sea of mud.

With characteristic zeal and energy Fr. Payeras undertook reconstruction, but at a different location three miles northeast of the original mission site in the Valley of Los Berros (watercress). In March 1813, Payeras formally petitioned the government to relocate at Los Berros. By the end of the month

Governor José Joaquin Arrillaga granted permission, and by the end of April Purisima was officially established there.

In nine months' time the Mission Indians had erected temporary structures and made a start on a new aqueduct system. A temporary church was constructed of poles plastered with adobe. Payeras contracted skilled artisans to direct and oversee the new construction. In October 1814, stonemason Ignacio Yguera was contracted to help in the overall construction and to devote his knowledge to building the mission church.

By the middle of 1815 much had been accomplished, including construction of a monastery building with a high central wall that divided it into two rows of rooms. Those provided rooms for the resident padres, servants, and guests, and spaces for workshops and a chapel. A covered corridor with colonnades ran along the front of the building. In 1816 a separate building for workshops, and soldiers quarters was constructed.

In the interim Fr. Mariano Payeras was named Father-President of the California missions on July 24, 1815. He held this office for four years and conducted mission business from Purisima. Building activities continued into 1817 with the foundation of a new church laid, and an improved water system with fountains and a lavanderia. Great progress was made at Purisima during the period 1817-1819, and the mission was once again a flourishing establishment.

With his tenure as Father-President of the mission completed, Payeras was chosen as Commisary Prefect in October of 1819. At the time, this was the highest office to be had amongst the California Franciscans.

The years 1820-1822 were busy years for Fr. Mariano Payeras. By late October 1820 he had visited Missions San Carlos, San Juan Bautista, Santa Cruz, San Francisco, San José, and San Rafael. In April of 1821 he was at Mission Soledad. By this time Fr. Payeras was in failing health, and although a sick man he continued to persevere in his work to benefit the missions and the Indians. In the spring of 1822 he was in the provincial capital of Monterey to take the Oath of Allegiance to the government of an independent Mexico. The new Mexican government, and the previous Spanish government, had never relaxed their vigil as to Russian incursions into northern California. At this time the Mexican government sent an imperial commissioner, Fr. Agustin Fernandez, to Monterey so that he might scrutinize the Russian site at Ft. Ross. Since Payeras was available it was decided he would accompany Fernandez to the Russian enclave, and they left on October 11th. The journey was a success and tensions were somewhat relaxed in regards this Russian incursion. In fact, Payeras even established tentative trading agreements with the Russians. Payeras's report of this journey is one of the best descriptions we have of Fort Ross and its operations.

In poor health for some time, and refusing to curtail his labors, Mariano Payeras soon fell victim to exhaustion. On April 28, 1823, he died at Purisima at age fifty-three. The next day he was buried under the church pulpit. His death marked the end of the relatively good days at Purisima, and the mission went into a long period of decline.

The year 1823 saw the last of construction at Mission Purisima, although in 1821 a campo santo had been joined to the church along with a distinctive campanario.

Mission Purisima now came under the administration of Frs. Antonio Rodriguez (1777-1824), and Blas Ordaz (1792-1850), and it was they who would preside over the final days of Purisima. In February of 1824 the mission experienced an Indian uprising. The revolt had been plotted by Chumash Indians at Santa Inés and Purisima, but before it was put down it had spread to other missions. The Indians wanted to free themselves from what they viewed as intolerable oppression. On February 21st the Indians revolted at Purisima. During the ensuing evening conflict one Indian was wounded, but four travelers were murdered as they approached the mission, unaware of the uprising. Next day the padres buried the murdered travelers, and fighting continued. The Indians gained complete control of the mission for almost a month before the governor was able to relieve the embattled mission. He raised a force of about a hundred men, mainly from the northern settlements, under the command of Lieutenant José María Estrada. Estrada's report of March 19, 1824, noted that one militiaman was killed and three wounded. Of the Indians, sixteen were killed and a considerable number wounded. Captain José de La Guerra arrived from the Santa Bárbara Presidio and took measures to punish the Indians. Seven Indians adjudged guilty of murdering the travelers were executed on March 26, 1824, and the Indian ringleaders sentenced to terms in the presidio jail. The remainder of 1824 was uneventful.

In December of that year Fr. Marcos Antonio de Vitoria (1760-1836) became Fr. Rodriguez's colleague. The death rate at Purisima compared to baptisms was still four to one. That year also brought a marked decline in harvests and livestock. Purisima as a viable mission was definitely in decline, and like other missions it witnessed an overall decimation of the Indian population. By the end of the decade Fr. Vitoria complained that he was unable to perform the necessary religious exercises because he was alone and had to devote most of his time and energy to caring for the sick.

The final blow to Purisima came in the early 1830's when the laws of secularization were issued. With the arrival of Governor José M. Echeandia, mission confiscatory decrees were issued on January 6, 1831. There was opposition to the decrees, and it was not until 1833 that a new governor, José Figueroa, actually contemplated secularization. On August 9, 1834, he

A carved wood confessional in the mission church of Purisima; priest sat in the enclosure to hear confessions of penitents who kneeled on either side and spoke through grilles.

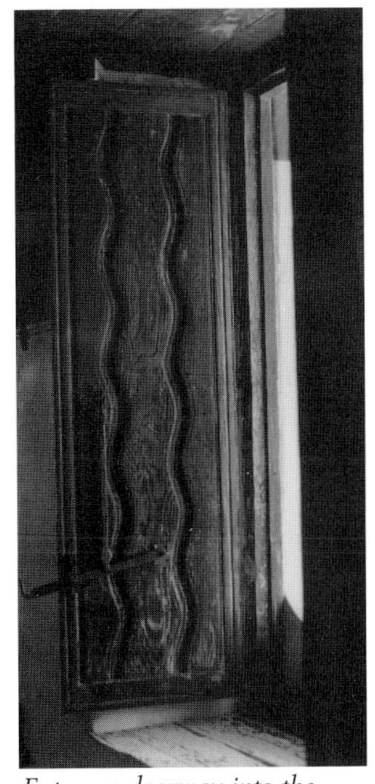

Entrance doorway into the padre's chapel in the monasterey building at Mission Purisima; note hand carved "River of Life" motif on door.

Nicho in the padre's chapel at Mission Purisima with a bulto of San Roque.

Detail of the bulto of San José in a nicho in the padre's chapel.

communicated authorization decrees to the padres, and on November 4, 1834, he published the final legislation. Thereafter secular commissioners were appointed to take over the missions. On November 30, 1834, Domingo Carrillo was appointed commissioner of Purisima. Mission days were over. When Fr. Marcos Vitoria officially delivered up Purisima on March 1, 1835, its assets were evaluated at $62,000. The following ten years saw the complete disappearance of Purisima as a mission establishment, with the resident missionaries retiring to Mission Santa Inés and the last religious service held in July 1836. Through a succession of administrators mission assets continued to disappear, and by February 1841 most of the mission properties had been disposed of. A proclamation by Governor Manuel Micheltorena restored the mission to the Church, but by this time Purisima was well beyond material benefit. In 1845, Governor Pío Pico, the last Mexican governor, authorized the mission to be sold, and in October the mission was put up for sale. On December 4, 1845, John Temple of Los Angeles purchased it for $1110.00. After the United States acquired California the Church began to press claims for the return of mission lands. It was not until January 24, 1874, that President Ulysses Grant deeded the mission to the Church. Little of the original Purisima lands were recovered. Much of those mission lands had been acquired by enterprising citizens, and they were able to retain their land titles. The land that was restored to the church consisted of a mere fourteen acres. On January 22, 1883, Bishop Francis Mora sold those holdings to Eduardo de la Cuesta. Later, Union Oil Company of California came in possession of the land and eventually returned it to the Church.

One by one, Purisima's buildings were reduced to ruins until by 1933 the monastery building was an unroofed heap of earthen rubble and the church a ruin marked by only stubs of its walls to indicate the building outline. Efforts had been made in 1905 to restore the monastery building, and local people had succeeded in interesting the Landmarks Club of California in preserving it. However the plan came to naught, and each year more of the adobe returned to the earth. Santa Bárbara County acquired five hundred acres of mission lands in 1933-34, and at that point much of it passed into public ownership. It was then offered to the depression era Civilian Conservation Corps as a restoration project. Santa Bárbara County and the State of California purchased an additional forty acres of the original mission site. Still later four hundred and seventy acres were added as a private gift. In 1935 the property was vested in the state and designated La Purisima State Historical Monument, to be administered by the Department of Natural Resources, Division of State Parks. For this grand project the Federal Government in cooperation with County and State agencies through the National Park Service and the Department of Interior, was able to furnish funds, professional advice,

Padre's chapel in the monasterey building at Mission Purisima with altar and nichos carved into the wall with polychrome bultos (left to right) San José, Our Lady of the Immaculate Conception, and San Antonio de Padua.

and labor. This consortium was thus able to supervise development and restoration of Purisima. It is presently a historical state park that encompasses over 1900 acres.

Site reconnaissance and excavation began in November 1934, and the land transfer that was completed in 1935 allowed archaeological investigation of the monastery. By the spring of 1937 restoration of this building was completed and plans for restoration of the entire mission establishment were put into effect. The restored monastery building is three hundred and eighteen feet in length, including the buttresses. The adobe walls are four and a half feet thick, and the building is fifty feet in width. In contrast, the restored church is one hundred and forty feet in length and twenty-five feet in width.

Of the five mission bells at Purisima noted in the inventory of 1835, one was taken to the first Catholic Church in Lompoc about 1875, but disappeared sometime in the early 1920's. It is possible that two of the other bells were taken to Mission Santa Inés. One original bell hangs in Purisima's campanario and is inscribed "Manuel Vargas Me Fecit, Ano de 1818, Mission de La Purisima De Le Nuebe California"; this bell was cast in Lima. Morever, an 1817 Vargas bell hanging in the church at Guadalupe is also undoubtedly from Purisima.

Mission La Purisima Concepción is the only California mission laid out in a single line instead of an enclosed quadrangle. As one walks along the dirt path, a portion of the original Camino Real, leading to the mission, the landscaped setting is as it was in mission days with fenced fields and grazing animals. The visitor immediately notes the distinctive color of the walls of the enclosed cemetery and campanario. This earth tone ocher color was attained by tinting the whitewash with iron oxide. The cemetery has a large wooden cross a memorial to the Indians buried there but is totally devoid of any landscape amenities. The campanario, architecturally distinctive with its platform and tiled roof, is modeled after the campanario at Mission Santa Inés. Attached to the bell wall is the whitewashed and brown-bordered church building. Entrance to the church is through a side door carved with the "River of Life" motif. As in its early days, there are no church pews for the mission Indians sat or knelt on the tile floor. A painted line down the middle of the room separated the men from the women. At the front of the church is the comparatively simple altar and frescoed wall, decorated with stenciled floral designs and faux-painted to resemble marble. Behind the altar, three nichos have been carved into the adobe wall. The central and largest nicho contains a large polychrome bulto of Our Lady of the Immaculate Conception. To her left is a smaller nicho with a bulto

An old sanctus bell in the padre's chapel at Mission Purisima.

Soldiers quarters at Mission Purisima; note footlocker, cots (one with a hat on it), musket, shield, and other equipment

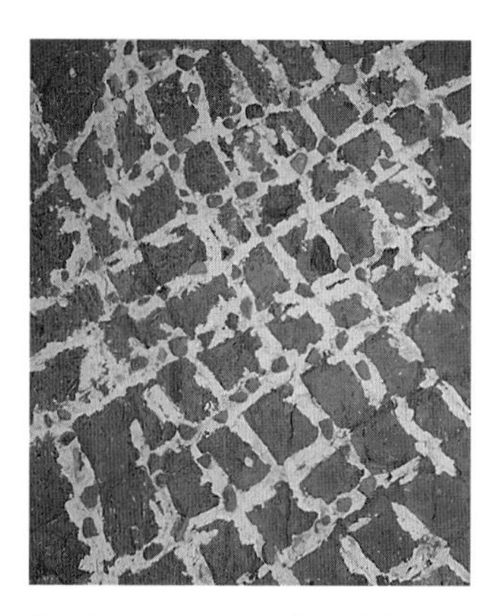

During restoration the adobe walls are diagonally scored, then lime mortar and rooftile fragments inserted into the gorves before the wall is finally plastered over.

of San José, and to her right is a nicho with San Antonio de Padua. Interestingly, the tabernacle on the altar closely resembles the one in the baptistry chapel at Mission Santa Bárbara. The carved and decorated pulpit, with a tall sounding board, sits high on the right sidewall. Oil paintings of the Stations of the Cross line the walls. The lighting fixtures and sanctuary lamp were copied from those at Mission Santa Inés.

Adjacent to the church is a long building that served as living quarters and as workshops of the blacksmith, carpenter, saddle-maker, potter, and weavers and as the kitchen. At the farthest end is the large buttressed monastery building. This building contains the padre's chapel, his living quarters, a library, and a few guestrooms. The relatively large chapel served for church services after the main church became unusable in 1826 when spring water bubbled up right under the church, damaged the church foundations and walls, and rendered the building unsafe. The padre's chapel was then enlarged and utilized as the main church from that time on (Boulé, 1988, p. 16). The chapel also includes a loft for singers and musicians. Fourteen simple wooden crosses on the walls mark the fourteen Stations of the Cross. Situated at the front end of the chapel is an altar with a richly decorated frontal done in polychrome gesso relief. Above and behind the altar are three nichos carved into the adobe wall. The large central nicho holds a polychrome bulto of Our Lady of the Immaculate Conception, to her left is a smaller bulto of San José, and to her right is one of San Antonio de Padua. All of the bultos are from Mexico. An old sanctus bell is situated to the left of the altar. A richly carved confessional is also present in the chapel. The interior walls of the chapel are not as ornately decorated with stenciled floral and geometric designs as those of the church and tend to reflect the chapel's overall simplicity.

Mission La Purisima Concepción can truly be referred to as a "Place in Time." It is the most accurately and fully restored of the twenty-one California Spanish Colonial missions. All the major buildings have been rebuilt and furnished as they were thought to have been during the mission's peak in 1820. In addition, the grounds have been planted to reflect the period, and authentic breeds of livestock graze there, watered from the original mission aqueduct system. The present day visitor to Mission Purisima is able to experience a real and profound feeling of just what the early California mission establishments were all about.

CHAPTER SIX

TWO MORE LINKS IN THE MISSION CHAIN:

SANTA CRUZ 1791 AND NUESTRA SEÑORA DE LA SOLEDAD 1791

Facade of the replica chapel of the old Santa Cruz Mission constructed in1931.

MISSION SANTA CRUZ:

Synopsis: Twelfth mission; founded first by Fr. Fermín Francisco Lasuén on August 28, 1791, and again on September 25, 1791, by the mission's first padres: Isidoro Salazar and Baldomero López; named for the Holy Cross; churches: 1791, 1795, 1858, 1887-present; adjacent pueblo of Branciforte established 1797; mission secularized in 1834 after an active mission life of forty-three years; put up for sale in 1846, but there were no buyers; earthquakes: 1840, 1857; mission church and some land restored to the Church in 1859 by President James Buchanan; one-third-size church replica constructed in 1931.

Location: Mission Santa Cruz is located adjacent to the Santa Cruz Mission Plaza at Emmet and High Streets in the city of Santa Cruz.

The mission site had been suggested by the Gaspár de Portolá Expedition of 1769. Santa Cruz, the Holy Cross, was the name given to this twelfth Alta California Spanish Colonial mission founded in 1791. The wooden cross on which Jesus Christ was crucified is probably the most enduring and holy symbol in Christendom. However the symbology did not come into common use until the time of the Roman Emperor Constantine who proclaimed Christianity the official religion of the Empire in the Edict of Milan in 315 A.D. According to legend the True Cross was acquired by Helena, mother of Constantine, in 326 A.D. A portion of the cross was placed in a jeweled reliquary. The remainder of the cross was later cut into many small pieces, and these amongst other objects of the crucifixion became the most venerated relics of the Church. The True Cross was of the Latin form, and though many variations are known, this is the type most generally found in the California missions. Large wooden crosses were set up at the time of the founding of all the Alta California missions, and usually a large wooden cross was also placed in the camposanto, since individual grave markers were not in common use. Within the mission churches small wooden crosses often served as the Stations of the Cross. There is sometimes mention of so-called Jerusalem Crosses. Those are of the usual form but are inlaid or veneered with mother-of-pearl. An example of this is present on the tabernacle in the baptistry chapel at Mission Santa Bárbara.

Fr. Fermín Lasuén had originally founded Mission Santa Cruz on August 28, 1791, saying, "I found the site to be most excellent as had been reported

Detail of San José bulto showing him holding his characteristic flowering staff.

to me. I found besides a stream of water very near, copious and important. On August 28th, the day of San Agustin, I said Mass and raised the Cross on the spot where the mission is to be" (Lee, 1992, p. 35). Later, on September 25th, the mission was again dedicated on the same site by Frs. Isidro Salazar (Ca. 1758-?) and Baldomero Lopez (1761-?). In attendance at this second founding ceremony were padres from Mission Santa Clara and the Commandante of the San Francisco Presidio. Since Governor Pedro Fages had left California in April 1791 and his successor José Antonio Romeu was in failing health when he arrived in the colony, the governors' high office was not represented at this dedication. The site was located on the side of a hill overlooking the San Lorenzo River. The first church was probably an enramada erected during the first month. However during the rainy season of that first year the San Lorenzo River flooded its banks and the padres realized the necessity to move the mission location to higher ground. Preparations were made to relocate, and on February 27, 1793, the cornerstone of the new church was set. When completed and dedicated in 1794 the new structure was one hundred and twelve feet in length, twenty-nine feet in width, and twenty-five feet in height. The foundations were of stone and measured three feet in height, above which the adobe walls were five feet thick. The mission church entrance and facade were simply decorated with plastered pilasters, squared off at the top. Above this was a triangular gable pierced by a small square window. To the right was an attached square three-tiered campanario with a dome surmounted with a metal cross. The initial roof, probably of thatched grasses, was replaced with fired red tiles in 1811.

The mission enterprise grew, and tradition has it that the grinding stones utilized in the gristmill were gifts to the mission in 1796 by the English explorer George Vancouver. By this time at least two sides of the typical mission quadrangle had been completed, and the Mission resident Indian population comprised about five hundred Indians. With a good climate, fertile soil, and industrious Indian laborers the agricultural enterprise was doing very well. In July 1797, Governor Diego de Borica decreed that Pueblo Branciforte would be established across the San Lorenzo River from the mission. Previous experience had shown that a colonial settlement placed closer than seven miles from a mission establishment was a decided negative factor to the padres' education and control of the Indian population. Thus it turned out in this instance. The governor had insisted that the new colonists to settle Branciforte were to come from Guadalajara, New Spain. When they arrived it was found that most were little more than prison convicts who had been given the opportunity to settle in Alta California in lieu of a jail sentence. They were definitely not people imbued with a love of agricultural pursuits. Rather, they much preferred to spend their time in gambling and loafing rather than pursue any physically demanding tasks. Some runaway Mission Indians, coaxed across the river to Branciforte, were soon caught in the grip of the aguardiente bottle and pressed into the service of the indolent Brancifortians. The padres further exacerbated the problem by punishing those Indians who succumbed to the settlers' enticements. The padres vigorously protested to the colonial government to remedy this intolerable situation, but to no avail. The strict punishments that the padres meted out to those wayward Indians had tragic consequences. In 1812, a group of missions Indians who had suffered floggings as punishment took matters into their own hands, when they kidnapped and murdered the mission priest, Fr. Andrés Quintana (1777-1812). This particular padre had accomplished a great deal in improving the conditions of the mission Indians and was for the most part well liked. His death was a great blow to the overall stability and progress of Mission Santa Cruz.

In 1818, the pirate Hippolyte de Bouchard threatened the California coast, even sacking the provincial capitol of Monterey. Orders were sent by Governor Pablo Vicente de Sola that the padres evacuate the mission site and move the Indians to Mission Soledad. Fr. Ramón Oblés (1786-?) complied with the evacuation order and requested the Branciforte Pueblo officials pack and remove the mission's valuables, while he took the Indians to safety. Instead, the "good citizens of Branciforte" rushed to the mission complex and proceeded to plunder it. In the ensuing melee some Brancifortians got into the mission's wine and brandy cellar, and it turned into one big drunken fiesta! The others vandalized the mission church and took for themselves those valuables they were supposed to keep from the pirates. Ironically, Bouchard and his men never actually threatened Mission Santa Cruz. When Fr. Oblés returned to the mission he was completely devastated by the theft and destruction that the Brancifortians had wreaked on the mission properties. Fr. Oblés wrote to the Father-President of the missions asking for permission to shut down Santa Cruz, but church officials prevailed upon him to remain and continue his efforts with the Indians.

Present-day small, tranquil mission garden at Santa Cruz, with flowing fountain and statue of the Madonna.

Mission records of 1831 show that in spite of everything the mission complex was still a viable agricultural enterprise. However, fewer than three hundred Indians remained to work the mission lands. Mission Santa Cruz was secularized in 1834, and the church properties valued at $79,000. Two years later the overall evaluation had managed to decline to $1000.00!

In 1840, a strong earthquake shook the area and toppled the campanario.

Of interest is that church records of 1835 indicate that Mission Santa Cruz possessed three mission bells that were valued at $3500.00, the highest value for any in the mission chain. Their whereabouts remain a mystery to this day, but they probably disappeared at this time. This earth tremor was accompanied by a tidal wave that caused great havoc to mission property. In 1846, Mission Santa Cruz was offered for sale at public auction, but no buyers came forward. Shortly thereafter the U. S. Government acquired the California Territory. In 1859 President James Buchanan restored the mission and approximately seventeen acres of land to the Church, a miniscule portion of the mission's original land grant holdings.

There does not appear to have been a priest at Mission Santa Cruz from 1844 to 1853, and the mission sank further into decline. The final blow occurred in February 1857 when a devastating earthquake destroyed the mission church and outbuildings. By 1858 the remaining Branciforte population had joined with later townspeople to become the city of Santa Cruz. They built a large wooden cross beside the mission ruins and constructed a new church called Holy Cross. This structure served as a parish church until it was replaced in 1887 by the church presently standing at the corner of the Santa Cruz Mission Plaza.

The city of Santa Cruz has completely covered the original mission lands with homes through the years. Yet a white painted Gothic-style church with a tall bell steeple was sited on the original mission location. It is located on one corner of Mission Santa Cruz Plaza that was attractively landscaped in 1989. To the right of the church, and also facing the mission plaza, is a one-third-size replica of the old mission church. This was built by Gladys S. Doyle in 1931 as a private endeavor to remind the townspeople of their spiritual and cultural heritage. After her death in 1933 she was buried in the baptistry.

The model used for the replica exterior is from an oil painting by French artist Trousset, which now hangs on the wall of the mission gift shop. This painting was executed after the 1857 earthquake with the help of locals who described the original mission complex to the artist. An original watercolor, also hanging in the gift shop, was painted by an artist the day after the 1857 earthquake occurred. It is a valuable asset because it is the only surviving record of the mission's interior. Interestingly, the ceiling and vigas are painted with chevron designs that are strikingly similar to that in Mission San Francisco (Dolores). The few religious relics, prayer books, a 1795 candelabra, original nails used in the construction, pieces of original adobe bricks, along with a few church vestments, are in glass covered cases in the small museum.

The exterior of the replicated church was built to resemble, as closely as possible, the original mission church. Duplication of the original church interior was not attempted. This is most apparent in the absence of Indian painted wall decorations, so common in most missions. In essence, the present interior conveys a more sombre contemporary church setting. Still, some artifacts of the old mission church are present. The most apparent is a 1797 oil painting of the Virgen de Guadalupe, hanging on the right sidewall of the sanctuary. The church altar is positioned in a recessed alcove in the front of the church. On the altar is the original tabernacle with embossed silver door. In three nichos carved into the wall, above and on each side of the altar, are three old polychrome bultos. In the center, above the altar is the bulto of San José, slightly below and to his left is the bulto of Virgen de La Purisima Concepción, and to the right of the altar is the bulto of San Miguel Arcángel. Small wooden crosses line the sidewalls and serve as the Stations of the Cross, along with a few old religious oil paintings. An attractive baptismal font, carved out of native stone, is presently situated on the sidewall to the right of the entranceway.

Present day Mission Santa Cruz is nicely represented by a one-third size replica of the old mission church. It is positioned in a lovely area along with a number of restored private homes, some of which are over a hundred years old, thus dampening the effect of urban encroachment on this quiet tranquil corner. This situation has been greatly enhanced since the mission church faces the attractively landscaped Santa Cruz Mission Plaza which, with its well kept lawns and large trees, offer an additional spiritual sanctuary. The small and intimate church replica has three daily services but is most frequently utilized for church weddings.

Overall view of the restored mission buildings at Mission Soledad.

MISSION NUESTRA SEÑORA DE LA SOLEDAD

Synopsis: Thirteenth mission; founded by Father-President of the California Missions, Fr. Fermín Francisco Lasuén, on October 9, 1791; named for Our Lady of Solitude; churches: 1791, 1797; floods: 1824, 1828, 1832; church collapsed in 1832 due to flooding, replaced by chapel same year; secularized in 1835 after an active mission life of forty-four years; sold in 1846; returned to Church in

1859; restored by "Native Daughters of the Golden West" 1952-1963; mission presently designated as a registered California State Landmark No. 233.

Location: Mission Nuestra Señora de la Soledad is located on Fort Romie Road, three miles southwest of the town of Soledad.

Our Lady of Solitude was chosen as the patroness of the thirteenth California Spanish Colonial Missions, founded on October 9, 1791 by Fr. Fermín Lasuén. Captain Gaspár de Portolá and Fr. Juan Crespí discovered the valley in which the mission is located during their 1769 expedition to find the elusive Monterey Bay.

Soledad is dedicated to Mary Mother of Jesus after His crucifixion, left in sorrow and loneliness after the loss of her Son, she meditates on those recent events. The title specifically refers to Mary's solitude on Holy Saturday. In all depictions, Mary is shown wearing a black or dark blue cloak that almost completely covers her. She may also have her chest pierced by one or seven swords, representing her sorrows.

The Sorrowing Virgin as a singular devotional figure does not commonly appear in Spain before the seventeenth century. Then, she was shown more frequently in sculptural works than in paintings. Still, devotion to Our Lady of Solitude is undoubtedly strongest on a personal level. Devotion to her is very strong in Mexico. Her feast was only officially recognized by papal decree in 1727.

In the California missions representations of Our Lady of Solitude are not very common, while practically every mission had one or more of the Virgin of Sorrows (Dolorosa), either in sculpture or painting. The dressed bulto of the Virgin, once at Mission Soledad and now in the Monterey Presidio Chapel, has been called both Virgin of Solitude and Virgin of Sorrows in different documents. Exceptional bultos of Our Lady of Solitude are presently in Missions San Luís Rey, Santa Bárbara, and Santa Inés. Oil paintings of Our Lady of Sorrows are generally head and shoulder images. The most important one is the historical painting which figured in the first Indian conversions at Mission San Gabriel. This original painting was stolen from the mission sanctuary some years ago but was returned to San Gabriel in 1991.

On the way north in 1769, Captain Gaspár de Portolá and Fr. Juan Crespí spent a day in the valley where Mission Soledad is now located. Legend has it that they tried to communicate with a local Indian who had approached them. In attempting conversation the only Indian word that appeared to be recognizable was one that sounded like "Soledad," the Spanish word for solitude, and it seemed to them a most apt description of this treeless, hot, unceasingly windy place.

Father Lasuén founded the mission on the Portolá-Crespí site on October 9, 1791. The location itself was ideal from the padre's standpoint since it offered an intermediate stopover between Mission San Antonio de Padua in the south and Mission Carmel in the north. Fr. Lasuén said Mass, and raised and venerated the Cross, and so began the history of Mission Nuestra Señora de la Soledad on that fateful October day. However, before Fr. Lasuén had founded the mission the requisite royal gifts to equip and furnish the mission were lost. This quandary compelled Lasuén to appeal to the other established Franciscan missions for the necessary start-up furnishings and sustaining supplies. This was only a minor preview of the troubles this Mission was to endure over the years.

Painted wall of the chapel at Mission Soledad with dressed bulto of Our Lady of Soledad in nicho with Indian-style painted wall deorations.

For the actual founding ceremony a brushwood enramada had been constructed, and it would be six years before this crude structure was replaced with a church of adobe walls and thatched roof. It has been suggested that building at Mission Soledad went so slowly because there were so few Indians, for they, of course, actually did the construction. In addition, there appears to have been an almost constant turnover in priests, even during the mission's early days. Records show that there were approximately thirty different priests at Soledad over forty-four years! The relatively harsh climate appears to have been the primary contributing factor. The winters were cold and damp, the summers unbearably hot, and in all seasons the wind blew constantly. Priests assigned to Soledad were soon faced with the reality of crippling rheumatism and respiratory problems. Requests for transfer to a more habitable mission were a continuing source of distress for the Father-President of the missions.

During those early days, Mission Soledad gained some degree of notoriety by having in residence two rogue Franciscan padres: Frs. Mariano Rubí (1756-?) and Bartolomé Gilí (1759-?). Their missionary careers began at the College of San Fernando in Mexico City in 1788. From the very beginning both carried on in a most un-Franciscan manner. Their notorious escapades at San Fernando included climbing the college walls after hours and spending the night on the town. Then they slept all day and avoided their regular priestly duties. Why the Franciscan College tolerated this sort of behavior is unclear. In any case, the malcontents were assigned to missionary duty in Alta California, Fr. Rubí in 1790, and Fr. Gilí the following year. Eventually, the two padres arrived at Soledad. Here, their unbecoming behavior and constant complaints, mainly about the unavailability of altar wine, was an unpleasant source of embarrassment (Wright, 1964, p. 63). Finally, Fr. Lasuén, as Father-President, agreed to their removal. Fr. Rubí departed Soledad in 1793. A year later, Fr. Gilí was placed on a ship returning to New Spain. The ship's captain refused to disembark his passenger at Loreto, Baja California. Instead he kept him on board the ship and carried him across the Pacific Ocean to the Philippines. One might say it was justifiable retribution!

A marked exception to the continued turnover of padres at Soledad was Fr. Florencio Ibáñez (1740-1818) who arrived at the mission in 1803, and

Holy water stoup with decorative wall paintings at Mission Soledad.

remained there for fifteen years giving devoted service to this lonely mission outpost. Those were the mission's good years. Crops grew well and harvests were sufficient. Fr. Ibáñez designed and built an efficient irrigation system that utilized water from two nearby rivers. By 1805 there were a little over seven hundred Indians at Soledad, the largest number of Indians ever in residence there. Infectious diseases like smallpox, measles, and influenza killed off some of the Indian population, but some simply ran away. After 1805 the Indian population at Soledad rapidly declined.

In 1814, the Spanish colonial Governor José Joaquin de Arrillaga, the official whom the Franciscans so admired, arrived at Soledad to visit his fellow Spaniard and old friend, Fr. Ibáñez. In failing health for sometime, Arrillaga seems to have had a premonition of his approaching death. Since he was unmarried and without family, he retired to Soledad to wait out his last days in the company of an old friend. He died at the mission on July 24, 1814, and Fr. Ibáñez buried him in the church. Only four years later Fr. Ibáñez went to his reward and was buried next to Arrillaga.

One of the worst problems at Soledad was disastrous flooding. The Salinas and Arroyo Seco Rivers were small in the summer, when water was most needed for the crops, but raging torrents in the winter, with sometimes catastrophic effects. In 1824 a flood destroyed the church where Arrillaga and Ibáñez were buried, and the church was never rebuilt. Instead, a smaller chapel was built as a replacement, but in 1828 another flood washed away the chapel. Again the chapel was rebuilt only to be swept away in another flood in 1832, to be rebuilt once again. Yet, in spite of those natural disasters, Soledad was always good sheep country. The mission had over six thousand sheep that made the mission viable, for at the time the value of sheep was double that of a horse (Stern, Miller, Hallan-Gibson, Neuerburg, 1995, p. 35).

The padre who experienced those natural disasters was Fr. Vicente Francisco de Sarría (1767-1835), a devoted religious who had served first as Father-President of the missions (1823-1825) and later as their Prefect. During the unsettled times in Mexico when no new padres arrived to relieve those in place, he volunteered to assume the post at Soledad. Here he served the Indians with complete and unwavering devotion and he struggled to keep the mission in habitable condition. By 1832, he and the few remaining mission Indians were on the verge of starvation. Alone at Soledad he watched and prayed as the mission's fortunes inexorably declined. In May 1835 his body was found at the foot of the altar. As a final act of devotion the few remaining mission Indians

Standing melted adobe ruins of one of the original walls in the mission quadrangle at Soledad.

placed Fr. Sarría's body on a litter and carried it one hundred miles to Mission San Antonio de Padua, where he was buried. When this burial party left Soledad the remaining adobe structures began their long return to the earth. Never again would there be a resident priest at Soledad—a sad ending for a lonely mission. The Mission records and valuables were transferred to Mission San Antonio de Padua. Secularization occurred in the same year, and to add insult to injury, the mission tile roof was removed and sold in order to pay a debt. In 1846 the mission was sold by Governor Pío Pico for $800.00. Yet in 1825 Soledad properties, aside from the church proper, had been appraised at $36,000.

The American traveler Henry Miller visited the mission site on June 25, 1856 and said

> *I arrived at Soledad at ten. The mission is a great heap of ruins with exception of one building amid a small church of modern date.... Although there is hardly anything else but ruins left, this Mission was once in a very flourishing condition. The plain on which it is situated is called "Llano del Rey", and the priests caused the Indians to make an aqueduct of fifteen miles length with which they could irrigate over twenty thousand acres of land, providing thus against the summer drought (Miller, 1997, p. 22).*

Miller made a drawing of the mission site, which is shown on page 21.

The mission was returned to the Bishop of Monterey in 1859, but by that time it was a complete ruin never again to be occupied by the Church. For ninety years Mission Soledad stood exposed to the elements slowly eroding away. In 1952 a group of state women called "Native Daughters of the Golden West" undertook to rebuild Mission Soledad and restore it to the condition of its early days. For the rebuilding and restoration, adobe bricks were prepared in the old manner, many of which were reconstituted from the remains of the original mission bricks. Those new adobe bricks have had a material added to them designed to prevent them from crumbling as easily as the original adobe bricks, which had a remarkable tendency to disintegrate with seasonal climate changes. The restored chapel was dedicated on October 9, 1955, and in 1963, seven rooms of the padre's quarters were restored and presently serve as a small museum and gift shop. Mission Nuestra Senora de la Soledad, now a California Registered State Landmark No. 233, is administered by a committee of local citizens.

The exterior of the Soledad Mission Chapel is marked by its overall simplicity. The walls are whitewashed, as are the interior walls, and contrast

Original mission bell cast in Mexico City in 1794, hanging on the left side of the chapel at Mission Soledad.

nicely with the red roof tiles. Attached to the chapel wall, adjacent to the entranceway on the left side, is the original mission bell. It hangs on a sturdy wood beam supported by an adobe pillar. The bell was cast by Pablo Ruelas of Mexico City in 1794.

As one enters the chapel his eyes immediately focus on the ceiling, which consists of lengthwise boards painted in tones of blue and gray. Those are supported by trusses painted with diagonal lines in gold, red, and blue. A linear series of electric chandeliers hang from the ceiling beams. Stenciled painted Indian-style decorations line the chapel walls above a light colored painted dado. At the front of the chapel is the altar, behind which is a painted wall reredos. Most imposing is a large square nicho carved into the center of the wall. Standing in the nicho is a large dressed bulto of Nuestra Señora de la Soledad, in sombre black lace from head to feet. The colorfully painted reredos is decorated with faux-painted red columns to resemble marble. The painted Ionic columns with gold- painted bases and capitals convey a rich texture to the reredos. The border of the nicho is brightly stenciled with a repetitive floral pattern. The top of the painted reredos is capped with a half-circle lunette with a Corazón de María in red pierced with the seven swords of Mary's sorrows. Original oil paintings of the Stations of the Cross hang along the sidewalls. The simple wooden pews, a gift from a local parish church, fit in nicely with the overall decor of the chapel. No daily services are held here since no priest has resided at Soledad since 1835.

For the last few years the mission site has been an outdoor laboratory for archaeology students from the University of California at Los Angeles. They have concentrated their efforts primarily on the old mission quadrangle behind the padre's quarters. We can hope that their findings will give us a better idea of the overall size of the mission complex and what was accomplished in this lonely spot over two hundred years ago.

For many missionary padres assignment to Mission Soledad must have been regarded as being sent to Siberia, with its unhappy history of natural disasters and its unhealthy climate. Even today it is a lonesome and forlorn place in which the presently restored mission stands out as an oasis with its well tended rose gardens.

CHAPTER SEVEN

AN AMBITIOUS SUMMER (1797) WITH FOUR NEW MISSIONS:

SAN JOSÉ, SAN JUAN BAUTISTA, SAN MIGUEL ARCÁNGEL, AND SAN FERNANDO REY DE ESPAÑA

Side view of Mission San José showing the church elevated above the sidewalk level and conveying a more massive appearance.

MISSION SAN JOSÉ:

Synopsis: Fourteenth mission; founded by Fr. Fermín Francisco Lasuén on June 11, 1797, as the most easterly located of the California missions; named for its patron San José, the foster father of Jesus; churches: 1797, 1809, 1869; smallpox and measles epidemic in 1805; Indian uprising in 1826; secularized in 1834 after an active mission life of thirty-seven years; sold in 1846; mission buildings returned to Church in 1859; devastating earthquake in 1868; restorations: 1915, 1950; rebuilding and complete restoration 1982-1985.

Location: Mission San José is located in the city of Fremont at the Junction of Highway 238 and Washington Boulevard.

San José was chosen as the patron of the fourteenth Alta California Spanish Colonial Mission by the Viceroy of New Spain, Marquis de Branciforte. The mission was founded by Fr. Fermín Lasuén on June 11, 1797.

José (Joseph), husband of the Virgin Mary and foster father of Jesus, is mentioned in the first and second chapters of Matthew and Luke in the New Testament. He was a carpenter and is described as a just man. According to one tradition he was already an elderly man when he married. His feast was introduced into the church calendar in 1479, and his popularity coincides with the discovery and colonization of the New World. He became a special patron of the converted Indians. Pope Pius IX declared him patron of the Church in 1870, and he later became a protector of workers and a patron of social justice.

Until the end of the sixteenth century San José was generally shown as a participant in biblical scenes such as the Nativity and the Flight into Egypt rather than as a single figure for devotion. In religious art he usually holds the Infant Jesus in his arms, or the Child Jesus holds Joseph's hand in a version of the Holy Family. Until recent times he never appeared alone, as his importance derives from being the foster father of Jesus. He generally holds a staff with blooming lilies, signifying his chastity, or with other flowers that blossomed on his walking staff when he was chosen as the husband of Mary.

Every California mission had an image of Joseph, either a sculpture or a painting. Bultos of him were generally on the main altar, unless there was a side altar specifically dedicated to him. He was often depicted carrying the baby Jesus, and one or both figures wear crowns.

On Trinity Sunday, June 11, 1797, Father Lasuén, accompanied by Sergeant Pedro Amador and five soldiers, sited Mission San José at a location fifteen miles north of the pueblo of San José. He raised and blessed the Cross, celebrated Holy Mass, and dedicated the mission to San José. The mission location was sufficiently distant from the pueblo to relieve any anxiety the padres might have had about close proximity of pueblo to mission and the potential bad influences the pueblo might have on the Mission Indian population. Unfortunately, the local Ohlone Indians, were either indifferent or outright hostile to Christian conversion.

The Indians' ancestral home was located to the east and south of San Francisco Bay and stood astride the approach to the San Joaquin Valley. Numerous hostile Indians lived in this area. The mission served as a halfway point between the pueblos of San José and San Francisco, and it became regional headquarters for the Spanish military in their forays against those hostile Indians since they harbored the numerous mission Indian runaways from Mission Dolores in San Francisco. As a result many battles between Indians and Spaniards occurred over a number of years.

The original mission church of San José was a crude enramada constructed on Mission Creek north of the present site, in September of that first year of 1797. Soon after it was completed a start-up herd of cattle arrived from Mission Santa Clara, as was customary when new missions were established. The early mission buildings, though crude, were laid out at San José in a rectangle instead of the typical mission quadrangle. The padres persisted in their conversion efforts, and after a discouraging first year began to have some success. By 1800 there were close to three hundred Indians living at the mission, and the agricultural enterprise was well underway, and the mission began to prosper. However, a devastating epidemic of smallpox and measles took an inordinate toll on the Indians in 1805. In eighteen months the Indian death toll was one hundred and fifty. The epidemic frightened the Indians, and many fled the mission, too afraid to remain. In 1806 Frs. Buenaventura Fortuny (1774-1840) and Narciso Durán (1776-1846) were assigned to Mission San José. For twenty-seven years they worked together harmoniously. A large new church had begun the year before they arrived following a church design attributed to a padre at Mission San Juan Bautista. During the construction, giant redwood logs, were dragged from a forest twenty-five miles north of the mission. These were cut into twenty-four foot lengths to support the roof of the church. When completed the building was one hundred and twenty-five feet in length, thirty feet in width, and twenty-four feet in height (Boulé, 1988, p. 12). The new church was dedicated on April 22, 1809.

Restored painted doorway decoration in the mission church of San José following the style employed by Mexican artist Agustin Davila in the 1830's.

Father Narciso Durán was an accomplished musician and was very adept at teaching others. During his tenure at San José he formed a thirty-piece orchestra. He fabricated his own musical instruments until real ones could be obtained from Mexico. Orchestra participants had uniforms and even a contrabass. The fame of the orchestra was so widespread that it was said Indians would walk miles to be present at a mission concert. In addition, Fr. Durán devised a system for showing the four choir parts in two colors (red and black) and two shapes (squares and diamonds) for each color. From this the Indians had little difficulty reading the music, which was hand lettered on large sheets of parchment. In time the Indians even mastered Gregorian chants. Fr. Durán was a very able and devout padre whom the Indians revered. He could drive a hard bargain with a ship's captain when it meant getting needed supplies for the mission, and he administered complex mission enterprises with great skill. In fact he was elected Father-President of the California missions three times (1825-27, 1831-38, and 1844-46). His administrative capability was immense, but it was his misfortune to head the missions when they were in terminal decline. Still, his leadership prolonged the life of the mission chain.

Bulto of San Antonio de Padua mounted on an elaborate wall pedestal in Mission San José; note painted background wall decoration faux-painted to resemble natural marble.

From 1810 until the early 1830's much progress was made at Mission San José both in agricultural and livestock enterprises and in the conversion of the Ohlone Indians. In 1810 the mission enterprise produced four thousand bushels of wheat and much produce. By the year 1832 livestock herds comprised thirty-seven thousand cattle, horses, and sheep, which grazed on mission lands that extended from present-day San José to Oakland. Indian housing continued to be built so that in 1825 there were close to two thousand Indians in residence. A dam and irrigation system had been built in 1819, and by the close of the following decade a tannery and soap factory were in operation. The inner mission patio was surrounded on three sides by buildings, with a ten-foot wall

Restored painted wall decoration, with crucifix, done in the style of the 1830's by artist/restorer Richard Menn during the 1982-1985 church interior restoration.

on the fourth side. The church was located front and center, not a corner anchor as at other missions.

It is interesting to note that in 1826, the English navy explorer Frederick William Beechey and his crew spent sometime visiting both Missions San Francisco de Asís and San José during their 52 days anchorage in San Francisco Bay. As a keen observer, Beechey was in an ideal position to report and contrast the status of the Indians at each mission. He was particularly appalled at the miserable living conditions of the Indians at Mission San Francisco, in contrast to the more civilized conditions he observed at San José. He perceptively noted: "In some of the missions much misery prevails, while in others there is a degree of cheerfulness and cleanliness which shows that many of the Indians require only care and proper management to make them as happy as their dull senses will admit of under a life of constraint" (Paddison, 1999, p. 184).

In 1826, Fr. Fortuny, Durán's colleague for twenty-seven years, was assigned to Mission Sonoma, and Fr. Durán was left alone to carry the burden. In that same year, soldiers attacked the Cosumnes Indians north of San José and killed forty individuals (Wright, 1964, p. 65). Three months later a force of soldiers and settlers under General Mariano Vallejo marched against the San José runaway Indians Estanislao and Cipriano and their followers. This was a particularly unfortunate situation because Estanislao was an unusually bright Indian and was a great favorite of Fr. Durán. In May of 1826 the Spanish force battled one thousand Indians in a three-day campaign that ended in complete victory for the Spaniards. Those Indians not killed on the spot were summarily hanged, with the exception of Estanislao who was brought back to San José. Fr. Durán secured his pardon and he lived at the mission until his death in 1836.

The Mexican War of Independence from Spain prevented new padres from coming to Alta California, and the College of San Fernando in Mexico City suffered because of the anti-Spanish sentiment rampant in the new Mexican republican government. That government requested the Zacatecan College to supply Franciscan padres for the California missions. In 1833, Governor José Figueroa arrived in the colony with a number of Mexican-born padres to take control of the Alta California missions. At that time Fr. Durán relinquished control of Mission San José and retired to Mission Santa Bárbara.

Mission San José was secularized in 1834 and came under the jurisdiction of administrator José de Jesus Vallejo, brother of General Mariano Vallejo. At this time mission properties were valued at $155,000. Under Vallejo the mission lands were divided into large ranchos, many of which were purchased by local Californios. In two years time mission assets had been completely dissipated. The mission Indians fled, many died of disease and starvation, the mission buildings decayed, and the livestock herds ran off or were appropriated. In 1846 Governor Pío Pico sold the remaining mission properties to his brother

Andrés and former colonial Governor Juan Bautista Alvarado for $12,000. This sale was later nullified by the U. S. Government, and in 1859 some twenty-eight acres of former mission lands were restored to the Church.

During the Gold Rush of 1849, H. C. Smith converted some of the standing mission buildings into lodgings and added a general store at the south end of the mission wing. The town and mission complex that grew up became a thriving supply center as gateway to the southern California mines. Prominent early pioneer families such as the Peraltas, Avisos, and Livermores established close ties to the mission community. By 1860 a Mexican cantina and hotel occupied some of the former mission buildings.

In 1852 the mission church was served by clergy from Mission Santa Clara, and the following year the church was designated as the area parish church called St. Joseph's. At that time a resident parish priest moved into one of the remaining buildings, and the old adobe church was utilized for another fifteen years until 1868.

Detail of the bulto (dressed) of Christ scourged (Jesus Nazareno) in a neoclassical balcony setting on a side altar at Mission San José.

On February 5, 1856, the American traveler Henry Miller arrived at the mission and said,

> *I went to the Mission San José, which is about fifteen miles from the town of San José on the north side of the Bay of San Francisco. The priest, a youth of about eighteen years of age, very politely showed me round the ruins which are remaining of this once flourishing Mission. The old adobe church is a large building, poorly decorated, and surrounded by ruins of a once massive edifice. This Mission is situated in a small valley surrounded by mountains, which are covered in the summer with grass and wild oats (Miller, 1997, p. 5).*

Miller also included a drawing of the mission site, which is given on page 7.

On October 21, 1868, a massive earthquake centered on the nearby Hayward Faultline virtually destroyed the mission buildings. The adobe walls caved in, the roof broke open, and the bells in the campanario tumbled down. After the earthquake only the padre's living quarters remained standing. Soon thereafter the mission church site was cleared of debris and a wooden, New-England-style steepled church rose on the original foundations and tile floor. This church continued to serve as the community parish church until recent times. By 1890, a Victorian-style rectory had been built over the area that had once been the padre's quarters and mission administrative building. Almost two decades into the twentieth century a restoration group called "Native Sons and Daughters of the Golden West" became interested in restoring some of the original mission complex. In 1915, and later in 1950, the group spearheaded a drive to save surviving portions of the mission wing and to convert it into a museum.

In 1956, the town of Mission San José, as it was then called, was incorporated into the city of Fremont. Some twelve years later the city initiated plans for the rebuilding and restoration of the San José Mission church. Saint Joseph's, the wooden church built after the 1868 earthquake, was moved to the city of San Mateo in 1982, after being empty and unused since 1965. The Victorian rectory had been moved to nearby De Anza Street in 1979. After extensive planning and archaeological investigations at the mission site, construction began in 1982 for what would be a replica of the 1809 Mission San José adobe church. The project took three years and five million dollars; the building was completed and rededicated on June 11, 1985. The reconstruction was funded from private and corporate donors, including the Diocese of Oakland, legal owner of Mission San José. During the restoration new adobe bricks were made in the old way, with asphalt added to retard erosion. For the rebuilding of the mission church over one hundred and fifty thousand adobe bricks were prepared, and the finished walls are four to five feet in thickness. The wood timbers utilized in the church structure were cut in the Oakland Hills and moved to the site. Archaeological excavation exposed the original tile floor and the grave of Robert Livermore, a prominent early Californian. Other renowned Hispanics were buried under the church floor, but only Livermore's grave was marked. Digging also exposed a fountain in front of the church that supplied hot water produced from a nearby natural hot spring.

The facade of Mission San José Church is very simple, with almost no decoration. The building is painted white and has only three outside windows, a small one over the entranceway and one on each side of the sanctuary. The entrance has massive dark wood doors topped by a wooden gable overlain with a red tile roof. Steps leading to the entrance are constructed of bricks cut in half-circles. The campanario is low, hardly appearing above the roofline, and contains four original bells. The church itself conveys a massive appearance as it sits elevated above the street level. The church building is one hundred and twenty-six feet in length, thirty feet in width, and twenty-four feet in height. Huge buttresses, four to five feet in thickness, on the outside walls add to the church's massive appearance. The under-roof is unique as it was formed by tying together 12,000 hazelwood branches with rawhide thongs.

Nothing specific was known about the interior church decorations before the arrival in 1835 of Fr. José Gonzáles Rubio. He undertook a total remodeling of the church interior, contracting with Mexican artist Agustin Davila to decorate the church and to paint the reredos. Church inventories of the time note that both the walls and the ceiling were entirely covered with painted decorations. The original Davila painted walls were recreated during the church restoration by Carmel artist Richard Menn and his associates. The only original

Davila work present in the church is the baptismal stand and font, decorated with various designs, in which 6500 Indians received the sacrament of Baptism between 1797 and 1934.

Two altars are prominent on the left sidewall of the mission church. The neoclassical altar nearest the sanctuary has a nicho with a large polychrome bulto of San Buenaventura that dates from about 1808 *(color page J)*. The side altar nearest the entranceway signifies martyrdom and features a large bulto of the scourged Christ (Jesus Nazareno); included in this altar are relics of Roman martyrs, and a nail said to contain, within its hollow center, metal filings from a nail of the True Cross. The two bultos survived the 1868 earthquake and were returned to the mission after restoration.

The focal point of the mission church is the main altar and its spectacular neoclassical reredos. The bright reredos is capped with a polychrome relief of God the Father, below which is a Dove representing the Holy Spirit. Both are set within stylized gilded rays of light. Below this is an oval oil painting of Jesus. The center of the reredos is supported by two square pilasters faux-painted to resemble marble, in addition to four rounded and fluted columns, all capped with gilded Corinthian capitals and bases. High in the center of the reredos is an arched nicho with candelabra on either side and at the base. The background is painted blue. Within the nicho is a large imposing polychrome bulto of the mission's patron San José. This bulto is from Spain and dates from the fifteenth century. Below San José *(color page M)*, in a glass enclosed nicho, is a smaller eighteenth-century Mexican bulto of the Virgin Mary. Large wooden candlesticks sitting on the altar have been painted to resemble silver. The ornately gilded altar features, on either side, cherubs holding candles. A large wheeled sanctus bell is situated on the right side of the altar. In front of the sanctuary is a hand-carved painted railing copied from a piece of the original railing.

Original hand-hammered copper baptismal font on wooden pedestal with original painted decorations by the Mexican artist Agustin Davila done in the 1830s.

Early nineteenth-century German oil paintings of the Stations of the Cross hang along the side walls. Close to the church entranceway, on the right wall, is the original hammered copper baptismal font. It rests on the wooden pedestal originally decorated by Davila. Overhead are massive redwood ceiling beams and a high vaulted ceiling, adding to the church's open and spacious feeling. Replicas of two of the original chandeliers hang from the ceiling.

As with any of the California missions, maintenance and restoration are a continual process. Most recently, the focus at San José has been on the seismic retrofitting of the last surviving portion of the 1809 adobe building. California State law and city ordinance required that all unreinforced masonry buildings had to be seismic retrofitted by the millennium, be closed, or be demolished. The Committee for Restoration raised close to a million dollars to comply with the mandatory public safety requirements.

Mission San José stands today as a wonderful example of community dedication and involvement in this beautiful restoration. It is with justified pride that the community can look back on the outstanding role they played in restoring a portion of their cultural and religious history.

View of the rather plain church facade at Mission San Juan Bautista; note campanario that was designed and built during the 1976 restoration.

Overall view of Mission San Juan Bautista as seen from the town square.

MISSION SAN JUAN BAUTISTA:

Synopsis: Fifteenth mission; founded thirteen days after Mission San José by Father Fermín Francisco Lasuén on June 24, 1797; named for its patron St. John the Baptist; churches: 1797, 1812; earthquakes: 1800, 1812, 1906; secularized in 1835 after an active mission life of thirty-eight years; mission buildings restored to Church in 1859; school and orphanage on mission property 1861-1906; smallpox epidemics in the 1870's; modernizations and restorations: 1860, 1884, 1906, 1929, 1949, 1976; church continually active since founding; largest church in the California mission chain; mission placed under jurisdiction of Maryknoll Fathers in 1928.

View looking down the arched corridor towards the front entrance at Mission San Juan Bautista.

Location: Mission San Juan Bautista is located four miles south of U. S. Highway 101, off California State Highway 156, on the town square of San Juan Bautista.

San Juan Bautista, Saint John the Baptist, was chosen by the Viceroy of New Spain, the Marquis de Branciforte, as the patron of the fifteenth Alta California Spanish Colonial Mission. It was founded on June 24, 1797, the Saint's feast day, by Fr. Fermín Lasuén.

John, called the Baptist, was the son of Zacharias, a priest in the temple of Jerusalem, and Elizabeth, a kinswoman of Mary. As a young man John went into the desert to live the life of a hermit. At the age of thirty he began to preach against the evils of the day and to baptize followers along the banks of the Jordan River. His message was one of penance and baptism, and before long he attracted large crowds. He baptized Jesus Christ, whom he regarded as the Messiah and spoke of Him as the Lamb of God. For political motives Herod Antipas arrested him, and later beheaded him at the whim of Salome, daughter of Herodias, Herod's wife.

Detail of the elaborately decorated pulpit, off of the central aisle in the mission church of San Juan Bautista; note the decorative painted column on which the pulpit sits, and other painted wall decorations.

From earliest Christian time John has held an esteemed position within the Church. Baptismal scenes appear as frescoes in the catacombs of Rome, and the religious iconography is among the earliest of Christian stories. Juan is generally depicted with unruly hair and beard and wearing an animal skin. In devotional art he is often shown baptizing Jesus on the banks of the River Jordan. He stands on the bank while Jesus is ankle deep in the water. A dove, representing the Holy Spirit, descends from above. As a single devotional figure he may be shown preaching and holding a staff topped with a cross. He sometimes carries, or is accompanied by a lamb, a reference to Christ as the Lamb of God. Occasionally, one may find paintings or sculptures of his head on a platter.

The baptistry of most California missions contained a painting of the Baptism of Christ, and a number of those images have survived. A single figure of San Juan Bautista with a lamb is the central bulto on the high altar at Mission San Juan Bautista. A small oil painting of San Juan Bautista kneeling with a lamb in front of a cross at the mission is probably one that was brought up from New Spain to the mission in 1805.

Mission San Juan Bautista was successful from the very beginning. Fr. Lasuén had chosen an ideal site, one that had abundant trees for timber and tule reeds for the necessary roofing materials. There were good limestone deposits only a mile away and local areas where harder rock was available for the foundations. Six months after the founding ceremony on June 24th, the church was complete along with quarters for the padres, soldiers, and Indians. They had also finished building a granary. The resultant church building was one hundred and sixty feet in length and paved with ladrillos, large kiln-baked tiles. Progress was continual so that by 1800 there were five hundred Indians in residence, and thought was given to the eventual enlargement of the original church building. During that year there were twenty days of earthquake tremors during which the buildings sustained damage. Accordingly the padres decided to add to the original building as they proceeded to repair what earthquake damage had occurred. It was not until 1803 that construction on the large new church began. This was initiated in a ceremony on June 13, 1803, when the colonial governor, José Joaquin de Arrillaga, and other dignataries were invited to witness the laying of the cornerstone. A story of this gala event was written,

View of a corner of the restored courtyard at Mission San Juan Bautista with typical mission-style architecture and well tended gardens.

placed in a bottle, and sealed in the cornerstone.

Building progress continued on this large second mission church, and in 1808, Fr. Felipe Arroyo de la Cuesta (1780-1840) was assigned to the mission. He convinced the builders that adding a third aisle to the church would be a decided asset to a growing mission congregation. When the mission church was completed in June of 1812 it was the largest Franciscan structure in Alta California. Ironically, by 1812 death and runaway Indians had reduced the mission Indian population to approximately 550, one-half of what it had been in 1805. In spite of the shrinking population a typical mission quadrangle was completed that year. Late in 1812, another massive earthquake hit the mission and there was substantial damage to the complex. Faced with the reality of living in an earthquake prone area the padres pragmatically decided that instead of rebuilding the church as it was, they would fill in the archways along the side aisles with brick. The result being that the church would now be long and narrow, as were most of the other Alta California mission churches. Thus the mission church became smaller in size but more earthquake-resistant.

As the village of San Juan Bautista continued to grow, two buildings were constructed around a plaza in front of the mission convento: soldiers' barracks in 1813 and a nunnery in 1815. In the mission church proper a red tile floor was laid over the sand base.

Fr. Arroyo de la Cuesta, who was in charge of the mission during this time, was an enthusiastic padre who wanted his church interior to be quite grand. He was constantly looking for furnishings that would enhance the interior of the church. He accomplished much in beautifying the church but did not direct his attention to painting the interior walls until 1816. Somehow he made contact with the American sailor Thomas Doaks of Boston who had jumped his ship, the Albatross, in Monterey and made his way to San Juan Bautista. He was the first American citizen to settle in Alta California. He was not an artist, but he volunteered to paint the church interior for room and board. Fr. Arroyo de la Cuesta recognized this offer as a better deal than that bid by a Spanish artist who commanded seventy-five cents per day, so he hired Doaks to paint the interior church walls and the reredos. Doaks' completed his paintings of the reredos in good style, as proven by the fact that his painted reredos of 1818 has never been repainted. However, his ceiling and wall frescoes have often been whitewashed. Doaks took out Spanish citizenship, established permanent residence in San Juan Bautista, and married the daughter of José Castro, a prominent local citizen.

An accessory altar dedicted to the crucifixion and located at the rear of the south nave in the mission church of San Juan Bautista.

When Fr. Arroyo was assigned to Mission San Juan Bautista in 1808 he was a renowned linguist able to deliver sermons in seven different Indian dialects. In 1815 he published a study of various California Indian languages which the Smithsonian Institution edited and republished in 1860. He was a forceful, imaginative padre with a richer educational background than most of his Franciscan colleagues. As a classicist, he enjoyed endowing his newborn Indians with the names of heroes from antiquity. Wright (1964, p. 70) noted that the American trader Alfred Robinson remarked that the region abounded in infant Alexanders, Ciceros, and Platos. Fr. Arroyo served Mission San Juan Bautista for twenty-five years, and made the mission a scholarly place.

In 1815, Fr. Estevan Tapis (Ca. 1756-1825) came to Mission San Juan Bautista. He had been Father-President of the California missions after Lasuén's death in 1803. Following this tenure his only desire was to be a mission priest. He and Fr. Arroyo worked together at the mission for ten years, and Tapis is perhaps the best known of the San Juan Bautista padres. He performed and composed music and taught the Indians to read music so that they could sing four-part harmony. The mission became quite famous for its music, and long after Fr. Tapis' death in 1825 at the age of seventy-one the Indian choir was still performing arrangements he had written for them. Fr. Tapis is buried in the mission church sanctuary.

By 1831 there were 1200 resident Indians and more than 18,000 head of various livestock. In all aspects it was a viable agricultural enterprise. However in 1833, Fr. Arroyo was forced to turn over the running of the mission to Mexican-born Zacatecan Franciscans. Just two years later, in 1835, the mission was secularized. A secular administrator was put in charge, and shortly thereafter the mission's total assets were completely liquidated. Following secularization, Fr. Arroyo joined his Franciscan brothers at Mission San Miguel and served there until his death in 1840.

During the Gold Rush days the village of San Juan Bautista was an important stagecoach stop. Still, in all this time the mission never lacked a spiritual guide or pastor. In spite of what was going on around them the padres steadily carried on their religious obligations. By 1839, the village had grown

The mission church sanctuary at San Juan Bautista showing the altar and reredos with six nichos holding bultos of San Juan Bautista, San Pascual, San Antonio de Padua, San Francisco, San Isidro and San Domingo.

up around the mission complex, and the mission church became the local parish church. On November 19, 1859, President James Buchanan restored title to Mission San Juan Bautista to the Church.

In 1860, Fr. Cipriano Rubio the church "modernizer" arrived at Mission San Juan Bautista. In carrying out his progressive remodeling ideas he built a rather strange, American Gothic style two-and-a-half-story wooden tower. This was to hold the church bells and to serve as his living quarters. Later he encased the structure in stucco. Luckily, this out-of-place campanario was damaged in the 1906 earthquake. Still, it was not until 1976, when major repairs were made to the mission, that a campanario more in style with the rest of the mission was designed and built. In the 1870's there were sporadic outbreaks of smallpox during a time of severe local drought. Illness and dryness conspired to reduce the town's population, and for a few years it had all the appearances of a ghost town.

During the latter half of the nineteenth century some of the mission buildings were put to various uses. Notable were a school and orphanage established on mission property in 1861 and carried forward until 1906. Throughout this period of change the mission church actively served its parishioners. Holy Mass has been said at Mission San Juan Bautista everyday since its founding in 1797 with very few exceptions.

The mission complex is located on a large town square with a luxuriously grassed plaza. There are well kept restored historic buildings on two sides of the plaza, as it was during the mission period. The mission convento has nineteen arches across the front of an unusually long corridor. The seventh and nineteenth arches are higher and squared-off, instead of being rounded. It has been suggested (Boulé, 1988, p. 11) those arches were constructed in this manner so that on feast days church parades with their tall banners would have easier access. Alternately, it could have been a simple matter of convenience so that large ox-carts could move materials and supplies into the patio area. Three additional rounded arches form the entrance to the front of the convento.

At the far eastern end of the corridor is the campanario that was built during the 1976 restoration project. It is two-tiered and has three bell openings, of which two of the bells are original. The church facade is relatively plain. The entranceway comprises three rounded arches, of which the center one is the largest. Above this is a large square-shaped window followed by the gabled red tile roofline. This is surmounted by a simple cross. There is the restored L-shaped church and a two hundred and thirty-foot long cloister as in mission days, when two sides of the quadrangle were adobe walls. Presently, the cloister has a gift shop and a fine museum. In 1976 the church interior side archways were rebuilt as they were in 1812, thus making the mission church once again the largest and only three-aisle church in the Alta California mission chain. The church proper is one hundred and eighty-eight feet in length, seventy-two feet in width, and forty feet in height, with three-foot- thick adobe walls. Large archways divide the center of the church from the sides.

A doorway in the mission church of San Juan Bautista; note Moorish-style arch and wall dado faux-painted to resemble marble, capped with a decorative painted border.

The interior church walls are painted with decorative elements in earth tones of brown, red, and grayish blue, adding overall interest to the church interior. The sidewalls have painted dados that rise about five feet from the floor and are faux-painted to resemble marble; the dados are capped with a border of various painted decorations in the Indian manner *(color page W)*.

The wooden altar and reredos are constructed in a rather simple style. The reredos has six nichos, each with a polychrome bulto. Red velvet hangs at the back of each nicho, contrasting and highlighting the bultos. Five of the bultos are half life size, but the bottom center nicho contains a life-size bulto of the mission patron San Juan Bautista *(color page J)*. Directly above him is a bulto of San Pasqual. San Antonio de Padua is in the upper left nicho, with San Francisco below; San Isidro stands in the upper right nicho, with San Domingo below. The sanctuary walls and ceiling are arched and painted in a light blue color, as are the wooden ceiling braces and horizontal boards.

There are a number of accessory altars in the mission church, two are dedicated to the Virgen de Guadalupe and another to the Crucifixion. All are done in the typical mission neoclassical style and have attractive painted decorations. Some of the decorative components are faux-painted to resemble marble *(color page F)*.

From the rear of the church, a door opens into a modest baptistry. The room is attractively painted with various decorative elements. In the center of the room are two large stone baptismal fonts, and on the wall behind the largest font hangs an oil painting of Christ's baptism *(color page I)*. One of the most furnishings in the church proper is the wonderfully decorated pulpit, with its sounding board above. It sits on a shortened faux-painted fluted column capped by a Greek Ionic capital. In general, the decorative elements present in the mission church are outstanding, and add much to the church's overall beauty.

Carved stone baptismal fonts in the baptistry of the mission church of San Juan Bautista.

The mission cemetery is situated in an olive grove beside the church, and here four thousand mission Indians are buried. One of the cemetery walls sits atop the infamous San Andreas Fault line, the seismic nemesis of so many California missions. Just north of the cemetery is one of the few remaining sections of the old Camino Real, along which the padres walked from one mission to another. The mission patio is beautifully landscaped with stately trees, rose gardens, and a well tended central lawn and walkways. Quiet areas are available where the weary visitor can sit and relax for a few moments. There is a nicely carved statue of a Franciscan padre with an Indian boy in a corner of the patio, and there are other sculptural pieces displayed within this tranquil oasis.

In August of 1928, Mission San Juan Bautista was placed under the jurisdiction of the Maryknoll Fathers, and today the mission is administered by the Diocese of Monterey-Fresno.

Modernization and restoration of the mission church has been an ongoing endeavor since 1860, when a wooden campanario was erected by Fr. Rubio. This was later stuccoed over. Some repairs and restoration were undertaken after the 1906 earthquake. Then, concrete buttresses were built and reinforced to support the forty-foot-high walls that mark San Juan Bautista as the tallest adobe structure in the mission chain. Again, in 1929, the campanario was remodeled to give it more of a mission flavor. A significant restoration project occurred in 1949-1950 when the William Randolph Hearst Foundation allocated substantial monies to restore many of the California missions. Until the 1949 restoration, the church interior retained Fr. Rubio's tongue and groove sheathing over the beamed ceiling, and his wooden flooring covered the original tile floor. Now, in the center aisle, one can see the tracks of bear and coyote that were apparently made when the tiles were fresh and still drying in the sun (Lee, 1992, p. 34). Finally in 1976 there was a major overall restoration of the mission complex. It was then that the church was restored to its 1812 three aisles, thus making it once again the largest church in the Alta California mission chain.

Today's visitor to the mission will be entranced with the overall beauty of the town square. It is California's only original remaining Spanish Plaza, and is now a State Historical Park. The land, with the exception of the mission, was acquired by the State in the 1930s. Presently, one can take a walking tour of the surrounding twelve block area and visit over thirty historic buildings. In this manner one gets an authentic first hand impression of what the San Juan Bautista Mission community was like before the turbulent Gold Rush days.

The San Juan Bautista mission complex is one of the most compelling and beautifully restored of the California missions. It is a must for anyone desiring to fully explore the spell of the Alta California Spanish Colonial missions.

MISSION SAN MIGUEL ARCÁNGEL:

Synopsis: Sixteenth mission; founded only a month after Mission San Juan Bautista by Father Fermín Francisco Lasuén on July 25, 1797; named for San Miguel, Saint Michael the Arcángel, by the Father-Guardian of the Franciscan College of San Fernando, Mexico City; churches: 1797, 1798, 1818; devastating fire in 1806; minor damage from 1812 earthquake; secularized in 1836 after an active mission life of only thirty-nine years; last Franciscan priest in 1841; mission illegally sold in 1846; resturned to Church in 1859; resident priest

The relatively plain facade of the 1848 mission church of San Miguel.

The front courtyard of the mission with fountain, portions of the arched corridor, and the church.

appointed in 1878; diocesan clergy 1879-1928; restorations: 1806, 1821-1822, 1886, 1901, 1928-1939; mission reassigned to Franciscan friars in 1928.

Location: Mission San Miguel is located eight miles north of the city of Paso Robles, off of U. S. Highway 101, in the village of San Miguel.

San Miguel, Saint Michael the Arcángel, was chosen as the patron of the sixteenth Alta California Spanish Colonial missions. It was founded by Father-President of the California missions, Fr. Fermín Lasuén on July 25, 1797. Fr. Lasuén was assisted in the founding ceremony by Fr. Buenaventura Sitjar from nearby Mission San Antonio de Padua.

Michael is one of the three arcangels mentioned twice in both the Old and New Testaments. He is the protector of the Chosen People, both Jew and Christian, militant leader of the Heavenly Hosts against Satan, and protector of Christians at the hour of death.

In devotional art he is generally depicted as a winged warrior subduing the devil. His sword or spear is often raised as in battle, and he usually carries a set of scales for the weighing of the soul at death. He appears as a beardless handsome youth who often stands on the figure of Satan, piercing him with a spear or sword.

Over the centuries numerous paintings and sculptures of him have been created. One of the most famous widely appealing, is by the Italian Renaissance painter Raphael and was a great influence on later artists. Representations of

side altar in the mission church of San Miguel dedicated to San Francisco; note original (1821-1822) wall decorations by Estevan Munras.

San Miguel are very common in Mexico where he has been a consistent patron for numerous churches. In Church theatrical productions he was a favorite character following the Conquest, and in California he had a leading role in the Christmas Pastorela. In 1779 he was designated as the patron of the Alta California missions.

Many of the California missions had carved or painted images of Miguel, and some had both. Early bultos of San Miguel still survive at Missions Carmel, San Antonio, Dolores, Santa Bárbara, Santa Cruz, and San Miguel. A bulto of him was lost in the 1926 fire at Mission Santa Clara. A fine oil painting of him hangs in the mission church of San Miguel. In religious art, one may find groupings of all the arcangels, but San Miguel is generally the leader among them.

Fr. Fermín Lasuén, accompanied by Fr. Buenaventura Sitjar, left shortly after establishing Mission San Juan Bautista to found Mission San Miguel. In addition to the padres of the founding party, there were eight soldiers, four of who were to serve as guards at the new mission. It was late in the afternoon when they arrived at the designated site, chosen two years previously by Fr. Sitjar. Located between Missions San Luís Obispo and San Antonio de Padua it was considered an excellent choice due to its location at the juncture of the Nacimiento and Salinas Rivers on a flat fertile area. The party camped that night under the stars, and the following morning they cleared the site. In addition they erected an enramada and living shelters for the padres and the soldiers. The next day, July 25, 1797, bells suspended from a large oak tree pealed to call the Indians to this event. Fr. Lasuén, the celebrant, offered the initial prayers, sang the "Veni Creator Spiritus," and blessed, water and the large wooden cross that had been erected. Then Fr. Lasuén venerated the Cross and sprinkled the surroundings with Holy Water. On the altar was an image of Our Lady, and it was here that Fr. Lasuén intoned the Litany of the Saints, chanted High Mass, and preached a sermon. The singing of the "Salve Regina" followed, and the Mass ended with the singing of the "Te Deum Laudamus". The priest took formal possession of the site and dedicated it to San Miguel Arcangel, the Most Glorious Prince of the Celestial Militia. San Miguel had been previously chosen as patron by the Father-Guardian of the Franciscan College of San Fernando in Mexico City. During this first afternoon, the two priests baptized fifteen Indians.

In the beginning, the established neighboring missions sent necessary supplies and converted Indians to assist in the formal establishment of the mission. Fr. Sitjar (1739-1808) was left in charge, and Fr. Antonio de la Concepción Horra (1767-?) was assigned to aid him. However, shortly after arriving at Mission San Miguel, Fr. Horra appears to have suffered a complete mental breakdown and did many erratic things which frightened the Indians. In time, Fr. Horra sank into insanity, and was returned to Mexico City under guard.

Sent to replace Fr. Horra in 1800 was Fr. Juan Martín (1770-1824) who was to become the presiding padre at Mission San Miguel for twenty-seven years. In August of 1799, Fr. Sitjar returned to mission of San Antonio de Padua, and Fr. Baltasar Carnicer (1770-?) came to assist Fr. Martín.

At the end of the first year an adobe chapel, thirty-four feet in length and twenty feet in width, had been built along with a few outbuildings. By the end of 1798 close to two hundred Indians lived at the mission, and the mission's agricultural enterprises were well underway. Progress was continual, so that by 1806 close to a thousand Indians were laboring at the various mission endeavors.

In August of 1806 tragedy struck when a devastating fire broke out and consumed two rows of buildings and part of the mission church roof. More immediate was the destruction of mission supplies and provisions, including the previous year's wheat production. Again, neighboring missions rallied to San Miguel's aid with needed food and provisions. By the end of the year most of the mission structures had been rebuilt, and some additions even made. After this disastrous fire baked clay tiles replaced the straw roofs of the mission buildings for added fire protection. In fact, the Indians at Mission San Miguel became so proficient at roof tile making they began to supply other missions with this commodity and were able to barter them for other needed supplies.

Large sixteenth century Spanish polychrome bulto of a militant San Miguel located in the mission museum; dimensions: 88 inches high, 56 inches wide , and 48 inches in depth, the gift of a church parishioner.

The years 1808 and 1809 saw new buildings added to the mission complex. The buildings were erected around a patio instead of the usual mission quadrangle. The tile making enterprise established at this mission prospered, and during these two years some 36,000 tiles were produced. In 1810 alone, 20,000 tiles were produced. Building construction continued and mission ranch lands were expanded.

In 1816 foundations were laid for the present church, and with Fr. Martín's excellent planning the structure was finished in 1818. The completed church is one hundred and forty-four feet in length, twenty-seven feet in width, and close to forty feet in height. The adobe walls are almost six feet thick and stand on a foundation of stones. During 1821 a Spanish artist from Monterey, Estevan Munras, reached Alta California from Peru (Neuerburg, 1989, p. 64). A young man and fellow Catalonian friend of Fr. Martín, he arrived at Mission San Miguel to decorate the church interior. During 1821-22 he and his Indian assistants painted almost every surface of the church interior with various symbolic and floral designs. Many of the designs he took from pattern books and stenciled on the walls. The painted reredos was a rich pastiche of both architectural and decorative elements. The result is that Mission San Miguel has one of the most richly decorated church interiors of all the Alta California missions.

Throughout the remaining mission period building and consolidation of the mission enterprises showed steady growth. The largest wheat crop was in 1805, and the peak overall agricultural production occurred in 1810. Livestock production grew steadily from 1797 and reached its peak in 1822.

Detail of the upper left side portion of the reredos showing colorful painted wall decorations in addition to the distinctive columns with lotus-like leaf configuration, and oval painting of the Franciscan coat-of-arms.

By 1832 after more than ten years of neglect by the Mexican government this production had dropped to one-tenth of what it had been at its peak. The greatest number of Indians at Mission San Miguel occurred in 1814 when there were one thousand in residence. The unfortunate years of Mexican rule saw the Indians flee the mission confines and scatter into the countryside to be wiped out by starvation, disease, and alcohol. There are some twenty-two hundred mission Indians buried in a small crowded Indian cemetery on the San Miguel mission property.

Fr. Juan Francisco Martín was born in Spain in 1770. He sailed from Cadiz, Spain in 1793 arriving at the College of San Fernando in Mexico City in September of that year. He came to Alta California in 1794 and served two years at Mission San Gabriel and one year at La Purisima. Assigned to Mission San Miguel one month after its founding in 1797, he spent the remaining twenty-seven years of his life there. He died in August of 1824 and is buried on the gospel side of the high altar.

Fr. Juan Cabot (1781-Ca. 1856), who had arrived at the mission in 1813 to assist Fr. Martín, continued to serve Mission San Miguel after Fr. Martín's death. In 1834 Fr. Cabot, old and in failing health, asked to return to Spain. He had served twenty-one years at Mission San Miguel and nine years at other Alta California missions. His brother, Fr. Pedro Cabot (1777-1836), took charge of the mission until the arrival of Fr. Juan Moreno (1799-1845) in 1835. By 1838, Fr. Moreno was living in virtual poverty at the mission; by October of 1839 he was forced to retire to Mission Santa Inés. The last of the Franciscan padres, during what has been referred to as the mission period, was Fr. José Ramón Abella (1764-1842), who remained at Mission San Miguel until his death. An independent Mexico was in control of Alta California by 1825. The libertarian government was determined to secularize all the Alta California missions as quickly as possible. In 1831, Governor José Maria de Echeandia illegally appointed José Castro as commissioner of Mission San Miguel. Accordingly, he was to inventory the mission's property and lands and to distribute these to the Indians. The padres, if they chose, could remain as curates, and a stipend taken from their revenues derived from the Indian's labor would help support them. The padres refused this offer. When José Castro came back to the mission accompanied by the governor, he made a speech to the Indians emphasizing the advantages of freedom that secularization would bring to them. When asked to vote on this issue the Indians overwhelmingly decided to remain at the mission with the padres.

The first administrator sent to San Miguel was Ignacio Coronel, who resigned almost immediately and was replaced by Inocente Garcia. The Indians thoroughly disliked Garcia, and many fled the mission during this time. Garcia was succeeded by José de Jesus Pico. Mission San Miguel was one of the last missions to be formally and legally secularized under Mexican law. The mission inventory of 1837 evaluated the properties at just $83,000, with debts of less than $1000.00. Even at this point Mission San Miguel was still a viable enterprise. It should be noted that there were other padres who remained at the mission until it had been formally sold, all of whom complained of the mission's poverty during those trying times.

Unusual octagonal-shaped pulpit in mission church of San Miguel with it's crown-like sounding board, suspended dove, and front panel with relief figure of the Virgin Mary; note rays of large stylized pecten shell on wall behind pulpit.

The dispersal of mission property and lands to politicos had begun by Governor Juan Bautista Alvarado in 1841-42 and continued with the last Mexican governor Pío Pico, until he was deposed by the U. S. Government on August 10, 1846. In 1845, before he was removed, Pico had issued a decree for all the Alta California missions to be sold. On July 4, 1846, Petronillo Rios and his partner, an Englishman named William Reed, purchased San Miguel illegally. This sale was later nullified by the U. S. Government, and mission lands and properties left in charge of the padres until further adjudication could take place.

William Reed and his family occupied the mission buildings as their home until 1848. Reed kept a small amount of gold from the mines in the Sierra Nevada, and as a practicing cattle and sheep rancher he always had on hand sums of money derived from livestock sales. In December of 1848 he entertained five persons at his home in the mission. Accounts vary as to just who those five people were. They might have been deserters from a British ship docked in Monterey, U. S. Army deserters, or riffraff caught up in the opportunities of the day. Nevertheless, Reed and his family entertained them as guests for a period of five days. Quite probably, Reed told them of his good fortune and of the gold and monies he had accrued. After taking leave of their host one afternoon, the men went far enough away to hide in an arroyo until darkness. They then returned to the mission, their objective to murder Reed, his family, and their servants. Eleven bodies were thrown in a heap on the floor of the convento living room, where two of Reed's mining friends found the bodies the following day. They spread the alarm and a posse, organized at San Luís Obispo, overtook the murderers close to Santa Barbara. One was shot, another jumped into the ocean and drowned, and the remaining three succumbed to the sentence of Judge Lynch. The bodies of the slain Reed family and their servants were buried in one grave at Mission San Miguel Cemetery.

From 1848-1870 portions of the mission complex were rented out as a saloon, a general store, dance hall, living quarters, and as an office for the Howe Sewing Machine Company. During this interval the church itself was maintained and religious services were ongoing. Mission San Miguel was

Overall view of the altar and reredos in the mission church of San Miguel; reredos and wall decorations were done in 1821-1822 by Estevan Munras and Indian assistants.

restored to the Church on September 2, 1859 by a proclamation signed by President James Buchanan, giving ownership to the Bishop of Monterey, Fr. Joseph Alemany.

In 1878, Fr. Francis Mora, Bishop of Los Angeles and Monterey, appointed Fr. Philip Farrelly resident priest to Mission San Miguel. He was the first resident priest after a hiatus of thirty-six years. In the following years attempts were made to prevent the mission from falling into ruin. Notable among those concerned with preserving the mission was Fr. José Mut, who followed Fr. Farrelly in 1886. He initiated repairs on both the mission church and convento. He remained at Mission San Miguel until his death in 1889, and he lies buried in the church cemetery. In 1901 repairs and restoration were again needed on the mission buildings. Fr. Henry S. O'Reilly, then resident priest, solicited and received donations that allowed him to complete most of the pressing and necessary repairs.

On November 13, 1912, two large marble slabs were placed over the graves of Frs. Martín and Ciprés within the church sanctuary. During the ceremonies a Requiem Mass was sung in plain chant, as the padres had taught the Indians. Fr. Zephyrin Engelhardt, renowned historian of the California missions, presented a sermon in which he spoke of the work of the early Franciscans and what that had attempted to achieve. Padres of the day chanted the "Libera" as the ceremony of the Absolution was performed over their graves. The resident priest at this time was Fr. W. A. Nevin, who was succeeded by Fr. Gabriel Ryan, who in turn was followed by Fr. Ascensio Segarra. Fr. Segarra remained at Mission San Miguel until August 1928, when Bishop John MacGinley of the Diocese of Monterey and Fresno returned the mission to the Franciscans. When this occurred, Fr. Angelus Bold was appointed first superior and pastor. He was followed by Fr. Modesto Muennemann, who actually initiated mission restoration. He departed in 1932 and was replaced by Fr. Fidelis Wieland, who in turn was succeeded by Fr. Tiburtius Wand. He brought to San Miguel many years of experience working with the Indians of Arizona and California. The entire mission restoration program was directed and achieved solely by the Franciscan Brothers without any State or Federal monies. The expert craftsmanship of Brother Benedict Schlickum and architectural and engineering knowledge of Fr. Thaddeus Kreye were invaluable contributions. Fr. David Temple, a specialist in California history and culture, coordinated the final restoration. Since 1928 the mission has been continuously maintained as a parish church and monastery.

During the early phase of restoration the most pressing concern were the termite-ridden wooden mission church beams, which the Indians had long ago carried from the Santa Lucia Mountains beyond the village of Cambria. The roof tiles were removed and steel girders placed under the insect-treated old beams. The original tiles were then replaced on the strengthened roof. Additional necessary improvements were also made, and the mission outbuildings repaired or restored. This major reconstruction and restoration effort was completed in 1939 by the Franciscan Brothers.

The first thing the visitor sees on arrival at Mission San Miguel is the Memorial Bell Tower. The tower honors Franciscan priests and brothers who served in World War II, especially Fr. Fidelis Wieland. He was a former pastor at Mission San Miguel who lost his life serving as a U. S. Navy chaplain in the South Pacific during the war. The tower was built in the late 1950's by Jesse Crettol and his assistants. It is four-tiered and constructed of burnt brick, and has five rounded arched openings in which ornamental concrete bells occupy each opening. The belltower is capped by a simple metal cross. The belltower closely resembles the campanario at Mission San Diego de Alcalá.

Relatively recent memorial belltower at Mission San Miguel, dedicated to the Franciscan priests and brothers who served in World War II.

The plain facade of the mission church is marked by a criss-crossed network of cracks on the walls. These, a result, of occasional earthquake tremors. The only break in the facade are the entrance doors, and above them a large rectangular window. Above this is the facade gable and overlying red tile roof capped with a metal cross. The entranceway is flanked by two large stately Italian cypress trees.

The church interior is resplendent with painted decorations, the 1820s work of Mexican artist Estevan Munras and his Indian assistants. Much of the painting was done with stencils. The motifs are neoclassical, but are more colorful than those generally found in non-frontier interiors *(color page V)*. The walls of the nave are divided by Doric columns, painted in blue, based on the columns of the Basilica Aemilia in the Roman Forum (Neuerburg, 1989, p.65). The last intercolumn areas have huge stylized sea shells painted in pink, green, and blue. The last one, on the right sidewall, serves as the background for the pulpit. A simple continuous marbleized dado runs along the bottom of the wall.

Behind a more contemporary altar is the colorful and exotic reredos. Estevan Munras constructed it of wood, cardboard, and cloth. Occupying a central position is a large polychrome bulto of the mission's patron San Miguel *(color page C)*. On the left is a smaller bulto of San Francisco, and on the right is one of San Antonio de Padua. All are original and placed on pedestals. The panels behind the bultos are painted with borders of roses and carnations. The columns on the reredos are painted to resemble Mexican onyx and have bizarre lotus-like leaf capitals, giving them an almost Egyptian appearance. They are painted in bright red and blue. Above the two smaller bultos, high on the reredos, are two oval paintings of the coats-of-arms of the first and third order of St. Francis. The paneled pedestal of the reredos has a strong marbelized design. On the frieze above the high entablure is a triangle with an all-seeing "Eye of God" surrounded by stylized clouds and rays of light. On the top, on

Relatively recent (1950s) stone campanario adjacent to mission cemetery; large bell weighs 2,500 pounds.

either side, are large lidded urns with painted flowers on their fronts, and behind them a horizontal flower garland.

To make themselves heard the padres relied on the height of the pulpit and the accompanying sound board. The octagonal-shaped pulpit at San Miguel is unique with its crown-like high sounding board, with a white dove suspended above it. The dove represents the Holy Spirit and refers to the Holy Scriptures that were read from the pulpit. The image of the Virgin Mary as the "Seat of Wisdom" is a somewhat unusual painted relief figure on the front panel.

Two side altars stand close to the sanctuary. The one on the right sidewall is dedicated to San Francisco and has a large polychrome bulto of him on the altar. Directly across the nave, stands a side altar dedicated to the Holy Mother.

The still radiant colors of the church interior have withstood time and the impulse of later "restorers" to improve on the originals. Visitors can still enjoy the purity of the original decorated church interior.

Carved wooden bas-relief panels depicting the Stations of the Cross line the walls of the church, as do a number of old religious oil paintings, some of which are indeed art treasures. From the door of the sacristy east along the north wall is a very old painting of San Miguel en Cielo (St. Michael in Heaven), next is one of San Antonio carrying the Christ Child, who holds a stalk of lilies in his right hand. Further is a Nuestra Señora de Soledad holding the broken body of Christ in her arms; next a depiction of San Buenaventura, then Nuestra Señora de Guadalupe; followed by E1 Bautismo de Cristo por San Juan and a painting of Mary Magdalene.

On the south wall, from east to west, hang oil paintings a of Santo Domingo, La Divina Pastora, San Mateo Apostol, San Rafael Arcángel, San Gabriel Arcángel, and San Miguel (Iversen, n.d., p. 20). This is truly a remarkable collection of devotional art treasures *(color page M)*.

The exterior mission convento comprises twelve rounded arches, none of which appear to be of the same width or height. Mission San Miguel has never had a distinct frontal campanario. Instead, bells were hung from a stout wooden beam suspended from one of the convento arches. The bell presently hanging in one of the archways was cast in Mexico City in 1800 and is dedicated to San Gabriel. Sometime in the 1950s a peculiar small campanario was erected adjacent to the cemetery above the roof at the rear of the church. This addition holds three bells, two small ones and a larger one that weighs 2,500 pounds. This large bell was recast in 1888 from six cracked and broken bells collected from other missions.

Original (1800) mission bell suspended from a corridor archway; bell is dedicated to San Gabriel Arcángel.

The courtyard in front of the convento has a lovely fountain and pool added in the late 1940s when the courtyard was developed. The fountain is modeled on the 1808 example at the front of Mission Santa Bárbara. There is also an inner patio with a well-kept garden containing thirty-four varieties of cactus.

Mission San Miguel is a remarkable and inspiring monument to the tenacity and industry of those early Franciscan padres who devoted their lives to the Christianizing of the California Indians. Although each mission has its unique and distinctive character, San Miguel has perhaps more than others preserved what might be described as its original purity and integrity. Of particular beauty are the church interior decorations done in 1821-22. These are simple, unpretentious, and refreshing in their clear proportions and their honesty. Who can visit Mission San Miguel and not come away with the lasting remembrance of those painted simulated doorways, archways, huge pecten shells, and columns painted on church walls, that are totally unaltered by latter day restorers?

View of the facade of the mission church of San Fernando Rey de España with it's rather plain architectural style.

MISSION SAN FERNANDO, REY DE ESPAÑA:

Synopsis: Seventeenth mission; founded only six weeks after Mission San Miguel Arcángel, by Father-President Fermín Francisco Lasuén on September 8, 1797; this was the fourth mission founded in 1797; Saint Ferdinand King of Spain (1217-1252) was chosen as the mission's patron; churches: 1797, 1799, 1806, 1974; earthquakes: 1812, 1971, 1994; minor fire 1905; secularized in 1834 after an active mission life of only thirty-seven years; mission illegally sold in 1846; last Franciscan priest left in 1847; last entries in register books dated 1852; portion of mission property restored to Church in 1862; last Mass at Old Mission in 1874; restorations: 1865, 1897, 1912, 1916, 1923, 1930-33, 1941, 1949, 1974, 1997; Oblate Fathers of Mary Immaculate assumed responsibility of Mission San Fernando in 1923.

Location: Mission San Fernando, Rey de España, is located at 15151 San Fernando Mission Boulevard, Mission Hills, in the city of San Fernando.

San Fernando Rey de España was chosen as the patron of the seventeenth

View of the distinctive convento building taken from Brand Park across the road; note original mission fountain that was installed here in 1922, and the life size bronze statue of Father Junípero Serra with his arm around the shoulder of mission Indian convert Juan Evangelista.

Alta California Spanish Colonial missions by the Viceroy of New Spain, the Marquis de Branciforte. The mission, founded by Fr. Fermín Lasuén on September 8, 1797, was the fourth Alta California mission founded that year. San Fernando was also the patron of the Franciscan College in Mexico City, which sent the missionaries to Alta California.

Ferdinand was born in Salamanca, Spain, in 1198. His father was King Alfonso IX of Leon, and his mother was Berengaria, daughter of King Alfonso III of Castille. Eventually Ferdinand became king of the united kingdoms of Castille and Leon. He was a good ruler who showed compassion for his subjects, avoiding overburdening them with heavy taxes. He waged successful campaigns against the forces of Islam, eventually expelling the Moors from all of Spain except Granada and Alicante. He captured Cordova and Seville and transformed their famous mosques into cathedrals of the Blessed Virgin. He led an exemplary life that focused on prayer and humility and was a member of the Third Order of Saint Francis. He founded the University of Salamanca. When he died in 1252 he was interred in the Cathedral of Seville. He was canonized in 1671 by Pope Clement X. In 1717 his mortal remains were placed in a magnificent reliquary above the altar of the Royal Chapel in Seville.

In devotional art, San Fernando is generally portrayed as a crowned king wearing a breastplate beneath his royal robes. He may hold a scepter, and a large decorated orb. Representations of him are rare before the seventeenth century. However, the eighteenth-century Spanish kings made much of him, and in Mexico and South America his image was placed on the reredos of the cathedrals of Mexico City, Puebla, and Cuzco.

Images of San Fernando in the Alta California missions are rare. An oil painting of him was billed to the Presidio Church of Monterey in 1791. According to an 1808 inventory, Mission San Fernando had both an oil painting and a life-size bulto of him. The bulto, still present in the mission church, occupies the central position on the magnificent reredos, but the oil painting is not mentioned on the last mission inventory of 1849.

In August of 1795, Fr. Vicente de Santa María (1742-1806), a resident missionary at Mission San Buenaventura, accompanied an expedition led by Ensign Don Pablo Cota, with five soldiers, which explored the interior country between Missions San Buenaventura and San Gabriel in search of a prospective site for a new mission. Fr. Santa María kept a diary of this trip and recorded his favorable impression of Francisco Reyes' Rancho Encino location. Father-President of the Alta California Missions, Fr. Lasuén, read Padre Santa María's description and was impressed enough to visit the site personally. Then, on September 8, 1797, the day of the solemn Feast of the Nativity Most Holy, Lasuén formally founded the mission dedicated to San Fernando, Rey de España. Lasuén blessed water, the location, and a large wooden cross, which the congregation venerated and raised aloft. He was assisted by Frs. Francisco Dumetz (1734-1811) and Juan Lopé Cortes (1772-?). Dumetz was the first padre assigned to the new mission, along with the soldiers to garrison the location. Lasuén chanted the Litany of the Saints, sang a Mass during which he preached a sermon, and concluded by singing a "Te Deum". In the same enramada in which he said Mass he also baptized ten Indian children. Mission San Fernando, thus established, would last until 1847. During those fifty years, fourteen Spanish Franciscans ministered at the mission. Among those who served at Mission San Fernando there were two padres, Frs. Marcos Vitoria and José Zalvidea recognized as saintly by their contemporaries; a learned gentleman, Pedro Cabot; a reformed alcoholic, Vicente Oliva, and a recognized womanizer, Blas Ordaz. The remainder were priests of rather ordinary merit (Nunis, Jr., 1997, p. 244).

Other end of convento building at mission San Fernando with El Camino Real Bell, erected by Mrs. A.S.C. Forbes in 1910, it was originally sited in front of the main entrance, but was later moved to this location.

By the time Mission San Fernando had been founded, the Indians of the surrounding region had already undergone a major shift in the subsistence practices to supplement their traditional hunting and gathering economy through growing their own crops, and tending the livestock of the pobladores of Los Angeles.

Fr. Dumetz was responsible for erecting the first buildings at Mission San Fernando. He supervised the building of the second church and the plan of the mission quadrangle. In 1804 he laid the foundations for the third church which was completed after his departure in late 1805. Fr. Pedro Múñoz (1773-1818) formally dedicated this third church on December 6, 1806. It is rectangular and is one hundred and eighty-five feet in length and thirty-five feet in width. The adobe walls are five feet thick at the base, tapering to three feet at the roofline. Mission San Fernando is somewhat different in the placement of buildings, as the church is widely separated from the convento, not adjoined to it as in most Alta California missions.

Fr. Pedro Múñoz in 1808 had a dam constructed to create a reservoir and an irrigation system installed. In 1811, an aqueduct a little over a mile in length was built to supply the mission fountain. The Great Earthquake of 1812 badly damaged the church walls, and thirty new beams, along with massive buttresses, were added near the sacristy to shore up the building.

Work on the convento building had begun in 1810 and took twelve years to complete. The building is not an integral part of the mission quadrangle. It is situated a short distance away, facing on the main colonial highway, the El Camino Real, with both the church and the quadrangle out of view.

Architecturally, it is more imposing than the church. The convento, sometimes referred to as the "long building," is two hundred and forty-three feet in length, fifty feet in width, and at the apex of the present two-story structure forty-five feet in height. At its completion in 1822 the building comprised twenty-one rooms. Those included quarters for two resident padres, guestrooms, a chapel, a kitchen, a dining room, storerooms, and a winery. On the front of the building twenty-one Roman arches support the sloping tiled roof. A long portico extends the entire length of the building. Indian-crafted wrought-iron grillwork, a specialty of this mission's Indian craftsmen, add to the stately appearance of the structure. Two pilasters support the main doorway. Above the doorway is a small shell-shaped nicho which once held a statue of San Fernando. The sala, is the largest in the Alta California missions, and the several windows and doorways in the sala are of Moorish design. The flat ceiling rests on square beams which are not supported on corbels but are fastened into the walls. The second-story addition was completed in 1820. From 1857-1861 its western rooms were used as a station for the Butterfield Stage Line, which operated between Los Angeles and San Francisco. In the late 1880s the rooms were utilized by the Porter Land & Water Company as employee quarters and for storerooms. On March 13, 1905, a story in the Los Angeles Times noted that the mission convento building had a narrow escape when squatters started a fire in the building (Weber, 1997, p. 40).

From its initial founding Mission San Fernando prospered so that by 1806 the mission enterprise was producing hides, tallow, soap, cloth, and other products in considerable quantity. The mission was located right on the El Camino Real leading to a growing Los Angeles; therefore it became a favorite stopping-off place for travelers on the highway, and Los Angeles was a ready market for its products.

Mission San Fernando's most successful year was 1819 when there were close to 22,000 head of livestock within the mission enterprise. Cattle raising was the largest endeavor, but the mission was renowned for its artistic works in wrought iron. There were also extensive grape vineyards; the vines were brought north by the padres from the Baja California missions. The orchards grew many varieties of fruit, and by 1832 there were 32,000 grapevines and 1600 fruit trees producing on mission lands. Settlers continued to encroach on mission lands, so disputes over land boundaries and water rights were ongoing. Most ominous however, was the constantly declining mission Indian population. Since the Indians were the prime labor force, a declining Indian population did not bode well for the mission enterprises.

The mission Indian converts spoke three dominant languages: Gabrielino Tongva, Tataviam, and Ventureno Chumash. By 1814, persons who arrived from the Antelope Valley region spoke a fourth language, Serrano. Speakers of all these languages intermarried with those who spoke different languages, so that by the end of the Mission Period, most families were of mixed tribal ancestry (Johnson, 1997, p. 252).

With the mission in decline by the 1830s, the final deathblow was dealt on August 9, 1834, with enforcement of the Laws of Secularization by the Mexican government. Within two months time the mission was taken out of the hands of the padres, and secular administrators were appointed; the first was Antonio del Valle. At that point the resident priest, Fr. Francisco Gonzáles de Ibarra left Mission San Fernando and returned to Mexico. The mission establishment quickly fell into chaos. A series of civil administrators controlled the mission properties after 1835. In 1838, Governor José Echeandia attempted to convert Mission San Fernando into a parish. This was unsuccessful, and it was also canonically invalid. The mission Indians were totally discouraged and embittered by what was happening, and many of them left the mission confines during these unsettling times.

Interior view of a doorway in the convento sala with unique painted frescoe of grape harvesting above the doorway; note richly painted wall dado.

While all of the difficulties relating to Mission San Fernando were being played out, another event of importance occurred on mission ranch land near Castaic on land that had been formerly granted to Antonio del Valle by Governor Juan Bautista Alvarado in 1839. Apparently, the majordomo of the mission, Francisco Lopez, on March 9, 1842, while digging up some wild onions, found gold flakes adhering to the plant roots. With further searching he found more gold, and subsequent investigations showed that the gold placer deposits extended for at least fifteen miles from a point on the Santa Clara River over the country drained by its upper waters. The news of this "gold strike" spread, and in a few weeks hundreds of treasure seekers invaded the area. In comparison to the later 1848 Mother Lode gold strike further north, this was nothing much. The amount of gold taken from the area has never been ascertained, although reports indicate one prospector realized some $80,000 from the precious metal (Weber, 1995, p. 36). Gold fever continued for about four years, but scarcity of water and the rather crude methods of extracting the gold made it all very difficult and uneconomical. With the 1848 Gold Rush at Sutter's Mill, interest in the small San Fernando deposits gradually died out. Unfortunately, there were those who believed that the mission padres had

View from the mission quadrangle at San Fernando with flowing fountain and side view of the mission church.

hidden away large amounts of gold for their own use. As a result, visitors to the mission ruins after 1874 came across large gaping holes within the mission church itself. As late as 1915 there were reports of tunnels dug right under the church altar searching for treasure that was supposedly buried with the dead padres under the church floor.

On March 29, 1843, Governor Manuel Micheltorena issued a decree restoring the missions to the padres. However, in October 1845 the new governor, Pío Pico, decreed that Mission San Fernando should be rented at the option of the government. The remaining Indians were given the choice of "freedom" or of working for the new tenants. By December 5th, Andrés Pico, brother of the governor, and Juan Manso took a nine-year lease on the mission and its properties, this for an annual stipend of $1,120.

By March of 1846 all of the missions were made liable to the laws of bankruptcy, and the governor was empowered to sell them to anyone. Under those laws Eulogio de Celis purchased the San Fernando Mission properties on June 17th for a mere $14,000.

When Andrés Pico's lease expired in 1854, he purchased a half interest in the Celis property for $15,000. For a number of years Pico and his family continued to utilize the mission convento building as one of their summer residences, and here they entertained many of the dignataries of the day.

Fr. Blas Ordaz, the last Franciscan to serve as residential priest, left in 1847. In the following years, the spiritual needs of the few people living at the mission were cared for by the priests from the Plaza Church of Nuestra Señora de Los Angeles. The last entries in the register books are dated 1852, and records indicate that Fr. Peter Verdaguer offered the last Mass in 1874.

On February 19, 1853, Bishop of Monterey Joseph Sadoc Alemany instituted a lawsuit against the U. S. Government to recover part of the mission's holdings, for the Church. The complicated and long drawn out legal proceedings were finally settled when on May 31, 1862, President Abraham Lincoln signed a proclamation restoring the requested properties to the Church. This decision had no effect on former mission ranch lands, which have remained in private hands.

There had been a number of attempts towards restoring Mission San Fernando even as early as 1865, when a journalist reported that the mission convento building had been newly repaired (Weber, 1997, p. 24). Most of those attempts were of minor importance. It was not until 1897, with the approaching mission centenary, that serious restoration was undertaken. The Landmarks Club of Southern California, under the aegis of Charles Fletcher Lummis, was especially active in mission restoration, having previously repaired Mission San Juan Capistrano. They now turned their efforts to Mission San Fernando. The Landmarks Club, with support of other civic-minded organizations, financed repair of the mission convento building in time for the mission's 1897 centennial. In addition to reroofing the building, they placed a temporary covering over the mission church to prevent further deterioration. In 1908, the Missionary Sons of the Immaculate Heart of Mary took charge of the nearby parish church of San Fernando. During their tenure, around 1912, several rooms in the convento were restored by the exiled Mexican Archbishop of Oaxaca, Eulogio Glllow y Zavalza, who unsuccessfully attempted to establish a seminary at the mission for clerical students expelled from Mexico.

On August 6, 1916, Lucretia del Valle organized a "candle sale" so that the Landmarks Club could strengthen the mission walls and replace the temporary central portion of the church roofing. At the appointed time some 6,000 concerned citizens assembled at the mission, and for one dollar each bought a candle that bore the name of the donor. Then, carrying the flickering candles at sunset they formed a long procession and marched through the old mission quadrangle. This must have been a truly memorable sight.

After 1923, when the Oblates of Mary Immaculate assumed responsibility for upkeep of the mission, much restoration work was done on the convento. The columns of the cloister were replaced, and a new foundation under the rear wall of the convento, with steel anchors to hold it, was put in place. An entirely new roof replaced the old patchwork roof that had previously covered the convento, and several rooms in the building were restored and reopened. Father Charles Burns, who was in charge of the mission from 1938-1944, initiated an ambitious restoration program to further restore both the convento and the mission church. Under the overall supervision of Dr. Mark Harrington of the Los Angeles Southwest Museum, the convento arches and the interior corridor were rebuilt. The church was refurbished, and one day short of the missions' 144th birthday, on September 7, 1941, Mass was celebrated in the church for the first time since 1874. Between 1945 and 1947, Harrington restored the old kitchen, the belfry, the majordomo's quarters, and the sacristy. The belltower was rebuilt and the mission bells hoisted into place. From 1947 to 1949, with funds from the William Randolph Hearst Foundation, Fr. Augustin O'Dea undertook the final stage of the restoration program, rebuilding the ruins of the Indian workshops that had originally connected the convento and the church.

Interior painted decorations had been known from photographs from 1875 and on, but in the mid-1930's, and especially in the 1941 restoration, traces of earlier, more primitive decorations were found and restored. However, in the church, less than one percent of the plaster on the altar wall survived, so restoration here was largely hypothetical. This was subsequently modified in 1957, and this was the version followed in the rebuilt replica church. The sidewalls had projecting pilasters painted to resemble stonework. It was found that the arches had a "River of Life" motif design, which was restored. Two different dado designs were discovered and partially restored in 1941. The design of the side altars was well enough preserved to allow accurate restoration. The recesses were framed by painted columns with leaf capitals, and an arch with voussiors above. Inside was a second pair of columns, painted in blue, topped with vases of flowers and arches of undulating leaf designs (Neuerburg, 1989, p. 66-67). Later restorations followed these design elements as closely as possible. One unique design panel is located over the exit doorway. Here the archway is painted with a colorful rendition of the "River of Life" motif, and below it, enclosed within the arch, is a stark black and white panel with all of the implements associated with Christ's passion.

Discoveries made in the 1920s and 1930s indicated that the mission convento building had been extensively decorated both inside and outside. Much was restored in the early 1940s, but during the extensive repairs after the 1971 earthquake they were plastered over. The interior of the sala had been decorated at least two times. At one time there was a wall dado of floral and vine motifs in red on pink. A more recent embellishment above the door opposite the entrance is a remarkable frescoe which shows a grape-harvesting scene. There are huge vines, large bunches of grapes, and very small human figures picking the grapes. It is framed with columns topped with vases. This particular frescoe had been replicated in 1987, and probably reworked during 1991-1994, when the late Dr. Norman Neuerburg supervised restoration of both the church and convento wall frescoes.

After the mission quadrangle was restored in 1950, St. Ferdinand's High School was built, and functioned at the mission during the early 1950's. This learning institution moved to new quarters in 1956 when it became Bishop Alemany High School.

On September 8, 1952, construction was begun on a diocesan seminary at Mission San Fernando. The completed Queen of Angels seminary was ready for occupancy by April 1954 and was officially dedicated on November 8, 1954. The seminary buildings blend in beautifully with the older restored mission buildings. The work of Christian education, begun by Father Junípero Serra so many years ago, continues in the same spirit at San Fernando.

Tragedy struck Mission San Fernando a little after 6 p.m. on February 9, 1971 when the massive Sylmar Earthquake (6.5 on the Richter scale) struck the mission complex and damaged the mission buildings severely. The church was damaged beyond repair, so that a replica church had to be built. This was completed and dedicated in November of 1974. Unfortunately, history repeated itself, for on January 17, 1994, at 4:32 a.m., another massive earthquake struck San Fernando. This temblor, now called the Northridge Earthquake, had its epicenter only three miles from the mission. Again, damage to the mission buildings was extensive, but within a few weeks the mission complex was once again functioning normally.

A day that is fondly remembered at Mission San Fernando is September 16, 1987, for on that day His Holiness Pope John Paul II dropped by for lunch! Ostensibly the papal visit was to meet with members of the National Conference of Catholic Bishops. This 5 1/2 hours visit was his second pastoral visit to the United States. At San Fernando, the Pope preached a homily to the assembled Catholic hierarchy of the United States during recitation of Lauds (Morning Prayer). A day later Pope John Paul II visited Mission Carmel and paid homage to Fr. Junípero Serra.

The church facade at Mission San Fernando offers little of memorable architectural style to enchant the observer. It is strikingly plain and unimposing, but it nevertheless has a distinct air of rugged architectural honesty and purity. The two-story campanario was restored in 1945-1946, and at that time had three bells, the largest of which weighs more than 700 pounds and is one of the originals from mission days. The other two are old bells imported from Spain. A unique carillon also hangs in the campanario. It consists of thirty-five bells, digitally controlled. The carillon had originally been at Mission San Fernando in the early 1930s, but over the years it has been changed, moved, and finally updated in the 1970s. It was rededicated at the mission on December 4, 1974. The carillon is now programmed to play the Angelus and other melodies and hymns in addition to Cantica del Alba, an ancient melody taught the Fernandino Indians by the mission padres.

Detail view of the Ezcaray altar at Mission San Fernando with bulto of Nuestra Señora del Pilar on marble support above the tabernacle.

The grounds of Mission San Fernando are beautifully landscaped and lovingly cared for. The quadrangle has a well-tended lawn with a flowing stone fountain at its center. It is built in the shape of a Moorish star, and is said to be a copy of an old fountain in Cordova, Spain. Behind the north wall of the church is a relatively small cemetery. According to church records, 2,425 people, mostly Mission Indians, were buried in the cemetery from 1798 to 1852. The cemetery continued to serve the area until 1917. A new mission cemetery, north and west of the original one, was dedicated on the Feast of All Saints, November 1, 1953.

The interior of the mission church is dominated by the strikingly beautiful Ezcaray altar, reredos, and pulpit. The pieces are Baroque and can be dated to

Ezcaray pulpit in mission church of San Fernando; note decorative wall frescoes.

1687, when Domingo Angel, a wealthy silk manufacturer from Burgos, Spain, had the pieces installed in the chapel attached to the congregation of St. Philip Neri at Ezcaray, Spain. The pieces are carved from blocks of solid walnut and surfaced with gold leaf. They are believed to be the work of a single master craftsman who began his work in 1608. The pieces represent a skill of workmanship and ornamentation rarely seen in this hemisphere.

In 1925 for reasons unknown, the chapel was dismantled and placed in storage. Some time later, all the altar and reredos pieces, an organ, pulpit, paintings, and two bronze bells were shipped to the United States. In 1934, Bishop John J. Cantwell of Los Angeles was contacted and offered the complete furnishings of the Ezcaray Chapel. For financial reasons the offer was declined, and the pieces were sold to a Pasadena collector. After his death, a consortium chaired by Edward T. Foley acquired the collection with the intention that it be used in a planned Los Angeles cathedral. Dr. Mark Harrington, who during this time supervised much of the restoration work at Mission San Fernando, suggested that the chapel pieces be temporarily stored at Mission San Fernando. The possibilities that the planned Los Angeles cathedral might never be built and that the mission might indeed acquire the pieces was uppermost in the minds of all concerned. Accordingly, the Ezcaray Chapel pieces were set up in the mission convento building and opened to public exhibit on June 18, 1941. In 1953 some of the pieces were assembled and used as a reredos for the chapel at the adjoining Queen of Angels Seminary, while some of the pieces remained on long term exhibit in the mission convento. In August of 1982, Msgr. Francis J. Weber attempted to have the Ezcaray pieces installed in the mission church. With diocesan agreement, and funding made possible through a grant from the William H. Hannon Foundation, this became a reality in early 1991. During the spring of 1991 the Ezcaray pieces were shipped to the Carmel studio of Richard Menn where they were repaired, cleaned, and regilded. During the week of November 3, 1991, they were returned to Mission San Fernando, and there reassembled for the first time in many years *(color pages F & R)*.

The 125-pound polychromed carved bulto of San Fernando was installed as the imposing focal point on the restored mission church reredos. San Fernando is shown being welcomed into heaven by God the Father (to his left), God the Son (to his right), and God the Holy Spirit, represented by a dove on the pinnacle of the reredos. The gilded stylized rays emanating from the life size bulto are reminiscent of the glory associated with eternal bliss.

At the right of the upper panel is a bulto of San Felipe Neri, the original patron of the Ezcaray Chapel. On the opposite panel is the bulto of a kneeling Santo Domingo, who holds a wooden rosary. Below, Blessed Father Junípero Serra holds a copy of his Marian Novena in his right hand, and a missionary crucifix in his left. Around his neck is the Cross of Caravaca. On the left is Mary Magdalene attired in the sackcloth traditionally associated with repentant sinners. There are also three painted scenes on the reredos. Above the tabernacle, Nuestra Señora del Pilar stands atop a marble column as she appeared to Saint James the Apostle. Immediately in front of her is a relic of San Fernando, displayed in a reliquary (Weber, 1997, p. 134-139).

Directly across the street from the mission convento building is Brand Park, a seven-acre public park. The land for the park was donated by the Mission Land Company and accepted by the Los Angeles City Council in 1921. Shortly thereafter a decision was made to move one of the mission's original fountains into the park area. This was accomplished on June 6, 1922. The next month, on July 4, 1922, the fountain was officially dedicated by L. C. Brand of the Mission Land Company. Sometime later, an imposing life size bronze statue portraying Fr. Junípero Serra, with his arm around the mission Indian convert Juan Evangelista, was sited adjacent to the old mission fountain. The tranquil park setting with its well-tended lawns, landscaped gardens, and stately trees provide a welcomed oasis to the mission visitor.

CHAPTER EIGHT

THE LAST OF THE SOUTHERN MISSIONS:

SAN LUÍS REY DE FRANCIA 1798,
AND SANTA INÉS 1804

Exterior view of Mission San Luís Rey de Francia showing, from left to right: the arched portico, church facade and campanario, and entrance to the old cemetery.

MISSION SAN LUÍS REY DE FRANCIA:

Synopsis: Eighteenth mission; last mission founded by Father-President of the Alta California missions, Fr. Fermín Francisco Lasuén, on June 13, 1798; named for its patron Saint Louis King of France (1215-1270); churches: 1798, 1802, 1815; secularized in 1834 after an active mission life of only thirty-six years; sold illegally in 1846; restored to Church in 1865; long period of deterioration from 1865-1892; rededicated by the Franciscans in 1893; restorations: 1893-1905, 1912, 1926, 1951, 1959-ongoing.

Location: Mission San Luís Rey de Francia is located above the town of San Luís Rey, five miles east of the city of Oceanside, off of State Highway 76.

San Luís Rey de Francia, Saint Louis King of France, was chosen by the Viceroy of New Spain, the Marquis de Branciforte, as the patron of the eighteenth Alta California Spanish Colonial missions. This, to recognize the relationship of France and Spain through the House of Bourbon. The mission was founded on June 13, 1798, by Fr. Fermín Lasuén.

Louis IX, King of France, was the son of Louis VIII and Blanche of Castille, sister of Saint Ferdinand, King of Spain. He was born in 1215 at Poissy, France. His father died when he was eleven years old, and his mother ruled as regent until his coming of age. He was a just and active ruler who preferred peace to war. He led two crusades: one to Egypt in 1248-1249, which ended in his imprisonment and the second to Tunis in 1270, which resulted in his death from pestilence. He led a holy and devout life, spending much time in prayer and caring for the poor. He was a member of the Third Order of Saint Francis and was eventually considered their patron. Pope Boniface VIII canonized him in 1297.

In devotional art, Luís is generally portrayed in royal garb, usually over armor, wearing a crown and with a scepter in his right hand topped with a fleur-

View of the restored arch and brick steps leading down to the lavanderia at Mission San Luís Rey de Francia.

de-lis. His left hand may hold a sword, a crown of thorns, or an orb. He is usually bearded. He is the patron of the French national church in Rome, Italy, and of the New Orleans and St. Louis Cathedrals in the United States. Devotion to him is most closely associated with the Third Order of Saint Francis.

Representations of San Luís Rey in the Alta California missions are rare. In 1791 an oil painting of him was billed to the Monterey Presidio. It is believed that an oil painting arrived for the founding of his mission, but this has not survived. A large polychrome bulto, which came from New Spain in 1808, is now centrally placed within the mission church reredos.

On February 27, 1798, the colonial governor, Diego Borica, issued a decree to supply soldiers to erect buildings for the founding of a new mission. The actual founding took place on the feast day of San Antonio de Padua, June 13, 1798. Fr. Lasuén, the celebrant, was at this time seventy years of age. Accompanying the Father-President were Frs. Noberto de Santiago (Ca. 1760-Ca. 1818), Antonio Peyrí (1769-?) and José Faura (Ca. 1773-?). Fr. Lasuén remained at the newly founded mission location for some time giving instructions and advice as to the best locations for various crops and the eventual positioning of the future mission buildings.

The mission is grandly sited on a low hill five miles east of the Pacific Ocean, overlooking a beautiful fertile valley. Mission San Luís Rey de Francia was a success from the very beginning. The Indians were friendly, industrious, and eager workers, and more importantly, very willing Christian converts. The first church was the typical initial crude enramada. The second church, completed in 1802 to accommodate a growing congregation, had a tile roof. By 1804 the inner patio had been enclosed. There were quarters for the padres, soldiers, and Indian women, and the overall agricultural enterprise was fully established. After only six years, produce crops averaged five thousand bushels per year, and there were over ten thousand head of various livestock.

Fr. Antonio Peyrí was an amazing man. Not only did he possess a true love and compassion for his Indian charges which they returned to him ten-fold, but he had a true inherent talent for planning, designing, and constructing the mission buildings. This came to fore when construction began on the present church in 1811. This church was completed and dedicated on the Feast of Saint Francis on October 4, 1815. The structure measured one hundred and eighty feet in length, twenty-eight feet in width, and thirty feet in height. Improvements and embellishments continued for another decade. The result was a magnificent mission complex, for by 1826 the mission quadrangle

measured five hundred feet along each side. In front of the patio is the cloister, uniquely distinguished by a long corridor that comprises thirty-two Roman arches. The cloister area had an infirmary, storerooms, and various Indian workshops. Orchards and gardens lay right outside the mission walls. One of the most interesting structures at Mission San Luís is the recently excavated large lavanderia (laundry) which stood at the bottom of a steep hill in front of the mission. It was also an area that was known as the sunken gardens because of the profusion of exotic plants that grew there. The water for the lavanderia flowed naturally from two springs and came out into small pools through Indian carved stone gargoyles. There was even a charcoal filter incorporated into the system to purify water for drinking after it had done the laundry. The area is presently distinguished by a unique brick arch and some fifty brick steps leading down to the lavanderia.

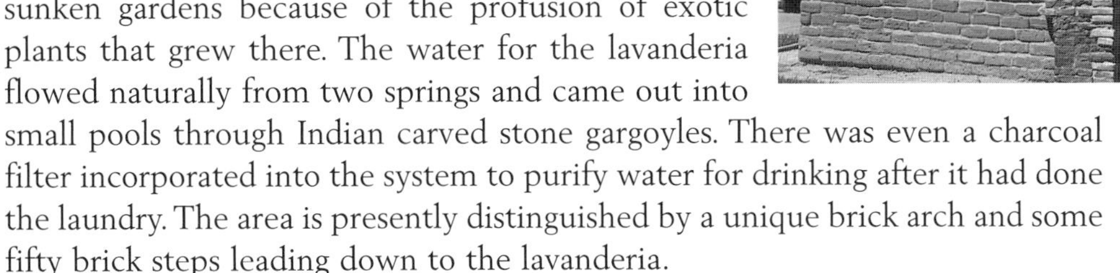

View through the partially ruined archway looking into the friary garden with mission buildings in the background.

By the early 1830s there were some 2,800 Indians living at the mission. The mission's agricultural enterprises extended in radius for fifteen miles. Mission San Luís Rey de Francia raised the most livestock and produced great quantities of produce during any single year. Life flourished at the mission until the Laws of Secularization came into play. At that point the mission's Spanish Franciscans were replaced by Mexican Franciscans from Zacatecas. Fr. Antonio Peyrí tried to work harmoniously with the Mexican padres, but by 1832, after serving the mission with great distinction for thirty-three years, he decided to return to Spain. On January 17, 1832, Fr. Peyrí sailed to Mexico aboard the American ship "Pocahontas" from San Diego Harbor. In the dark of night he left Mission San Luís, his home for so many very productive years, to avoid making sad good-byes to his loving Indians. By morning his ruse was discovered, and a large group of mission Indians rushed to San Diego Harbor to persuade Fr. Peyrí to return. They arrived just in time to see his ship pulling out of the harbor with Fr. Peyrí, arms extended, giving his blessing to those with whom he had spent so many fruitful years.

Detail of Indian carved stone gargoyle from which flowed natural spring water into the catch basins of the lavanderia.

Two Luíseño Indian converts accompanied Fr. Peyrí on this voyage: Pablo Tac and Agapito Amamix. In 1834, they entered the College of Propaganda in Rome and began studying Latin. Agapito became ill and died in the college villa in 1837; he was buried at the monasterey church. Pablo Tac continued his studies, and on February 2, 1839, he took vows to pursue the missionary field, but became ill and died on December 3, 1841. This young convert left behind an extraordinary literary legacy. With the help of Cardinal Giuseppe Caspar Mezzofanti, Chief Custodian of the Vatican Library, Pablo created a vocabulary and dictionary of the

Nicho on back wall of the baptistry at Mission San Luís Rey de Francia with a large polychrome bulto of San Juan Bautista.

Luíseño language. It is believed to be the earliest existing written work by an Alta California mission Indian. Pablo Tac's work was published in 1958 under the title *Indian Life and Customs at Mission San Luis Rey de Francas* by Minna and Gordon Hewes (Barrow, C. S. (Ed.), 1998, pp. 16-17).

Secularization of the mission was formally accomplished in 1834, with the stipulation that the mission lands were to be turned over to the Indians. Unfortunately, Mexican officials and settlers bought or sold mission lands, and many kept the money for themselves. Mission San Luís Rey de Francia was officially surrendered to Mexican officials in 1835. Its condition then deteriorated rapidly. Governor Pío Pico, the last of the Mexican governors, sold what was left of the mission complex in 1846 for $2,437, although true inventoried value was estimated at over $200,000! The mission buildings were stripped and abandoned until the arrival of U. S. troops in late 1846. The famous Indian scout Kit Carson, along with General Kearny and his soldiers, encamped on mission grounds.

On September 12, 1856, the American traveler Henry Miller visited Mission San Luís Rey. He stated (Miller, 1997, p. 55-57) that

> *I arrived at the Mission San Luís Rey in the afternoon, being built on a tableland over looking an extensive valley. The mission buildings have a very imposing appearance and are built in the ancient Spanish style. On the well-preserved church are two bellfrys (sic) of considerable height. The adjoining building forms a large square, to which you arrive by a large door under the porch of the building in front, which is composed of thirty-two arches, resting on solid square pillars. The building in the interior, forming the large square, is constructed in the same style, with a porch running all around, all the buildings being covered with tiles. In the middle of the square is a mount of earth, with a low wall round it, out of which grows a beautiful black pepper tree full of fruit, clad in the finest green. The interior of the Mission is in very good condition. Near the buildings are a few huts in which live some Indian families.*

On the following day, Miller did a sketch of the mission buildings which appears on page 55 of his book.

Shortly before his assassination, President Abraham Lincoln signed the proclamation restoring Mission San Luís Rey de Francia to the Bishop of Los Angeles. For the most part the mission remained abandoned for almost thirty years.

During this time of abandonment, historian H. L. Oak, accompanied by the renowned California historian H. H. Bancroft, visited the mission site on February 26, 1874. Oak (1981, pp. 28-29) noted that

> *The ruins....stand on an elevation overlooking the valley in all directions. They face the south....The church is thirty by one hundred and sixty feet on*

the interior with wings extending some twenty feet farther....It is built of burned bricks, each about six by ten inches and of great hardness....plastered on inside and out with a white, hard lime cement, and the interior frescoed in bright colors. The roof is of tiles. The floor is of white cement....The ceiling is of cloth, and that over the altar rises in an octagonal dome. Square pillars and arches project slightly from the surface of the walls and ceiling, support and ornament the interior. A wooden saint still stands in one of the many niches of the altars. A vase-shaped baptismal font of adobe or concrete stands in the small western wing....The church is still used for service at the monthly visits of the priest from San Diego....The interior of the church shows but little signs of decay, the fresco painting being comparatively intact and fresh....The walls are said however to be unsafe, and the tile roof insecure. The courtyard is about two hundred and fifty by two hundred and eighty feet and is surrounded by a portico of eighty-eight spans or arches each of about twelve feet supported by square pillars twenty-two inches square, each with a cornice and foundation projecting two or three inches.

On page 30, Oak enclosed a sketch of the overall ground plan of the mission complex.

In 1892, a group of Mexican Franciscans from Zacatecas arrived at the mission to escape religious persecution in their homeland. They were joined at the mission by Fr. Joseph Jeremiah O'Keefe, an Irish-born Spanish-speaking priest. Under his supervision the Mexican padres began the massive task of seriously restoring the complex. The overall goal of this endeavor was to establish a Franciscan missionary college. The first year was spent in building quarters for the Mexican priests and brothers working on the restoration. On May 12, 1893, the mission was rededicated by Bishop Mora, and the second phase of restoration began. This included rebuilding of the mission quadrangle as permanent living quarters, which was completed in 1905. In 1895, Fr. O'Keefe became the Mission Superior and continued supervising the overall restoration, and in 1912 he convinced the Franciscan Order to assume the care and rebuilding of the mission complex. During his nineteen years at Mission San Luís he made many improvements and in essence really initiated the first major restoration of the mission. Fr. O'Keefe remained at the mission until 1912 when he asked to spend his remaining years at Mission Santa Bárbara, where he died August 13, 1915.

Detail of the reredos in the mission church of San Luís Rey de Francia with six bultos on pedestals; top row: San Miguel Arcángel, San Luís Rey, San Rafael Arcángel; bottom row: San José, Crucifix, Our Lady of the Immaculate Conception.

In 1913, at the request of the Franciscans, the Sisters of the Precious Blood were called from Dayton, Ohio, to establish a school at the mission. As educational needs changed the Sisters purchased land adjacent to the mission and in 1928 opened the Academy of the Little Flower. In 1948, they added more classrooms, and the school prospered. However, due to the Sisters' advanced age and their inability to find other teaching sisters, they found they could no longer support the school. As a result the academy closed in 1977. The following years have seen gradual yet extensive restoration activity, which continues today. In 1926 a corner of the campanario collapsed and was repaired. During the 1920's and 1930's the mission grounds were utilized as scenic backgrounds for a number of Hollywood motion pictures. Then in 1957, the TV "Zorro" series was filmed at the mission.

Fr. Ferdinand Ortiz continued with the restoration of the church, and studiously followed Fr. Peyrí's original design. This phase of restoration included a new roof, ceiling beams, and a cupola, all of which was completed in 1931. For the mission Sesquicentennial (150th anniversary) celebration on July 18, 1948, Fr. Finbar Keneally arranged a spectacular fiesta pagent, including a wonderful outdoor Mass celebrated by thousands of the faithful. In 1950 the San Luís Rey Franciscan College opened and operated for nineteen years before its closure in 1969. In 1951 the mission was again rededicated after major restoration of two wings of the quadrangle. In all aspects of restoration, the mission depends almost entirely on volunteers and their contributions since the mission does not receive any State or Federal aid. The mission complex also houses a large retreat center built in 1970 that offers year- round activities to the immediate community and surrounding areas.

During the 1970s and 1980s the church parish experienced rapid and sustained growth. It services almost ten thousand Catholics, who now include Anglos, Hispanics, Samoans, Hawaiians, Filipinos, and Vietnamese. Through the Diocese of San Diego the parish first leased, and then purchased the land and buildings adjacent to the old mission from the Sisters of the Precious Blood. Currently, the expanded parish is located on this property east of the mission.

In 1970 the U. S. Department of the Interior designated the mission church as a National Historic Landmark. During the following decade a new $3.5 million dollars church was built. In addition, restoration continued with the rebuilding of the long-destroyed front colonnade of the mission, and construction began to make the church more earthquake safe and to add new quarters for the padres, and new cemetery facilities. The original mission cemetery is enclosed behind a high adobe wall to the right of the church facade. A large cross, built in 1830, stands in memory of those buried in the mission campo santo area, and is dedicated to the Luíseño Indians. By 1832, church records indicate that the mission had registered 2,718 deaths.

The mission bicentennial celebrations took place June 11-28, 1998. On June 13th, there was a Mass of Reconsecration of the mission church with the Vatican Choir (Capella Guilia) a spiritual highlight of the festivities.

Mission San Luís Rey de Francia is imposingly located on a low hill overlooking a beautiful fertile valley. The visitor is immediately entranced with the long arched front corridor and the beautifully proportioned mission church facade. In earlier time the trim of the church facade and cloister balcony were painted gold, but some years ago it was repainted a soft white. Twelve of the original thirty-two Roman arches form the front corridor of the two-story cloister. Today, church offices, a gift shop, and an outstanding museum occupy the first floor *(color page X)*.

To the right of the front cloister is the wonderfully restored old mission church. The pilasters on either side of the double-door entranceway are enclosed by two other pilasters that extend upward to the roofline, and within them are two niches with terra cotta statues. Above the entranceway is an ocular window. The top of the facade has been shaped with curved and coiled edges to form a tall triangular shaped wall above the roofline, and topped with a metal cross. In the center of the facade there is a niche with a statue of the mission's patron, San Luís Rey. To the right of the church facade is a three-story domed campanario capped with a metal cross. The dome is painted light blue. The church adobe walls vary in thickness from six to nine feet.

The interior of the old mission church is one hundred and eighty feet in length, twenty-eight feet in width, and thirty feet in height. The walls of the church are richly decorated with Indian-design painted frescoes *(color page N)*. These have been copied from pictures of the original fresco decorations. Just inside the church and to the left is the domed baptistry. The walls are decorated with a border of painted floral and geometric designs, below which is a red and black painted wall dado. An Indian-made adobe and brick pedestal sits in the center of the room and holds the original hand-hammered copper baptismal font *(color page S)*. On the wall behind the font is a colorfully painted nicho with a large polychrome bulto of San Juan Bautista.

On the right side church wall, opposite the baptistry, is the Madonna Chapel, formerly the mortuary chapel. It is a relatively large room with a high domed ceiling. The walls are brightly painted with Indian decorations. The altar sits in a recessed alcove and is done in typical neoclassical style, topped with a partially closed arch and supported by four painted columns topped with gold painted Corinthian capitals. Enclosed in the center nicho is a large polychrome bulto of the Madonna.

Oil paintings of the Stations of the Cross line both walls of the church interior. They were painted by Mexican artists in the 1780s (Boulé, 1988, p. 13).

Other than the mission church of San Juan Capistrano, San Luís is the only other Alta California mission church built on a cruciform plan. Each transepts holds a side altar. Above the transept is an octagonal dome built of narrow wooden boards that rise to an eight-sided window tower. This domed ceiling is

Detail of one of the neoclassical side altars in the mission church of San Luís Rey de Franica; center nicho with bulto of Saint Francis, to his left a bulto of Our Lady of Sorrows, and on the right a bulto of Our Lady of Solitude, note the painted decorations, especially the "money chain" motif on each side.

unique among the Alta California mission churches. A painted wooden pulpit and its funnel-shaped sounding board sit high on the left side wall close to the sanctuary: it is the original.

The original mission church reredos was demolished by treasure seekers sometime during the lengthy period the church was without a resident priest. During restoration, no attempt was made to duplicate the original reredos, since no pictures or drawings of the original had survived. Instead, the present reredos was constructed so as to fit in with the neoclassical style of the side altars. The reredos has six pedestals standing out from the back of the reredos. The top center one is occupied by a large polychrome bulto of Saint Louis IX, King of France and patron saint of the mission. To his left is a smaller bulto of San Miguel Arcángel, and on the right side is a small bulto of San Rafael Arcángel. Below the top row and in the center is a large square area that holds an imposing crucifix. To the left of the crucifix is a large polychrome bulto of San José, and on the right side is a bulto of Our Lady of the Immaculate Conception. The reredos has six classical urns spaced across the top.

One of the most outstanding attributes of Mission San Luís Rey de Francia is its richly decorated church interior. The original painted fresco decorations were done between 1815 and 1830 and were largely intact when the Franciscans returned in the early 1890's. Since then they have been repainted at least three times. The Indian-style fresco decorations are diverse and very colorful, employing floral and geometric design motifs. The pilasters on the sidewalls are faux-painted to resemble marble. A marbleized cornice circles the church interior above a large-scale lambrequin frieze in red and gold, and with gold tassels. A black lower wall dado with a dark red scalloped outline, similar to that of the lambrequin, is topped by a floral and geometric border (Neuerburg, 1989, pp. 70-71).

Flanking the border of the side altars are painted money chains, looking like lines of coins. The pediments of the side altars are coyingly painted with angels, and on one of these, two angels are holding a royal crown aloft. On a pilaster in the rear nave is a holy water font within a painted shell-like nicho. The decorative painted frescoes in the mission church are diverse, boldly painted, and eye-catching.

ASISTENCIA SAN ANTONIO DE PALA:

Under the prudent guidance and leadership of Padre Antonio Peyrí, the first padre at Mission San Luís, the old mission prospered beyond reasonable expectations. Within a favorable time period Fr. Peyrí was able to found and support an asistencia, San Antonio de Pala, to serve the Luíseño Indians twenty-five miles farther inland. On Saint Anthony's Day, June 13, 1816, the asistencia was formally established. Within two years time the Indians completed construction of a quadrangle measuring two hundred thirty-six feet by one hundred and eighty one feet. The roofs of the buildings were framed with cedar beams cut on nearby Mt. Palomar. Fr. Peyrí designed all the buildings and in addition supervised the construction of an aqueduct. Visitors of the day often remarked on the asistencia's overall prosperity and smooth running operation by the Indians.

This asistencia functioned after the disastrous 1834 secularization of the mother mission, mainly due to traveling priests who looked after the spiritual needs of the Indians, and the maintenance of the asistencia buildings. On Christmas Day of 1899, the buildings suffered serious earthquake damage. Preservationists took an active interest in the welfare of San Antonio de Pala, and under their direction the asistencia was restored by 1903 (Drain, 1994, p. 122).

A distinctive feature of the asistencia is its free-standing two-story campanario with its original bells. Inscriptions on the larger of the two bells note that it was cast in 1816 by Cervantes and includes the Latin text of the prayer generally sung in the Church on Good Friday: "Holy God, Holy Mighty One, Holy Immortal One, Have Mercy On Us." The winter floods of 1916 washed away the campanario's foundation and it fell, along with the bells. Within a years time a new replica campanario was built *(color page B)*.

The interior of the asistencia church has been decorated numerous times. For the most part, the painted fresco decorations survived intact until 1903 when they were whitewashed over. Fortunately, photographs taken in the 1880s and 1890s, showed that all four walls were decorated (Neuerburg, 1989, pp. 32-33). Today the sidewalls are painted with arches held up by painted columns and carry various painted Indian floral and geometric designs *(color page T)*. A repeated wall design is that of a cross standing on top of a stylized hill, a motif that is also inscribed on both campanario bells. All of the devotional statues in the church are modern; a few of the old original ones are in the asistencia museum. A photograph of the altar area taken in May 1990 shows a central nicho carved into the wall behind the altar, with a large statue of San Antonio de Pala. The painted shell-like nicho is bordered by a painted money chain. On a pedestal to the left is a large statue of Our Lady of the Immaculate Conception, and to the right is a large Sagrada Corazón.

The asistencia prospered with over thirteen hundred Indian converts, until beginning a decline in 1846 when some of the buildings fell into ruin. The church was partly restored in 1903 and the original quadrangle fully restored in 1959. Two of the strongest design and architectural components of the church are the exposed wood framing of the roof and the varied Indian-painted wall decorations.

San Antonio de Pala is one of the few surviving asistencias that were founded as sub-missions. It is located in what was the major grain-producing areas for Mission

San Luis and was established here to serve a large and very cooperative Indian population. It was very close to being destroyed when greedy and outright dishonest secular administrators rushed in to gobble up this prime land. As a result, the Indians were in essence dispossessed from their lands. After American occupation most of the asistencia land and property fell into private hands. In 1903 the property was restored to the Indians and the Church, only because the Landmarks Club of California was able to purchase the property from a private owner

An overall view of the facade of Mission Santa Inés, showing the arched corridor, church and the unque attached campanario.

MISSION SANTA INÉS, VIRGEN Y MARTIR:

Synopsis: Nineteenth mission; founded by then Father-President of the Alta California missions Fr. Estevan Tapis on September 17, 1804; named for its patroness Saint Agnes, a Roman maiden martyred in the fourth century; churches: 1804, 1812, 1817; earthquake: 1812; Indian uprising: 1824; secularized in 1834 after an active mission life of thirty years; site of California's first seminary: 1844-1881; illegally sold in 1846; mission property restored to the Church in 1862; seminary transferred to Christian Brothers 1877-1881; collapse of part of mission complex in 1884; collapse of campanario in 1911; mission assigned to Capuchin Franciscan Order of the Irish Province in 1924; restorations: 1812-1817, 1818-1820, 1824, 1851, 1882-1898, 1904-1924, 1926, 1947, 1954, 1970's, 1989, 1992 and ongoing.

Location: Mission Santa Inés is located on the eastern edge of the town of Solvang, at 1760 Mission Drive, three miles east of the town of Buellton off State Highway 246.

Santa Inés, Virgen y Martir, Saint Agnes, Virgin and Martyr was chosen as the patroness of the nineteenth Alta California Spanish Colonial missions. It was founded on September 17, 1804 by Padre Estevan Tapis (Ca. 1756-1825), then Father-President of the missions.

Agnes was a Roman maiden martyred in her early teens around 304 AD during one of the persecutions of Christians by Roman Emperor Diocletian. The oldest stories of her life are contradictory, but all attest to her resolve to retain her virginity as a spouse of Christ. For her refusal to offer incense to the pagan gods she was put into a fire but remained untouched by the flames. She was then beheaded. Her remains were placed in a grave in one of the catacombs outside of Rome. In the reign of Constantine, a basilica was placed above her tomb. In the seventh century the basilica was replaced by the present day structure, S. Agnese Fuori le Mura (St. Agnes Outside the Walls).

Soon after death her cult enjoyed wide popularity and she was venerated for her purity. In the earliest representation of her, on a marble slab in her basilica, she is shown in prayer with her hands outstretched. In the apse of the church, a seventh-century mosaic shows her attired as a Byzantine princess with flames at her feet. In the sixth century church of Saint Apollinare Nuova, built by Emperor Justinian in Ravenna, Italy, she appears in a mosaic frieze among the virgin martyrs, with a lamb at her feet. The lamb, 'agnus' in Latin, became one of her attributes, and she is generally shown carrying one on her left arm. On her Feast Day, January 21st, two lambs are blessed, and their wool is utilized to make palliums for the new archbishops of the year. She may also carry a martyrs palm or a sword, referring to her manner of execution. A baroque statue of her surrounded by flames, is on an altar in the church of Sant' Agnese on the Piazza Navona in Rome, Italy, above the supposed site of her martyrdom.

There is a large oil painting of Santa Ines by the Mexican artist Andrés López at Mission Santa Inés dated 1803. This painting shows the saint carrying the lamb and holding both the palm and lily. Nothing is known of the provenance of the painting at the mission showing her martyrdom, although it appears to be a seventeenth-century work. There is also no documentation for the bulto of her on the mission church reredos, but it appears to be typical of late-eighteenth-century Mexican work that has been modified during the nineteenth century. It was restored in 1953. In the mission gift shop, on a pedestal along the east wall, a statue of Santa Inés, probably of a more recent date, showing her with a halo, with her attributes in reverse position from the bulto on the reredos. She is also clothed more richly.

The founding of a mission between La Purisima and Santa Barbara had been foremost in the minds of the padres for several years. They believed an inland mission north of Santa Barbara would aid their missionary work in the region. They would be able to take advantage of the friendly Chumash Indians' disposition to Christian conversion. The Tulares, a hostile Indian group located

Altar and reredos in the mission church of Santa Inés, originally painted by the mission Indians in 1825 and totally repainted in the 1970's; note bulto of mission patroness in the center nicho.

to the northeast, lay beyond the region of Chumash control, so a new mission sited in the Santa Ynez Valley would secure the area as a buffer zone. Fr. Fermín Lasuén, Father-President of the Alta California missions, directed Fr. Estevan Tapis of Mission Santa Bárbara, and Captain Felipe de Goycoechea of the Santa Bárbara Presidio, to explore the area for possible future mission sites. Fr. Tapis recommended a Chumash village site called Calahuasa. Fr. Lasuén then requested that Governor Diego Borica recommend this as a suitable location for a new mission. The governor then forwarded on his recommendation to the Viceroy, Don José de Iturrigaray, for his approval. In the meantime Fr. Lasuén died at Mission San Carlos on June 26, 1803, and Governor José Joaquin de Arrillaga succeeded Governor Borica. Following the death of Lasuén, Fr. Estevan Tapis became the new Father-President of the Alta California missions, a position he would hold until 1812.

The initially recommended mission site was finally approved and the founding ceremony took place at the designated site on September 17, 1804. The celebrant was Father-President Estevan Tapis, along with the Commander of the Santa Bárbara Presidio, Don Raymundo Carrillo, and Frs. Marcelino Ciprés (1769-1810) of Mission San Luís Obispo, Romualdo Gutiérrez (Ca. 1782-1845), and José Antonio Calzada (1760-1814) of the new Mission Santa Inés. Fr. Tapis blessed water, the site, and the large cross that was planted and venerated. The group, along with Indians from Purisima, Santa Bárbara, and Santa Inés, sang the Litany of All Saints at the temporary enramada. Tapis then sang High Mass, preached a sermon, and concluded the service by singing the "Te Deum Laudamus", and a final "Salve" to the most Holy Virgin. Twenty-seven Indian children were baptized, and fifteen male adults submitted themselves for instruction in the faith. An adobe church was built during that first year, but details regarding it are lacking.

In 1804, a row of buildings was constructed measuring 232 feet in length, and 19 feet in width and height. This wing included a temporary church that was 86 feet in length, in addition to padre quarters, a sacristy, and a granary. With the help of the Chumash Indian converts from Missions Santa Bárbara and Purisima this wing had been completed in six months' time, prior to the formal founding of Mission Santa Inés.

At the end of 1805, Frs. Calzada and Gutiérrez began building another row of buildings similar to the initial one. It measured 145 feet in length by 19 feet in width and height. By 1806 another building 368 feet in length had also been constructed. A corridor, covered with tiles, was added to this; it measured 75 feet in length and 6 feet in width. With the completion of this addition the typical mission quadrangle was completed with each side comprising 350 feet. In 1807, new quarters were built for the padres and by 1810 additional buildings for the soldiers and their families. For the padres Mission Santa Inés was a lonely place; visitors were so infrequent that the mission bells would ring to announce the event.

At ten o'clock on the morning of December 21, 1812, a massive earthquake destroyed almost all of the previous building accomplishments. The mission complex was devastated in this tragedy, but under the guidance of Frs. Francisco Xavier Uría (1770-1834) and Ramón Olbés (1786-?) a temporary church was erected outside the mission quadrangle. Reconstruction continued for four years, and a new church facing east was built of adobe and brick. It measured 140 feet in length, 25 feet in width, and 30 feet in height, with heavily buttressed walls 5 feet thick. Heavy sugar pine timbers from the slopes of the Figueroa Mountains 30 miles away supported the tiled roof. The new church and buildings were dedicated on July 4, 1817. This date was probably deliberately chosen, for on that date Franciscans everywhere celebrate the Feast of the Anniversary of the Dedication of All the Churches of the Order.

Mission Santa Inés continued to grow and develop both its agricultural and livestock enterprises. An 1817 mission inventory lists 12,000 various livestock animals and almost 9000 bushels of sundry produce. The mission attained its greatest Indian population in 1817 with just under 1000 Indians in residence. Ironically, as the number of mission livestock animals grew, along with crops produced, the mission Indian population steadily declined.

When Mexico won her independence from Spain in 1821, and two years later became a republic, a difficult period began for the Alta California missions. In Mexican eyes the missions were identified with Spanish imperialism. As a result the Alta California missions were ignored and allowed to deteriorate. During this time missions, presidios, and settlers were not supplied from Mexico. In order to fill this gap the missions unwillingly became the overall supplier for themselves, the military, and the settlers. This was an undesirable situation at best. Many of the mission soldiers not having received their pay for an inordinate time took out their frustrations on the Indians. Finally, on Sunday February 21, 1824, the mission Indians at Mission Santa Inés took matters into their own hands and revolted against the soldiers' brutal treatment of them. They set fire to the mission buildings, and only when the roof of the church was ablaze did they realize the ramification of their deeds. After all, it was the soldiers they were angry with, not the padres. The Indians themselves finally put out the church fire, but by then many of the mission outbuildings had been burned to the ground. The Indian uprising quickly spread to Missions Purisima and Santa Bárbara and took additional lives and time before it was put down. Once again,

A preserved portion of the 1836 wall that divided the mission into two areas, one for the secular adminstator, the other for the padres.

Doorway from patio courtyard into mission church; note "river of life" motif carved into the door.

over an eight-year period, the mission was rebuilt. However, from that time on Mission Santa Inés would never again be a prosperous working mission.

By 1834, the Laws of Secularization were put into effect, causing the mission system per se to draw rapidly to a close. The missions were transferred from the jurisdiction of the padres to secular administrators. In essence, the Mexican government was attempting to eliminate all Spanish influence by reducing the missions to parish churches. In reality, secularization was but a blind to cover up a gigantic scheme to defraud the Indians of their rightful property. For the time being the secularization decree was not put into effect at Santa Inés, and Fr. José J. Jimeno (1804-1856) kept control of the mission, but without compensating salary. In July of 1836, José M. Ramirez, who had come to Alta California with Governor José María de Echeandia in 1825, appeared at the mission to be received as commissioner for the mission and all its properties. Apparently he turned over his commission almost immediately to José M. Covarrubias, who had been appointed mission administrator. A mission inventory was drawn up and signed by both Fr. Jimeno and Covarrubias, and with this the mission was confiscated and in control of a government agent. The appointment of Covarrubias caused the padres a good deal of trouble. He was a member of a group of politicos led by Pío Pico, whose stated aim was to wipe out all the Alta California missions. Covarrubias had married into Pico's family and so could be depended upon to carry out his aims. Right after taking control of the mission, Covarrubias had a dispute with Fr. Jimeno about the use of the mission courtyard. According to the law, the clergy was allowed the use of one-half of the buildings fronting on the courtyard, and the use of that much of the yard nearest the church. The remaining half was at the disposal of Covarrubias and his family. Dispute over usage continued and finally Fr. Jimeno had the Indians build a wall between the area they used, and the part Covarrubias claimed. The tile capped wall was built of large boulders laid in adobe mortar and ran for nearly 300 feet, thus dividing the mission into distinct church and secular areas. Inventories of church property and produce continued to decline from 1836 to 1839, but by then many of the mission Indians simply fled the mission. There were no longer enough Indians to attend to the crops, the livestock and the maintenance of the mission buildings.

On August 25, 1842, Governor Manuel Micheltorena arrived at San Diego from Mexico. He carried with him instructions from the general government to restore management of the missions to the padres. In 1843 he attempted to slow down the secularization process, and in so doing transferred 35,500 acres of land from Mission Santa Inés to Bishop Francisco García Diego y Moreno, the first appointed Bishop of Alta California. The bishop had arrived at Santa Bárbara in January 1842 and made that mission his residence. He had brought along some students for the priesthood who were quartered with him at Santa

Bárbara and continued their studies there. In 1844 the bishop and his students moved to Mission Santa Inés with the purpose of using the Micheltorena land grant to establish the first college seminary in California. The seminary, Our Lady of Refuge of Sinners, was originally located in the Santa Inés mission compound but was later relocated to the College Ranch near Santa Ynéz where it continued to function until 1881.

In 1846 the sympathetic Governor Micheltorena was replaced by the last Mexican governor, the infamous Pío Pico, who immediately accelerated the secularization process. In June 1846 he illegally sold Mission Santa Inés to Covarrubias and José Joaquin Carrillo for the sum of $7000. This took place just three weeks before the United States absorbed California, and the sale was later declared invalid.

In rooms behind the museum at Mission Santa Inés is Our Lady of the Angels chapel with a beautiful contemporary stained-glass window.

The college seminary continued under the supervision of Frs. José Joaquín Jimeno (1804-1856) and Francisco Sánchez (1813-1884) until May 7, 1850, when management of the mission fell to the priests of the Congregation of the Sacred Hearts of Jesus and Mary (Picpus Fathers of South America). The arrival and short stay of the Picpus Fathers at Santa Inés marked the close of the mission period and the end of Franciscan management. Father Eugene O'Connell succeeded the Picpus Fathers in the summer of 1851. He made the first real attempt at maintaining the mission buildings and made badly needed repairs and improvements.

Regardless, the overall condition of the mission complex continued to decline. On July 3, 1856, the American traveler Henry Miller visited Mission Santa Inés. He noted (Miller, 1995, p. 35):

> *I left early in the morning en route to the Mission "Santa Ynez" which is distant from the Mission La Purisima about 7 leguas in a southerly direction. Passing through a hilly country, well timbered, with the river to my right, I arrived at that Mission. It is built on the edge of a tableland. The church, which has a belfry with two bells in it, is in good condition together with the adjoining house; the rest is a great heap of ruins. The walls of some of the buildings are of an enormous thickness, built of adobe. There is a school established here, called a college, with the priest, an old Spaniard, presiding. I had some conversation with him and the schoolmaster, an old Irishman, who was dressed in ragged clothes, horribly dirty. I counted 9 or 10 boys as dirty and ragged as their preceptor, who are most part children of families residing in Santa Bárbara. After having taken a sketch, which was not a pleasant task, being all the time exposed to a burning sun, I left, taking the road towards Santa Bárbara, which is 12 leguas distant from this place.*

Miller's sketch of Mission Santa Inés is given on page 34.

The United States government formally restored the mission to the Church

Seventeenth century Mexican bulto of Our Lady of Solitude in the chapel of the Madonna at Mission Santa Inés, crucifix above nicho is an eighteenth century Mexican woodcarving; note various painted wall decorations.

in a proclamation signed by President Abraham Lincoln on May 23, 1862. Possession was given to the Bishop of Monterey, Joseph Sadoc Alemany, and to his successors.

On March 11, 1874, historian H. L. Oak, accompanied by the renowned California historian H. H. Bancroft and his daughter, visited Mission Santa Inés. Oak (1981, p. 70-72) stated,

> *There is no settlement here the only inhabitants being the padre, Juan Basso, and a Frenchman who keeps a store to supply the sheep herders who live at different points in this part of the valley. The buildings face the east and except the Church and the adjacent front court building are in a state of complete ruin....The church walls are built of brick, or at least are faced with bricks on the exterior, and plastered inside and out. These walls and those of the front court building are about six feet thick. The roof and part of the walls of the north wing are fallen. The east wall of this wing and another detached wall six feet thick and six feet distant from the first serve as a bell-tower each supporting two bells. The floor of the church is of square flags of stone (actually clay tiles) about 18 inches square. A gallery crosses the front end, which is reached....by a wooden staircase on the inside. The western end is where the altar is, inside of a railing, it is frescoed or ornamented on the walls and ceiling, which is of timber and boards whitewashed in other parts of the room....On the east and west of the front court building, but fallen on the southern half of the latter is a portico of brick arches each of ten feet supported by pillars of brick square and with cornices.*

Oak included a ground plan sketch of the entire mission complex (page 71 of his book).

Both of the previous firsthand accounts show the general deterioration of the mission buildings. This was made abundantly clear when on a first Sunday in October, Fr. Juan Basso (1863-1865), celebrated Holy Mass for the congregation, and after reading the Gospel he ascended the pulpit to preach the sermon. While speaking the pulpit was suddenly wrenched from its wall holdings and fell to the floor. Fortunately, it did not turn over, but the astounded padre found himself on the steps of the sanctuary. What better testament to the overall condition of the mission buildings? The pulpit was never replaced. Thus Mission Santa Inés lacks a prominent feature found in all of the other Alta California missions.

In 1877, supervision of the seminary was transferred to the Christian Brothers, who remained until 1881 when financial difficulties led to their departure. At that point the bishop sold off 20,000 acres of mission land, reducing the mission land holdings to approximately 16,000 acres.

In 1882, the Thomas J. Donahue family came from Ireland to live at Mission

Santa Inés for the next sixteen years. The family, whose father was a stonemason, resided in the southern half of the rectory, and on their own continued to make stopgap repairs and minor restoration to some of the mission buildings. The continuing deterioration of the buildings was beyond the capability of a single family and the structures continued their slow decline. The southern section of the front corridor collapsed in 1884, and soon thereafter adjacent buildings fell into ruin.

A new episode in the history of Mission Santa Inés began in July 1904, with the appointment of diocesan priest Father Alexander Buckler as pastor of the mission. He was a native of the Lower Rhine region of Germany. He began a concerted effort to both restore and maintain the mission buildings and their contents. He reroofed the church and what remained of the convento, reinforced the walls and foundations of the church, and built a new water and drainage system. In those endeavors he was aided by the numerous homeless men he housed and fed on the mission grounds. With their help he turned the mission ruins into what one might call a fair facsimile of what Mission Santa Inés had been. All who came to the mission marveled at "Padre Alejandro's Tramps" who brought some order to the ruins. During an exceptionally heavy rainstorm in 1911, the campanario collapsed. In 1912, Father Buckler built a new tower, adding a third arch, instead of building a replica of the original campanario.

Polychromed bulto of Our Lady of the Rosary in the mission church of Santa Inés; this Mexican baroque sculpture dates from the mid-eighteenth century.

Another of Father Buckler's achievements at Mission Santa Inés was the preservation and restoration of a large collection of church vestments. The mission collection comprises early church vestments from the 15th century to 1718 because Santa Inés became a repository for church vestments from earlier missions in Baja California and Mexico. Father Junípero Serra collected many vestments from the early missions of Baja California, and among the mission collections is a vestment he wore. The fine preservation and restoration of this irreplaceable collection is due almost solely to a twenty-year labor of love by Mamie Goulet Abbott, the niece of Father Buckler.

Father Buckler retired from Mission Santa Inés in 1924 due to failing health. At that time Bishop John J. Cantwell of Los Angeles offered the mission to the Provincial of the Franciscans. They declined the invitation, whereupon the bishop offered the mission to the Capuchin Franciscan Order of the Irish Province. The Capuchins accepted the invitation, and one of their first concerns was the installation of modern plumbing and electric lighting to improve mission living conditions. The inner patio garden at the mission was given a more formal appearance in 1926 when the Capuchins planted a hedge in the shape of a Celtic cross.

The Capuchins began a full mission restoration in 1947, funded in part by a grant from the William Randolph Hearst Foundation which allowed major restoration to begin. When the roof was removed from part of the mission they

Outdoor devotional site at Mission Santa Inés dedicated to the Virgin of Guadalupe and showing the Indian boy Juan Diego paying homage to the Holy Mother.

discovered several rooms that had been utilized as living quarters during the previous century. They also discovered an open balcony with rooms behind it, above the arches. They made extensive repairs to the roof and remodeled sections of the southern end of the building. The building was restored to its original two-story configuration, as it was prior to the 1812 earthquake. The campanario was remodeled to its original design before its collapse in 1911. The restoration work confirmed the mission originally had 22 Roman arches along its front, not 21 as previously believed. One of the mission bells was sent to Rotterdam for recasting and was returned in time to ring out the 150th anniversary of the mission in 1954. Many additional restoration projects were initiated, including a new heating system to preserve the collection of devotional art in the mission.

Repair and restoration of the mission museum occurred during the tenure of Father Timothy O'Sullivan (1950's-1960's), in addition to other innovations he began. The Chapel of the Madonna adjacent to the museum was created during this time. The polychromed Madonna bulto is a 17th-century Mexican sculpture of Our Lady of Solitude. The crucifix above the Madonna is an 18th-Century Mexican woodcarving.

The entire mission was repainted and weatherproofed. An improved irrigation and drainage system was installed in the newly landscaped patio gardens. Two new bronze bells named "Santa Inés" and "Saint Francis" were cast and installed in the campanario in 1984.

A church fiesta in August of 1989 celebrated years of hard work culminating in a million-dollar renovation and restoration project for the mission's east wing. A primary goal was the reconstruction of the nineteen arches that form the facade of the building. When this was completed the mission appeared as it was prior to the 1834 secularization. Restoration effort on mission artifacts and paintings became a focus in 1992 and is ongoing.

Two wonderful additions have been made to the outside of the mission complex, specifically at the east end. An outdoor shrine dedicated to the Virgin of Guadalupe with the Indian Juan Diego kneeling at her feet is an exceptional devotional site. Another, is the outdoor area devoted to the fourteen Stations of the Cross. Each station has been thoughtfully partitioned and nicely landscaped, and has a large wooden cross with an attached painting on the crossbars, representing each sorrowful event. The surrounding grounds are well tended and offer a sanctuary where the pilgrim can personally experience a time of tranquil devotion. Presently, the mission convento has a very well-supplied gift shop and an outstanding museum displaying a well-organized collection of mission artifacts *(color page I)*.

Between the museum and the church is a 12 feet thick wall into which the entranceway to the church has been cut. Upon entering the church one is immediately impressed with a pervasive warm feeling, for here is an intimate place of devotion that is obviously cherished by a loving congregation. Along the nave there are tromp-de-oeil paintings on which elaborate architectural details and various designs have been applied. Most of the original Indian painted decorations remained untouched until the 1970s-1980s when they were totally repainted *(color page N)*. The visitor's eyes are directed to the front of the church with its painted altar and reredos, originally done by mission Indians in 1825. In a central nicho is a polychrome bulto of the mission's patroness, Santa Inés, which probably came from Mexico in the early 1800's *(color page K)*. Oil paintings of the Stations of the Cross line the church sidewalls. They were painted in the late 17th century and are copies based on engravings from the church of Santa Maria del Giglio in Venice, Italy. On the right side of the nave, in the area that had originally been a doorway to the cemetery, stands a large polychrome bulto of Our Lady of the Rosary. This is a beautiful Mexican Baroque period piece from the mid-18th century. In a small baptistry area along the right sidewall is the original hand-hammered copper and zinc baptismal font sitting on a pedestal. Above it, on a shelf, is a carved bulto of San Juan Bautista; behind that is a colorful painted scenic decoration. The church ceiling has the original beams, and the tile floors are also original. Five Franciscan padres are buried under the tile floor of the church.

On east side of Mission Santa Inés is an outdoor area devoted to the fourteen Stations Of The Cross, each with a painting depicting a particular event and offering a tranquil site for the visitor; photo shows Station V "Jesus is helped by Simon".

The exterior facade of the mission church is quite plain. A small metal cross above the main entrance is the only decoration *(color page U)*. Above this is a large rectangular arched window, above which is a triangular-shaped gable that reaches up to the overhanging tile roofline. The double wooden doors are carved with the "River of Life" motif. The church and convento are painted a light tan color with dark brown trim.

Attached to the right of the church is the restored campanario, which holds three of the original bells. They hang in pierced arches in two rows two bells below and one above, in a shaped arch capped with a metal cross. Pediments decorate either side of the arch. The bells were cast in Peru in 1807, 1817, and 1818.

Behind the campanario is the mission cemetery. Here the graves, some marked with wooden crosses, hold the remains of 1600 mission Indians.

In back of the convento is a beautifully tended patio, in the center of which is a flowing fountain. Lovely rose bushes abound. On one side of the patio is a fragment of the 1836 wall which divided the mission into two areas, one for the secular administrator and the other for the padres. The presently restored mission complex forms an L-shaped cluster of buildings, which only suggests the size of the original mission complex.

The Capuchin Franciscan Fathers are indeed good custodians of today's Mission Santa Inés.

CHAPTER NINE

CLOSING THE MISSION CHAIN:

SAN RAFAEL ARCÁNGEL 1817, AND SAN FRANCISCO SOLANO 1823

(Left) View of the plain facade of the replica San Rafael Mission Chapel; note star-shaped window above chapel entrance.

(Right) View of the present-day parish church of San Rafael, located adjacent to the mission chapel; note distinctive bell tower.

MISSION SAN RAFAEL ARCÁNGEL:

Synopsis: Twentieth mission; originally founded as a hospital and asistencia of Mission Dolores by four padres: Frs. Vicente Francisco Sarría, Ramón Abella, Narciso Durán, and Luís Gil y Toboada, on December 14, 1817; named for its patron Saint Raphael Arcángel, the "Healer of God"; asistencia chapel built in 1818; raised to full mission status in 1822; Indian uprising in 1829; secularized in 1834 after a brief mission life of only seventeen years; abandoned 1844; offered for sale in 1846; small portion of mission land returned to Church in 1855; razed in 1870; replica chapel constructed in 1949.

Location: Mission San Rafael Arcángel is located in the city of San Rafael, at the corner of Fifth Avenue and Court Street, approximately fifteen miles north of San Francisco.

San Rafael is one of the three Arcángels mentioned by name in the scriptures and venerated liturgically. His name means "Healer of God," so he was an appropriate patron for a hospital and asistencia to which persons could go to recover their health. Rafael appears as one of the protagonists in the Old Testament apocryphal Book of Tobit. Tobit, a just man who had a son Tobias, had been blinded by the excrement of a bird. Tobit sent Tobias, accompanied by Rafael in disguise, on a journey to retrieve a debt owed to him. When the pair reached the River Tigris a fish jumped out at Tobias, and he caught it. Rafael instructed him to cut out the heart, liver, and gall. In time, they arrived at the house of Raguel, the father of Sara, to whom Tobias was betrothed. Sara, however, had previously had seven husbands, but because the Devil lusted after her, all of them died before the marriage was consummated. Tobias burned the liver and heart of the fish with ashes of perfume, and the odor caused the Devil to flee. As a consequence his wedding night with Sara was happily consummated. After they collected the debt owed to Tobit they returned home; Tobias put the gall on his father's eyes and cured him of his blindness. It was then that Rafael revealed his true identity.

In devotional art, when Rafael is represented alone, he is generally portrayed as a young man dressed as a pilgrim. He is winged and carries a fish in his left hand and a traveler's staff with a water gourd tied to the top of it in his right hand. He is the patron of travelers, a protector against eye diseases as well as other illnesses, and a protector against monsters.

There are a number of oil paintings and bultos of San Rafael Arcángel in the Alta California missions. A bulto originally sent to Mission San Juan Capistrano in 1800 has recently been restored after having been found in fragments in the sacristy of the ruined church. Another bulto of Rafael, now on the reredos of Mission San Luís Rey de Francia, probably came from the San Diego Presidio. A large oil painting dating from 1818 is presently in the mission chapel of San Rafael. A fine eighteenth century Mexican oil painting of Rafael, presently at Mission San Miguel, originally came from Mission San Antonio de Padua. In the mission church of Santa Bárbara there is a large mid-eighteenth century Mexican oil painting in which all three Arcángels appear. At Mission Santa Inés there is a unique primitive oil painting of Rafael done by a Mission Indian sometime in the early nineteenth century.

San Rafael did not begin as a mission but became one later on. San Rafael was conceived and built as a sanitarium to aid and succor the sick Indians from Mission San Francisco de Asís (Dolores). Converted Indians at Mission Dolores were dying faster than at any of the other Alta California missions due to the inclement foggy, damp, and windy year-round climate. The mission padres were determined to find a sunnier, more hospitable location for their sick charges. The site they chose was an ideal location across San Francisco Bay and north of Mission Dolores, where rolling hills east of the site protected it from the cold, damp winds. Best of all it was indeed a sunnier location!

This sub-mission or asistencia to Mission Dolores was founded in joint celebration by four Franciscan padres on December 14, 1817, Frs. Narciso Durán of Mission San José, Ramón Abella of Mission Dolores, and Frs. Luís Gil y Toboada, and Vicente Sarría. All participated in raising the Cross and performing the ceremonies marking the establishment of this asistencia to Mission Dolores. San Rafael Arcángel, as patron saint of good health, was appropriately chosen as the patron of this asistencia. On the founding day twenty-six Indian children were baptized, and two hundred adult Indians agreed to take instruction in the faith.

The more sickly of Mission Dolores Indians were immediately transferred to the new asistencia, along with a few converts gathered from surrounding areas. By the end of the first year there were more than three hundred Indians in residence.

Fr. Gil was assigned to be in charge of this new asistencia both because he had more knowledge of medicine than most other padres and because he was an accomplished linguist familiar with a number of local Indian dialects.

Since San Rafael had been conceived as a hospital and sanitarium, no effort was made to construct anything but a small building that would serve as an auxiliary sanitarium with a small chapel at one end. In a short time, the Indians erected a structure that measured eighty-seven feet in length by forty-two feet in width. The overall space was divided into a hospital, chapel, store rooms, and padre's quarters. The asistencia records were housed at Mission Dolores, and initially the Indians of San Rafael counted as part of the Mission Dolores population. There was no campanario; instead, three bells were hung from a stout wooden frame, and no attempt was made to erect subsidiary buildings to form a typical mission quadrangle.

Close-up view of the original mission bells mounted on a sturdy wooden frame just to the left of the chapel entrance at Mission San Rafael.

By 1819, under the solicitous care of Fr. Gil, the sick Indians began to recover. Ironically, it was Fr. Gil who became a sick man. That year he was assigned to another mission and was replaced at San Rafael by an outstanding padre, Fr. Juan Amorós (1773-1832). Not only was Amorós a well educated man for the times, but he was a devoted and energetic worker loved by both the settlers and the Indians—no small feat for an Alta California missionary! Fr. Amorós established and developed fine vineyards and orchards at the asistencia, and his fruit orchards were especially renowned for their marvelous pears. In addition, he also developed the typical mission enterprises, including the not so familiar one of boat building. This was an important endeavor at San Rafael where trips back and forth across the bay were of primary importance. Fr. Amorós rejuvenated the San Rafael Indian community, and before long close to one thousand Indians resided at the asistencia. As a result of the care given to the Indians and the rapid growth of the facility, San Rafael was raised to full mission status on October 19, 1822. Under Fr. Amorós' excellent leadership the mission Indian population reached 1140 by the end of 1828.

It should be remembered that by establishing another mission so far north, the Spaniards were served with an additional lookout post to observe the activities of the Russian enclaves at Fort Ross, farther north along the coast, and their inland expansion at Bodega Bay. Mission San Rafael admirably served this function, as did Mission San Francisco Solano at Sonoma. As a result Mission San Rafael became a stopping off place for soldiers traveling north. Visits of the military provided Fr. Amorós with a welcome break at this lonely missionary outpost. He also welcomed the military for the pragmatic reason that there was a constant fear of Indian attacks. Visitors of the day told of seeing guards on twenty-four hours duty, alert for any impending attack. One Indian troublemaker was named Marin. Early on he had been baptized by Fr. Amorós, but he later renounced the padre and joined with another Indian troublemaker called Quintin. Both caused the good padre much trouble over the years, but Marin returned to the fold and lived at San Rafael until his death in 1834. California eventually named a county after him, and Quintin gave his name to the infamous prison known as San Quentin.

The long foreseen Indian attack materialized in February of 1829. Loyal mission Indians took Fr. Amorós to a hiding place and formed a human shield around him to protect him from the attackers. They eventually hid him in the marshes and saved his life, but fighting continued between the soldiers and hostile Indians. When Fr. Amorós finally returned to the mission he found it was badly damaged and needed extensive repairs. Once the repairs were completed the mission continued to grow, but Fr. Amorós, after thirteen years of devoted service to the mission Indians, sickened and died in 1832. His tenure at Mission San Rafael was very productive, and he was almost solely responsible for all the accomplishments this small mission would ever have. He was buried in the mission chapel.

Mission San Rafael had its best year in 1832 with a produce crop of almost 20,000 bushels and various livestock herds numbering 5500. However it was during this time when, by law, Mexican Franciscans from Zacatecas replaced Spanish-born Franciscans in all the Alta California missions. At Mission San Rafael a Mexican padre, Fr. José Mercado, was sent to replace Fr. Amorós. This was a most unfortunate choice since Fr. Mercado was a man of violent excesses along with an uncompromising nature. One who would not tolerate anything he regarded as insubordination. He was a source of contention to the soldiers and the provincial government. In one instance, he accused a visiting Indian group of theft and then armed his own mission Indians, ostensibly to prevent any reprisals. His armed Indians were then accused of wrongly attacking another group of visiting Indians on Fr. Mercado's command, an attack that left twenty-one dead Indians. For this intolerable act Fr. Mercado was exiled to Mission Soledad as punishment. Still, the damage done to the mission by this problem padre caused great disruption to the everyday life of the mission Indian community.

Secularization was put into effect at Mission San Rafael in 1834. At that

Detail of the mission chapel reredos at San Rafael and center nicho with carved oak bulto of mission patron.

point, inventoried value of the mission was placed at slightly over $15,000, which was primarily the property value. The mission chapel value was listed at less than $200.

At this time, General Mariano Vallejo was in charge of all the military in Alta California. During his military service he came to know the missions very well, and more importantly, he was familiar with all of the loopholes in the laws of secularization. One important provision of those laws was that the padres were no longer in control of the Indians. Without the padre's advice and help, the Indians were unable to grasp the fact that land turned over to them had to be farmed or it would be lost. General Vallejo fully understood this and proceeded to confiscate unused Indian land, adding it to his own extensive land holdings. Since he was the officially appointed mission administrator he continued to confiscate mission equipment, supplies, and even the Indians themselves, whom he incorporated as peons into the work force of his large rancho in Sonoma. He did not leave anything behind; even the fruit trees and vineyards were taken up and replanted on Vallejo's ranchos.

In 1840, only one hundred and fifty Indians remained at Mission San Rafael, and by 1844 the mission was abandoned. What was left of the abandoned property was sold in 1846 for $8,000, but this sale was later declared illegal when the United States absorbed California. Captain John C. Fremont used the mission as his headquarters during the Mexican War in late 1846. In 1855, the U. S. Government restored six and one-half acres of mission land to the Church, but by this date the old mission adobe building was in ruins. Church services were conducted four miles from the old mission site at the St. Vincent Orphanage. During the 1860's the once flourishing mission orchards were used as camping grounds for squatters and derelicts. By 1870 the last mounds of melted adobe were cleared away to make room for the expanding city of San Rafael. In 1909, the Native Sons of the Golden West erected a mission bell and sign at the old mission site.

All that remained at the old mission site was a solitary pear tree from the original mission orchard. In conjunction with the 1949 construction of a replica chapel on the original asistencia site, Msgr. Thomas Kennedy transplanted a small tendril from this tree, nurturing it and replanting it as a living symbol of Fr. Juan Amorós' spirit that so infused the early mission Indians at Mission San Rafael.

It was a difficult task to build the replica chapel, since so few paintings or drawings of the old mission chapel were available. One exception to this was the mission painting done by the renowned California artist Henry Chapman Ford in the 1880's (see Johnson, 1968, p. 299). As a guide, this painting shows clearly just how architecturally plain the old mission chapel was.

The 1949 restoration of the mission chapel was helped in part by a grant from the William Randolph Hearst Foundation. The walls of the chapel were constructed of hollow concrete and then stuccoed over to resemble the original adobe texture. This replica chapel is approximately the same size as the original 1818 structure. The chapel facade is quite plain. The arched entranceway has concrete pilasters on either side. Over the doorway are two star-shaped windows, a smaller one above the larger, reminiscent of the Moorish star window on the facade of Mission Carmel. Three of the original mission bells hang from a stout wooden frame to the left of the chapel entrance. The interior sidewalls of the chapel are hung with contemporary hand carved bas-relief depictions of the Stations of the Cross. Hanging from the vaulted beam ceiling are wrought iron chandeliers fabricated to resemble the old mission candleholders.

The altar and reredos are contemporary in style and are painted a soft earth tone color with selective gilding. In the center arched nicho stands a tall bulto of the mission's patron, San Rafael Arcángel. The interior of the nicho is painted blue, and the top of the nicho has a gilded carved shell design. The reredos is topped with a gilded cross and a gilded vase on either side. The panels of the reredos have gilded stylized floral reliefs. On both sides of the reredos are oval nichos carved into the chapel wall. Each contains tall carved wooden bultos sitting on pedestals. In the nicho on the left side is a polychrome bulto of the Virgin of Guadalupe, and on the right side is a bulto of Saint Joseph. All the bultos are carved from oak wood.

The pulpit is situated at the right front of the arched sanctuary, and is decorated with a bas-relief carving of San Rafael Arcángel. Several deeply inset windows along the right sidewall of the chapel bathe the interior in a warm, sunny glow.

Attached to the left of the chapel building is a wing comprising a large gift shop and a small museum entered through the gift shop.

The present-day large parish church of San Rafael is sited to the left of the mission chapel, and faces the main street. Its exterior is characterized by an imposing tower with an oval nicho over the entranceway. In front of the nicho is a beautiful large bronze sculpture of a winged San Rafael holding up a cross in his right hand. The church was built in 1919 and has been remodeled and restored in 1926, 1949, and 1993.

MISSION SAN FRANCISCO SOLANO:

Synopsis: Twenty-first and last of the Spanish colonial Alta California missions; only mission established during California's Mexican period; dedicated on July 4, 1823, by Fr. José Altimira; named after Peruvian apostle St. Francis Solano; churches: 1824, 1832; Indian uprising in 1826; secularized in 1834; razed in 1838; present chapel built in 1840; offered for sale in 1846, but there were no buyers, finally sold in 1881 to a private party; mission purchased by California Landmarks League in 1903; damaged in 1906 earthquake; restorations: 1911-1914, 1943-1944; property deeded to the State of California by Landmarks League in 1926; mission presently administered as a museum by the State of California, and officially known as Sonoma Mission State Historic Park comprising the mission, soldiers' barracks, and General Mariano Vallejo's home.

View of the front of the Sonoma Mission, San Francisco Solano, with it's tiled roof, and exterior corridor supported by wooden posts instead of the usual mission adobe/brick arches.

Location: Mission San Francisco Solano is located off of State Highway 12 in the city of Sonoma, facing a corner of the Sonoma Pueblo Plaza.

San Francisco Solano, Saint Francis Solanus, was chosen as the patron of the twenty-first and last of the Alta California colonial missions. The mission was dedicated on July 4, 1823, by Fr. José Altimira (1787-1860?). Originally, this was supposed to be a site for the "New Mission San Francisco de Asís," but this intended move and designation was not approved by the Father-President of the missions. Instead, the mission came into being as Mission San Francisco Solano.

Francis Solano was born in Montilla, south of Cordova, Spain, of noble parents in 1549. His birthplace is presently renowned for the famous Amontillado sherry wines produced in the area. Francis joined the Franciscans at age 20, and was ordained a priest at age 27. He was noted not only as a preacher, but also as an accomplished musician (violinist). He served as a missionary to South America, primarily in Peru and Paraguay. He was an outstanding linguist and was able to preach to the Indians in various dialects. His final assignment was as superior of a monastery in Lima, Peru, where he died in 1610. His beatification occurred in 1675, his canonization in 1726. He is presently regarded as the Apostle of South America.

Detail of the entrance to Mission San Francisco Solano, with stout wooden timber frame holding one of the missions' original bells cast in 1829.

In devotional art, he is generally depicted in a Franciscan habit, carrying a cross. He is sometimes portrayed holding a violin. On the stone relief eighteenth-

Dressed bulto of Our Lady of Sorrows sitting on a pedestal on the left side of the altar in the chapel at Mission San Francisco Solano; note background painted decorative nicho with floral designs.

century reredos presently in the church of Cristo Rey, Santa Fe, New Mexico, he is shown performing a baptism. A 1743 dressed statue of him is present in the Monastery of San Francisco in Lima, Peru. A large 1764 oil painting of him preaching by the Mexican artist José de Páez, adorns the cloister of the College of San Fernando in Mexico City. Interestingly, this painting would have been familiar to those padres passing through the college on their way to assignments in Alta California. Fr. Junípero Serra was in residence at the college when the painting was done, and he held San Francisco Solano in special esteem.

Only a few images of San Francisco Solano made their way to the missions of Alta California. Oil paintings of him originally present at Missions San Carlos and San Francisco Solano disappeared long ago. A Mexican oil painting of him shown preaching to the Indians, done in the late 18th century, was listed on Mission Santa Bárbara inventories of 1854 and 1858, but has recently disappeared. An oil painting of San Francisco Solano is present in Mission San Fernando Rey de España. A small bulto of him was sent to Mission Santa Clara and survived the fire of 1926; it is presently on one of the side chapels of the mission church. A large handsome bulto of him now on a side altar at Mission San Francisco de Asís (Dolores), possibly arrived from Mexico along with the reredos around 1810.

Mission San Francisco Solano had its inception in a bit of religious and political chicanery. Fr. José Altimira was one of the last of the Alta California Franciscan padres born in Spain. He arrived in Monterey in August of 1819 and was assigned to Mission San Francisco de Asís. He was a young missionary possessed with a burning desire to make a great harvest of Indian conversions. Unfortunately, Mission Dolores was a poor site for numerous promising Indian conversions. Altimira saw himself as another Father Junípero Serra. He believed that the poor conditions existing at Dolores presented him with an excellent opportunity for a radical change in the overall missionary situation. Since he personally regarded Mission Dolores as a failed missionary enterprise, he reasoned that the best way to solve the problem would be to join Mission Dolores with asistencia San Rafael and then establish a completely rejuvenated mission in the fertile Sonoma region. This mission to be named the "New San Francisco de Asís Mission." Unbeknownst to the religious authorities, Fr. Altimira took his plan to Governor Luís Arguello, who thought it had some merit because be believed that by interposing an additional Spanish settlement/mission between the Russians at Fort Ross and Spanish Alta California he could keep closer watch on their expansionist activities. Since the governor was sympathetic to Altimira's plan for a new mission for his own motives, he gave his approval. After spending some days in search of a suitable mission site, Altimira and a small group of men found a desirable spot 20 miles north of San Rafael. On July 4, 1823, Altimira conducted his own personal founding ceremony and bestowed the name "New San Francisco Mission." He returned to Mission Dolores and prepared for the transfer. Then in the following month, August, he returned to the site with soldiers, Indians, and some supplies and began to prepare the site for the building of a church. By now, Fr. Amorós of San Rafael and Father-President Fr. José Señán strongly opposed the steps Altimira had taken without prior church approval. The young headstrong Altimira was ordered to stop construction at the mission site. He complied with the order but was furious. He then wrote an angry letter to the governor complaining of his difficulties with his fellow padres. After a number of letters had been exchanged, a three-way compromise was reached by the parties. Mission Dolores and San Rafael were to stay in place, and asistencia San Rafael would be accorded full mission status. Permission was granted to Fr. Altimira to complete the building of his mission, but it was to be named "San Francisco Solano", not "New San Francisco de Asís."

Large dressed bulto of San José sitting on a pedestal on the right side of the altar in the chapel at Mission San Francisco Solano.

The obstinate padre set about to prove the merit of his new mission. He built a wooden church and dedicated it in April 1824. Upon its completion, only Mission Dolores made the customary donation of goods and livestock that was generally given by other missions when a new mission was established. Ironically, the Russians at Fort Ross donated supplies and materials to this new mission endeavor.

By October of 1823, the mission buildings Fr. Altimira had started earlier were completed, and he laid out an area to mass-produce adobe bricks. He built kilns and even laid the foundations for a new church. In the early years he established thriving agricultural and livestock enterprises and initiated an ambitious building program. At the end of the first year close to 500 Indians were at the mission, although many of those were from Missions Dolores and San Rafael. By 1825 the padres quarters had been completed, along with housing for the soldiers and a granary. In 1826, an adobe wall capped with tile enclosed the completed mission quadrangle. Once the mission was fully established, Fr. Altimira found that he had most everything he needed to make a success of the mission except for that one crucial component, his lack of leadership. The mission Indians did not hold Padre Altimira in high esteem since he believed that teaching them Christian doctrine was more effective when accompanied by flogging and restraint. As a consequence some of the Indians fled the mission rather than serve under this misguided padre. By 1827 the mission Indians were in a state of revolt, and a few even set fire to some of the mission buildings and supplies. It became abundantly clear that although Fr. Altimira had much ambition, he was totally inept at working with and for the Indians. Eventually, in January of 1828, he had to flee for his own safety first to Mission San Rafael, and then to Mission San Buenaventura. Sometime later, without informing anyone or consulting his superiors, he left for Spain aboard

Interior view of the restored chapel at Mission San Francisco Solano showing wooden altar railing, altar, painted wall decorations, and two dressed bultos on either side of the altar.

an American vessel. The historian Bancroft reported that as late as 1860, Padre Altmira was living at Tenerife on the Canary Islands (Geiger, 1969, p. 9).

Fr. Buenaventura Fortuny (1774-1840) who had been a co-worker with Fr. Narciso Durán at Mission San José, replaced Fr. Altimira at Mission Solano. He arrived at the mission to find the Indians confused and demoralized. However, Padre Fortuny was an excellent and benevolent priest with a great capacity for leadership. Within two years time he had the mission running better than ever. He laid the foundations for a larger adobe church on the east side of the mission quadrangle, which was completed in 1832. By that time he had completed thirty buildings within the mission quadrangle. In addition he had close to 1000 Indians working some 10,000 acres of mission lands and maintaining various enterprises. Fr. Fortuny retired at this time after serving the mission for seven years.

The mission remained under Spanish Franciscan jurisdiction until 1833, when Mexican Zacatecan Franciscans took over the running of the mission. The Mexican padre in charge, Fr. José Gutiérrez (1801-1850) seems to have been another of those unfortunate choices. He was neither astute nor evenhanded in running the mission and working with the Indians, nor was he wise in his dealings with General Mariano Vallejo, the military commander in the area and a Sonoma landowner. Vallejo attempted to undermine Gutiérrez's influence over the Indians; in response the padre took to the whip as a means of insuring his authority. Those actions played directly into Vallejo's hands, and he informed the governor regarding conditions at the mission. This hastened mission secularization, which occurred in 1834. At this point the last of the Mexican padres at Mission San Francisco Solano fled to Mission San Rafael, refusing to obey secular authority. Thereupon Vallejo, the former commander of the San Francisco Presidio, who was well versed in all the loopholes in the Laws of Secularization, moved in and confiscated mission properties. The wily Vallejo publicly announced that he was holding the mission properties for the benefit of the Indians. However when the official appraiser arrived to inventory mission properties, Vallejo ran him off. Somehow most of the original mission lands and properties found their way into General Vallejo's ranchos.

Detail of the painted chapel pulpit at Mission San Francisco Solano with sounding board, painted wall dado, stations of the cross, and a candelabra hanging from beamed ceiling.

With the founding of the town of Sonoma in 1834, the old mission chapel became a parish church and remained so until 1881. In 1838 the large adobe mission church collapsed and was razed by the settlers of Sonoma Pueblo. In the process they removed the mission tiles and wooden beams and used them to improve their own homes. Accordingly, when the protective tiles were removed from the tops of the adobe bricks, the eventual rains melted the adobe into its initial mud, pebbles, and straw. Within just a few years most of the mission buildings were in ruins. Fortunately a chapel built on the west side of the mission quadrangle in 1840 served as a parish church until 1881. Early in 1846, the infamous Governor Pío Pico offered the few remaining mission properties for sale, but there were no takers.

Right across the way from the mission, on the Sonoma Plaza, a momentous event in California history took place on June 14, 1846. A group of American settlers and rogues, disgruntled with Mexican actions in regards their property, formed a revolutionary government. They rallied around the Sonoma Plaza flagpole and raised a new flag declaring California a free and independent republic. They captured General Mariano Vallejo, put him in jail, and consummated their so-called Bear Flag Revolt. The landing of U. S. Marines at Monterey and the beginning of the Mexican War quickly put an end to California as an independent republic.

With the outcome of the war, California statehood, and the building of a new Catholic Church a few blocks from the mission chapel, very few people cared or were interested in what would happen to the Sonoma mission. The property was sold in 1881, and the private owner established a saloon right in front of the mission chapel entrance and actually stored his liquor and hay in the chapel. The property continued to deteriorate, and the exterior of the chapel appeared in various guises over the years. It has been remodeled with and without a New England style belltower, with squared windows and with arches of red brick. By the turn of the century the buildings were in sad shape. Then in 1903, the California Historic Landmarks League purchased the property with the intention of restoring it. The chapel suffered extensive damage in the 1906 earthquake and was not repaired by the League until 1911 when they received financial help from the State of California. The tile roof was replaced in 1913 and the chapel remodeled in 1914. In 1926 the mission property was deeded to the State of California by the Landmarks League. Additional renovation and restoration of the chapel took place over the years culminating in the extensive restoration during 1943-1944. Today the mission stands as part of the Sonoma Mission State Historic Park.

The present day mission structure is of adobe brick that has been plastered

The interior courtyard of the restored two story soldiers barracks off of the Sonoma Pueblo Plaza with reconstructed caretta in foregorrund.

white inside and outside. It measures 105 feet in length by 22 feet in width. The only decorative elements on the chapel facade are the dark brown wooden beams above the squared-off recessed entranceway. Above the entrance is a large recessed square window with a dark brown wooden lintel capping it. In front of the chapel entrance and to the right is a stout wooden frame on which hangs an original mission bell cast in 1829.

The interior walls of the restored chapel are decorated with a continuous painted dado in colors of blue, gold, red, and brown, comprising stylized geometric and floral designs *(color page Q)*. The actual designs are modeled from pieces of the painted walls that were retrieved from the chapel wall ruins prior to restoration. Oil paintings of the Stations of the Cross hang on both sides of the walls, and replica candle chandeliers hang from the frescoed beamed ceiling. The ceiling above the altar is painted with a large "Eye of Heaven." There are no pews in the chapel. On the right sidewall, about halfway towards the front of the chapel, is a large pulpit on a pedestal with a flight of stairs for access and a sounding board above; this ensemble is colorfully painted in blue and gold.

At the front of the chapel is a blue painted wooden railing separating the sanctuary from the nave. Behind the railing is the altar, the front of which has gilded relief designs. Sitting on the altar is a uniquely decorated tabernacle with a bas-relief image of San Juan Bautista. On top of the tabernacle is a crucifix, and on either side are small polychrome bultos of the Holy Mother and San José. On a shelf behind the tabernacle stand six painted wooden candlesticks. The wall behind is faux-painted in a pseudo-neoclassical style with four blue painted columns topped with gold painted capitals of a combination Corinthian and Ionic style. High on the wall, and in the center, is an oil painting of San Francisco Solano shown in a standing pose holding a crucifix in his left hand. On the wall, on either side of the altar, are faux-painted nichos. In front of each, on pedestals, is a large dressed polychrome bulto. On the left side is Our Lady of Sorrows, and on the right San José.

The wing that served as the padre's quarters is about the same size as the chapel and forms an L-shape with it. This area presently serves as a small museum. In what was the padre's dining area is a permanent collection of paintings of all the Spanish Colonial Missions of Alta California painted by Chris Jorgensen between 1903 and 1905. Interestingly, the painting of the Sonoma mission shows it adorned with a wooden belltower.

The corridor on the exterior of the building has a series of wooden posts anchored to the brick floor, instead of the usual arches, supporting the tiled roof.

The patio adjacent to the chapel has been nicely landscaped and has a flowing fountain in the center. To one side of the patio is a reconstructed horno oven typical of those used to do much of the mission cooking.

Across the street from the mission is the reconstructed and restored two-story soldiers' barracks with a small museum and a large gift shop. In the barracks courtyard sits a replica carreta, the primary transportation vehicle of the day, as pulled by a team of oxen over the El Camino Real so long ago.

EPILOGUE

The history and evolution of the Alta California Spanish colonial missions is a fascinating story punctuated by a series of identifiable events.

It all began with Father Junípero Serra's founding of Mission San Diego de Alcalá on July 16, 1769. During a life of sixty-five years some twenty additional missions were established from San Diego to Sonoma. All by those indefatigable Franciscan missionaries imbued with a religious fervor to both Christianize and educate the indigenous Indian "tribes" of Alta California. In this remote outpost of Spanish Empire the padres attempted to bring to a stone-age people a Eurocentric form of religion and lifestyle they deemed superior to what they encountered in this backwash area. In this overall process they attempted to convert a multi-complex and varied native population into a subservient Christianized population. In many instances the indigenous Indian populations had little in common with each other. Still, they did possess a "culture" of which the padres showed little interest in exploring, and dismissed out-of-hand as unessential to their over riding missionary goals. One cannot deny the altruistic ambition of those religious zealots, and what they were striving to accomplish for their own ends. Unfortunately, they also brought with them a fixed mind-set towards the native populations, which left little room for mutual understanding and compromise. Perhaps their most devastating "gift" to the native populations was the introduction of common European diseases the newcomers brought with them. Smallpox, measles, mumps, influenza and syphilis, against which the Indians had no immunity and no traditional medicines or cures. Those diseases swept through the missions and Indian villages in devastating epidemics with appalling death rates. In all instances both the padres and the Indians were helpless in the face of those disasters. Yet in the beginning, the padres were able to mold the natives into cohesive groups where the rudiments of an alien religion were taught to them. Within this setting they were also able to teach them a wide variety of European skills and trades, which in essence totally changed their original way of life. The ultimate result was the establishment of religious enclaves in which the Indian converts became little more than an indentured population, raising all the food and supplying the total labor force for their new masters.

The first few years of mission establishment, along with the incorporation of the Indian labor force into the system, were indeed difficult times for all. In many cases the forces of nature were most inhospitable to mission development and expansion. Events such as floods, fires, and earthquakes were all too common during those early years. Indian revolts and uprisings also played a role, but these were put down quickly by the superiority of Spanish arms and determination. By the early 1820's most of the mission padres had converted thousands of Indians to Catholicism, and their agricultural, livestock, and workshop enterprises were fully developed and self-sustaining. The missions became miniature cities in themselves supplying all the needs of the padres, soldiers, settlers, and the Indians. The most troubling threat to the mission system was the escalating native death rate, which in some instances reached an astonishing ratio of four deaths to one birth. The viability of a continued Indian labor force was obviously close to collapse. Concurrent with this was Mexico's ten years battle with Spain for independence, which culminated in 1821. Throughout this long struggle, and afterwards, the Mexican government almost totally ignored mission needs. Thus the mission system, as it had then evolved, found themselves as the sole supplier of food and other necessities for not only the missions and their Indian charges, but for the military, and the increasing numbers of settlers. For the missions, this was an undesirable situation at best.

Adding to all of this was the spectre of secularization on the horizon. The Laws of Secularization required that all the missions and their assets were to be turned over to the Indians. This totally unrealistic decision was promulgated in the late 1820s, carried out during the early 1830's, and for the most part finalized by 1834. Since the native populations possessed no clear notion and understanding of individual land ownership and usage, they fell prey to unscrupulous land speculators and corrupt politicos. It was at this point in time that many Indians fled the missions entirely, or exchanged indenture to the padres for that of the newly established secular patrons. The padres found themselves helpless to aid the Indians in the face of secularization, and could offer little help or succor to their former charges. Accordingly, by 1836 the mission system per se had entirely collapsed. Somehow, during the next ten years, most of the mission lands, livestock, and properties fell into private hands. Without a caretaker Indian labor force to work the lands, and maintain the buildings, the missions fell into ruins. In only a few instances were the mission churches able to serve an almost non-existent Indian population. By 1846, with American occupation and eventual annexation of Alta California, a new era had begun.

In the late 1850s and early 1860s the U. S. Government returned minuscule portions of mission land grants to the Church. At that point many of the missions were only ruined buildings surrounded by piles of melted adobe mud.

After the 1850s, American settlers from the east arrived in ever-greater numbers to settle these new fertile lands. To them, the missions were compelling ruins, which they found to be romantic relics of bygone days. Those newcomers needed something to hold onto in this strange new land, and as their senses absorbed the mission ruins they invented a needed history. They examined the historic record, as it was known then and selectively eliminated things that did not fit their preconceived interpretations. Thus with carefully selected history they created the myth of the missions as peaceful places ruled by benevolent padres and inhabited by docile Indians. The human tragedy of the system was entirely overlooked.

From about 1870 to 1900 the mission ruins became compelling attractions for first the artist, and later on the photographer. The artist's paintings, watercolors, and etchings of the mission ruins had wide distribution and became a magnet for tourists. This was also true of the mass-produced stereopticon views with which the photographers flooded a receptive eastern market. In due course, tourists poured into California eager to see the mission ruins for themselves. The artists, photographers, and tourists were of great significance because they called attention to those historic monuments to seemingly more glorious days. Even the Church became acutely aware of the mission as an integral part of their religious heritage. Accordingly, during the late nineteenth and early twentieth centuries the Church itself began to take the lead in mission restoration. Admittedly, mission restoration was not an all-embracing church policy; instead it seemed to develop within the mind of individual padres who had become greatly concerned by a continuing loss of church history. In a number of situations it was the will and determination of an individual padre who called attention to the over riding need for mission restoration. Some of them were aided by outside private help, and contributions from private organizations, but the actual initiation of restoring each of the mission churches was almost solely the product of one mans compelling imagination and determination.

By the 1920s mission revival, with all of its ramifications, was in full swing, and this gave great impetus to eventual restoration of Alta California's Spanish colonial missions. This has been accomplished over the years, and today the missions stand as monuments to the restorer's art and talent. Perhaps more importantly, they are now pristine tourist attractions that draw hundreds of thousands of visitors to them each year. The spell of the Alta California missions as tourist destinations should however be tempered by the fact that these carefully restored buildings do not actually portray history. As we visit them today, they are rather in the manner of theme parks, using what might be considered the ornaments of history, to create a present-day world of somewhat belated fantasy.

PERTINENT VISITOR INFORMATION

Entrance fees collected at a number of the restored Spanish Colonial missions are used to maintain and refurbish the mission property. When writing to a mission it is perhaps best to include a stamped, self-addressed envelope and a nominal amount of money (check) to pay for brochures, etc., you might request. As California's population continues to grow, telephone area codes and numbers may also change. It is wise to call ahead for any special arrangements that may be needed, such as facilities for the handicapped and for group tours. Most missions offer self-guided tours, and some offer special docent tours. These can be arranged at the mission entrance. This information provided is accurate at time of printing, February 2001, and may change in the future.

Mission Basilica San Diego de Alcalá
10818 San Diego Mission Road
San Diego, California 92108
(619) 281-8449; Daily 9-5

San Diego Presidio Location/Junípero Serra Museum
2727 Presidio Drive
San Diego, California 92103
(619) 297-3258; Daily 10-5

St. John the Baptist Catholic Church
(Site of Asistencia Santa Ysabél)
23010 SR-79
Santa Ysabél, California 92070
(760) 765-0810; Daily 8-5

Mission Basilica San Carlos Borromeo de Carmelo
3080 Rio Road
Carmel, California 93923
(831) 624-3600; Mon.-Sat. 9:30-4:30, Sun. 10:30-4;
June through August open to 7PM; closed Christmas Day

Monterey Royal Presidio Chapel
(San Carlos Cathedral)
500 Church Street
Monterey, California 93940
(831) 373-6711; Open Daily

Mission San Antonio de Padua
Hunter-Liggett Military Reservation
P. O. Box 803
Jolon, California 93928
(831) 385-4478; Mon.-Sat. 10-4:30, Sun. 11:30-4:30;
closed Tues.-Wed. and major holidays

Mission San Gabriel Arcángel
537 West Mission Drive
San Gabriel, California 91776
(626) 457-3048; Daily 9-8 (closed 1-2); closed major holidays

Asistencia Nuestra Señora de Los Angeles
535 North Main Street
Los Angeles, California 90012
(213) 629-3101; open Daily

Mission San Luís Obispo de Tolosa
782 Monterey Street
San Luís 0blspo, California 93401
(805) 543-6850; Mon.-Sat. 9-4, Sun. 8:30-5; closed major holidays

Mission San Francisco de Asís (Dolores)
3321 16th. Street
San Francisco, California 94114
(415) 621-8203; Daily 9-4; closed major holidays

Mission San Juan Capistrano
P. O. Box 697
San Juan Capistrano, California 92693
(949) 248-2040; Daily 8:30-5; closed major holidays

Mission Santa Clara de Asís, Virgen y Martir
Santa Clara University
P. O. Box 3217
Santa Clara, California 95053
(408) 554-4023; Daily 8-7

Mission San Buenaventura
211 East Main Street
Ventura, California 93001
(805) 643-4318; Mon.-Sat. 10-5, Sun. 10-4; closed major holidays

Mission Santa Bárbara, Virgen y Martir
2201 Laguna Street
Santa Bárbara, California 93105
(805) 682-4713; Daily 9-5; closed major holidays

El Presidio Real de Santa Bárbara State Historic Park
123 East Canon Perdido Street
Santa Bárbara, California 93101
(805) 966-9719; Daily 10-5; closed major holidays

Mission La Purisima Concepción de María Santisima
State Historic Park
2295 Purisima Road
Lompoc, California 93436
(805) 733-3713; Daily 9-5; closed major holidays

Mission Santa Cruz
126 High Street
Santa Cruz, California 95060
(831) 426-5686; Tues.-Sat. 10-4, Sun. 10-2;
closed major holidays but opened Monday of holiday weekends

Mission La Soledad
36641 Fort Romie Road
Soledad, California 93960
(831) 678-2586; Daily 10-4, except Tues.

Mission San José
43300 Mission Boulevard
Fremont, California 94539
(510) 657-1797; Daily 10-5

Mission San Juan Bautista
P. O. Box 400
San Juan Bautista, California 95045
(408) 623-4528; Mon.-Sat. 9:30-5, Sun. 10-5, closed major holidays

Mission San Miguel Arcángel
775 Mission Street
San Miguel, California 93451
(805) 467-3256; Daily 9:30-4:30

Mission San Fernando Rey de España
15151 San Fernando Mission Boulevard
Mission Hills, California 91345
(818) 361-0186; Daily 9-4:30; closed major holidays

Mission San Luís Rey de Francia
4050 Mission Avenue
San Luís Rey, California 92068
(760) 757-3651; Daily 10-4:30; closed major holidays

Asistencia San Antonio de Pala
Pala Mission Road
Pala, California 92059
(760) 742-1600; Daily 10-4:30

Mission Santa Inés, Virgen y Martir
1760 Mission Drive
Solvang, California 93463
(805) 688-4815; Daily 9-7 (except Labor Day through May 9th, when it is 9-5:30); closed major holidays

Mission San Rafael Arcángel
1104 Fifth Avenue
San Rafael, California 94901
(415) 454-8141; Daily 11-4; closed major holidays

Mission San Francisco Solano State Historic Park
114 East Spain Street
Sonoma, California 95476
(707) 938-1519; Daily 10-5; closed major holidays.

COLOR PORTFOLIO

View of the mission church of San Gabriel taken from the park area across from the mission, and showing the scaffolding on the church exterior during restoration after the 1994 earthquake.

Section in the well tended patio garden of the mission church of San Gabriel dedicated to the Virgin of Guadalupe.

Free-standing campanario of Asistencia San Antonio de Pala; the bells were cast in 1816.

Large memorial cross built of floor tiles excavated from the original Spanish Presidio, and dedicated in 1913; cross is located close to the Serra statue, at Presidio Park, San Diego.

The Stations Of The Cross are located outdoors, within the courtyard of Asistencia Iglesia de Nuestra Señora de Los Angeles, de la Mission San Gabriel, Archángel, and are represented by simple wooden crosses; this image marks the VII Station when Christ falls for the second time under the weight of the cross.

Detail of the central portion of the reredos at the mission church of San Miguel with large polychrome bulto of patron San Miguel; topping the reredos is the all-seeing Eye-Of-God.

A side altar in the mission church of San Juan Capistrano with an ornately decorated nicho with a large polychrome bulto of San José.

Altar and reredos of the mission church of San Carlos Borromeo, carved by Califronia Mission restorer Harry Downie.

The magnificent Ezcaray altar and reredos in the mission church at San Fernando; note imposing bulto of mission patron, San Fernando Rey de España, on center of reredos.

One of a number of side chapels in the mission church of San Juan Bautista; this one is dedicated to the Infant of Prague.

View of the altar and painted reredos of the mission church of Santa Bárbara church with large 1793 polychrome bulto of mission patroness in the center, and above it a large crucifix from the mid-eighteenth century.

Detail of the central portion of the Mexican Baroque altar and reredos at the mission church of San Francisco de Asís.

Detail of the frescoe painting of the baptism of Christ on the wall of the small baptistry in the mission church of San Gabriel Archángel.

In the baptistry of the mission church of San Juan Bautista, on the wall above the baptismal fonts hangs an oil painting depicting the baptism of Jesus Christ; this oil painting probably came to the mission from New Spain in 1805.

Detail of the upper portion of the reredos with polychromed bulto of San Miguel, and a portion of the ceiling painting showing the Holy Trinity in the mission church of Santa Clara de Asís.

Oil painting in the Santa Inés Mission Museum portraying a typical baptismal ceremony during old mission days.

View of the altar in the shrine at the rear of Father Serra's church at Mission San Juan Capistrano dedicated to St. Peregrine, patron of cancer sufferers.

Detail of the large bulto of San Juan Bautista occupying the central nicho on the bottom row of the reredos in the mission church at San Juan Bautista.

Detail of the large polychrome bulto of San Buenaventura on a side altar of the mission church of San José; bulto carved in Mexico around 1808.

Detail of the bulto of Santa Inés, patroness of the mission as displayed in the center nicho on the mission reredos; note painted architectural designs and the shell-shaped top of the nicho.

A twelve inches high polychrome papier-mache portrayal of Father Junipero Serra standing watch over the vigil candles within the mission church of San Diego de Alcalá.

Detail of the lovely dressed bulto of Dolorosa in the mission church of San Antonio de Padua; note frescoe Indian style geometric wall decorations.

Detail of the reredos in the mission church of Our Lady of the Angeles showing the centerpiece oil painting of Nuestra Señora de Los Angeles, below which is the enclosed monstrance.

Detail of the large polychromed bulto of San Miguel with sword raised for battle, presently sited in the museum at Mission San Miguel.

Detail of reredos nicho in the church of San José with imposing fifteenth century Spanish bulto of the mission patron.

View of a very fine painted wall dado border in the mission church sacristy of Santa Inés, consisting of a Greek key design with a stylized row of daisies above rosebuds below.

Painted decorative frescoed dado in the baptistry of Mission San Luís Rey de Francia that utilizes a combination of Indian floral and geometric designs.

Various Painted Wall Decorations Found Throughout the Spanish Colonial Missions

Stylized painted floral frescoe design on a wall in the mission church of San Luis Obispo.

Typical Indian-style painted dado decoration on the walls of the mission church of San Buenaventura.

Painted Agnus Dei (Lamb of God) on the wall of the mortuary chapel in the mission church of San Carlos Borromeo.

Detail of the beautiful jeweled-like mosaic of "The Annunciation," on the facade of Our Lady of Angels Church in Los Angeles.

Decorative painted sidewall in the La Purisima mission church, of which the central design is an enlarged pecten sea shell, closely resembling the painted wall decorations present in Mission San Miguel.

Portion of an elaborately decorated door frame in the nave of the mission church of Santa Bárbara.

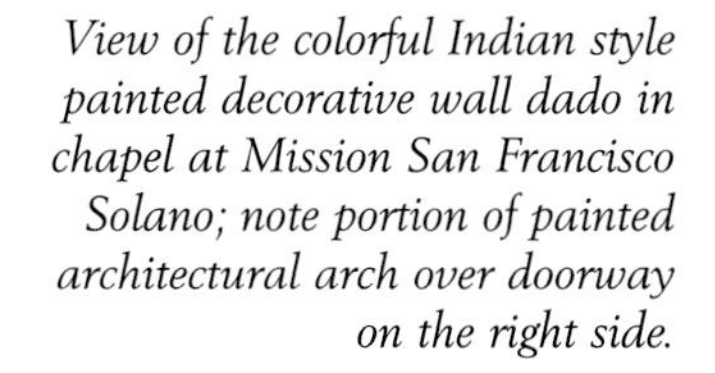

View of the colorful Indian style painted decorative wall dado in chapel at Mission San Francisco Solano; note portion of painted architectural arch over doorway on the right side.

Detail of the painted chancel railing and the richly painted wall designs in the Santa Bárbara Presidio Chapel; red and gold design on top is a facsimile of the ornate silk brocades used in the churches during festival occasions.

Typical Indian-style painted geometrical wall decorations in mission church of San Fernando.

Original hand-hammered baptismal font in the San Luís Rey church baptistry.

Baptismal area in asistencia chapel of San Antonio de Pala; note Indian painted wall frescoes.

A quiet devotional area in the mission church of Carmel; note blue painted wall dado overlain with a thin gold border, and capped with floral decorations.

Small baptismal area in the nave of mission church of Santa Inés, with original Indian hand-hammered copper/zinc baptismal font still in use today; note bulto of San Juan Bautista on shelf above the font.

View of the pulpit of the mission church of San Diego de Alcalá; with overhanging umbrella marking Pope Paul VI designation of the church at Mission Basilica in 1976.

Decorated doorway in Mission San Miguel Church leading to the inner patio; note original painted and cracked walls.

Colorful California poppies blooming admidst the weathered adobe ruins at Mission Soledad.

Holy Water stoup cut into the mission church wall at San Juan Bautista and painted with Indian-style decorations.

Period church vestments worn by the padres of Mission San Luís Rey de Francia, as dispayed in mission museum.

View of the confessional at the rear of the mission church of San Antonio de Padua; note painted wall dado, and geometric border design encompassing holy water stoup.

APPENDIX

APPENDIX A

GOVERNORS OF ALTA CALIFORNIA: THE SPANISH GOVERNORS

1. Gaspár de Portolá, governor of Las Californias, Alta and Baja, 1768-I770;
2. Felipe de Barri, governor of Las Californias, residing at Loreto, Baja California,1770-1775;
3. Felipe de Neve, governor of Las Californias, residing at Loreto, Baja California from March 4, 1775; at Monterey from February 3, 1777, to September 10, 1782;
4. Pedro Fages, September 1782, to April 1791;
5. José Antonio Romeu, April 16, 1791, to April 9, 1792;
6. José Joaquin de Arrillaga, governor ad interim, April 1792, to October 1794;
7. Diego de Borica, governor, October 1794, to January 1800;
8. José Joaquin de Arrillaga, governor ad interim, 1800 to 1804; Constitutional governor from 1804 to 1814;
9. José Arguello, acting governor from 1814 to 1815;
10. Pablo Vicente Sola, governor from August 15, 1815, to November 22, 1822.

THE MEXICAN GOVERNORS

1. Pablo Vicente Sola, holdover from the Spanish regime until November 1822;
2. Luís Arguello, acting governor, 1822-1825;
3. José María de Echeandia, 1825-1831;
4. Manuel Victoria, 1831-1832;
5. Pío Pico (twenty days), 1832;
6. José María de Echeandia (in the south only), 1832-1833;
7. Agustin Vicente Zamorano (in the north only), 1832-1833;
8. José Figueroa, 1833-1835;
9. José Castro (acting governor), 1835-1836;
10. Nicolás Gutiérrez (acting governor four months), 1836;
11. Mariano Chico (acting governor three months), 1836;
12. Nicolás Gutiérrez (acting governor three months), 1836;
13. Juan Bautista Alvarado (first revolutionary, then constitutional governor), 1836-1842;
14. Manuel Micheltorena, 1842-1845;
15. Pío Pico, 1845-1846.

APPENDIX B

THE TWENTY-ONE ALTA CALIFORNIA SPANISH COLONIAL MISSIONS
(with founding dates and their founders)

1. San Diego de Alcalá, July 16, 1769, Junípero Serra;
2. San Carlos Borromeo de Carmelo, June 3, 1770, Junípero Serra;
3. San Antonio de Padua, July 14, 1771, Junípero Serra;
4. San Gabriel Arcángel, September 8, 1771, Pedro Cambón and Angel Somera on Junípero Serra's instructions;
5. San Luís Obispo de Tolosa, September 1, 1772, Junípero Serra:
6. San Francisco de Asís, October 9, 1776, Francisco Palóu, on Junípero Serra's instructions;
7. San Juan Capistrano, founded October 9, 1775 by Fermín Lasuén, then abandoned; dedicated November 1, 1776 by Junípero Serra;
8. Santa Clara de Asís, Founded January 12, 1777 by José Marguia and Tomás de Peña, under direction of Junípero Serra;
9. San Buenaventura, March 31, 1782, Junípero Serra;
10. Santa Bárbara, Virgen y Martir, December 4, 1786, Fermín Lasuén;
11. La Purisima Concepción de María Santisima, December 8, 1787, Fermín Lasuén;
12. Santa Cruz, August 28, 1791, Fermín Lasuén;
13. Nuestra Señora de la Soledad, October 9, 1791, Fermín Lasuén;
14. San José, June 11, 1797, Fermín Lasuén;
15. San Juan Bautista, June 24, 1797, Fermín Lasuén;
16. San Miguel Arcángel, July 25, 1797, Fermín Lasuén;
17. San Fernando, Rey de España, September 8, 1797, Fermín Lasuén;
18. San Luís Rey de Francia, June 13, 1798, Fermín Lasuén;
19. Santa Inés, Virgen y Martir, September 17, 1804, Estevan Tapis;
20. San Rafael Arcángel, December 14, 1817, Vicente Sarría along with Ramón Abella, Narciso Durán, & Luís Gil y Toboada;
21. San Francisco Solano, July 4, 1823, José Altimira.

APPENDIX C

FATHER-PRESIDENTS OF THE ALTA CALIFORNIA MISSIONS 1769-1846

1. Fray Junípero Serra 1769-1784
2. Fray Francisco Palóu 1784-1785
3. Fray Fermín Francisco Lasuén 1785-1803
4. Fray Estevan Tapis 1803-1812
5. Fray José Señan 1812-1815
6. Fray Mariano Payeras 1815-1819
7. Fray José Señan 1819-1823
8. Fray Vicente Francisco Sarría 1823-1825
9. Fray Narciso Durán 1825-1827
10. Fray José Bernardo Sánchez 1827-1831
11. Fray Narciso Durán 1831-1838
12. Fray José Joaquin Jimeno 1838-1844
13. Fray Narciso Durán 1844-1846

GLOSSARY

ADOBE: Sun dried mud brick comprising a mixture of clay, straw, ash, and water; generally formed in rectangular wooden molds; the basic building material of the Alta California missions.

AGUARDIENTE: A strong alcoholic beverage generally referred to as "Mexican brandy."

ALAMEDA: A public thoroughfare usually lined with cottonwood or poplar trees.

ALCALDE: A magistrate or judge.

ALTA: Upper, as in Alta California.

ALTAR: A raised structure serving as the center of worship on which the eucharistic components are consecrated.

ARROYO: A dry stream or river bed.

ASISTENCIA: A sub-mission serving resident converted Indians but with no resident padre, generally serviced by a padre from the nearest mission.

AXUNTAMIENTO: A town council.

BAJA: Lower, as in Baja California; the peninsular part of Mexico directly south of Alta California.

BALUSTRADE: A low barrier generally comprising decorative carved and painted wooden spindles and a railing they support.

BAROQUE: Artistic expression prevalent in the 17th century, usually characterized by dynamic forms and elaborate ornamentation.

BASILICA: A Roman Catholic church that has been granted certain ceremonial privilages; a minor basilica is a church of special historical and religious importance.

BIRETTA: A unique hat worn by Catholic priests with three ridges on the top.

BULTO: A carved, painted, three-dimensional sculptural figure, generally of a saint, an angel, or Jesus Christ.

BUTTRESSES: Supporting structures, sometimes massive, built into a standing wall to steady and strengthen it.

CALIFORNIOS: Native-born Californians of Hispanic heritage.

CAMPANARIO: A bell tower or belfry which may be free-standing or attached to the church structure.

CAMPOSANTO: A cemetery; consecrated ground for burial, which may or may not be an integral part of the mission grounds.

CANTINA: A place that serves refreshments; a saloon or tavern.

CAPELLA GUILIA: The boys' choir of St. Peter's, Vatican City.

CAPILLA: A chapel.

CARRETA: A wooden two-wheeled cart, generally pulled by oxen; the main mode of transporting goods and materials in colonial Alta California.

CENOTAPH: A monument, sometimes quite elaborate, erected in honor of someone whose mortal remains are elsewhere.

CHAMFER: In architecture, a beveled edge.

CHANCEL: The area in a church containing the altar, seats for the clergy, and choir.

CHUMASH INDIANS: California Indians indigenous to the Santa Barbara Channel area perhaps the most advanced and receptive to Christian conversion of the Alta California Indians.

CLOISTER: In architecture, an area comprising a covered passageway on the side of a courtyard; a designated space for meditation.

COMMANDANTE: A military commander.

COMPOUND: As used in this book a term that describes the mission and its buildings.

CONCHA: A shell-like ornamental design, often above a window, a nicho, or a door.

CONVENTO: The padre's residence within the mission compound.

CORBEL: In architecture, a support that projects from the wall and supports a heavy beam; corbels are generally carved or painted.

CORINTHIAN: The most ornate Greek order of capitals on the tops of columns, characterized by elaborately carved acanthus leaf designs.

CORNICE: A molded and projecting horizontal component that crowns an architectural embellishment.

CORRIDOR: A gallery around the inner patio which may be arched or colonnaded.

COUNCIL OF TRENT: The gathering of the hierarchy of the Roman Catholic church, held in Trent, northern Italy, intermittently from 1545-1563, to undertake reform in the Church and provide guidelines to initiate the counter-reformation.

CUPOLA: A small rounded structure built on top of a roof or campanario.

DADO: A painted decorative border on the lower portion of the interior church wall.

DISTEMPER: Paint made by mixing pigment with water, egg yolks, and glue; used as a vehicle for mural or fresco paintings.

EL CAMINO REAL: Literally, the Royal Highway; in colonial Alta California a primitive narrow dirt cart track that linked the missions from San Diego to Sonoma.

ENRAMADA: A temporary brush shelter comprised of tree branches thatched with wild grasses or reeds; generally the first temporary mission church.

ENTABLURE: The upper portion of a wall that is supported on engaged columns or pilasters.

ENTRADA: An entrance or admission.

ESPADAÑA: The uppermost decorative crown of a church façade, often pierced to hang bells.

FAUX: False, like wood painted to resemble marble.

FINIALS: The crowning ornaments, as decorative vases or other ornamental architectural elements.

FONT: A carved stone or hammered metal receptacle to hold the water used in baptisms.

FRAY: "Brother"; a title preceding the first name of a priest, padre, or friar.

FRESCO: A painting that had been freshly laid down on moist lime plaster with color pigments suspended in a liquid medium.

FRIAR: "Brother", as in the Franciscan order.

FRIEZE: A sculptured or ornamental band, as on a building or in a church interior.

GENTE DE RAZÓN: Educated people; non-Indians whose way of life followed Spanish customs.

GESSO: Gypsum prepared with glue for use as an undersurface in painting, or with starch added for forming bas-reliefs.

HORNO: A large bee-hive shaped outdoor oven.

IONIC: A Greek order of architectural capitals characterized by their horizontal spiral volutes.

JACAL/JACALON: A hut constructed of logs set upright in the ground and interwoven with brush, and with a thatched roof; jacalon is a larger more elaborate jacal.

JUECES DE PAZ: Justices of the peace.

LADRILLO: A tile floor; but can also refer to a brick floor.

LAMBREQUIN: A short decorative painting of drapery atop a wall or below a cornice.

LANTERN: A structure with glass or open sides above an opening in the roof to let in light or air; a small tower that can be one stage of a cupola.

LAVANDERÍA: A laundry, or a wash basin area.

LEGUA: A measure of length varying from 2.4 to 4.6 statue miles.

LUNETTE: A small painted decorative object shaped like the crescent moon.

MAJORDOMO: A steward or overseer of a working enterprise.

MEZCLA: A mixture of concrete or mortar, often tinted with oxblood, used as a floor.

MISSION: A religious establishment usually staffed by two padres for the propagation of the faith, with the overall goal of converting the Indians to Christianity. It usually comprised church, cemetery, workshops and storehouses, living quarters, and all of the accoutrements of a working agricultural and livestock enterprise.

MONSTRANCE: An elaborate, finely crafted metal receptacle sometimes encrusted with gems, for displaying the consecrated Eucharist; many were distinguished works of art in precious metals.

MUDÉJAR: Artistic architectural motifs inspired by the Moors who lived in Spain and Portugal during the 13th and 14th centuries.

NAVE: The principal interior area of the church where the congregation worships.

NEOCLASSICAL: Art and architecture that constitutes a revival or adaptation of classical styles.

NICHO: A recess in a wall or reredos designed to hold a free-standing statue of a holy person or some other devotional object.

OCULAR: Like an eye in form and function; in the Alta California missions the term usually refers to an eye-shaped window above the main doors.

PADRE: Literally, "Father"; a Roman Catholic priest.

PALISADE: A row of large pointed stakes set into the ground to form a fence for fortification or defense.

PALLIUMS: A white woolen band with pendants in front and back worn over the chasuble by a pope or archbishop as a symbol of his religious authority.

PASTORELLA: "The Shepherd's Play"; a dramatic presentation in which shepherds go to Bethlehem to offer gifts to the Christ Child.

PEDIMENT: A triangular space formed by the gable of a two-pitched roof; prominent in classical architecture.

PILASTER: A fake pillar which can be made of various materials and generally found on the facades of some Alta California mission churches.

PLAZA: A rectangular central public area in a mission, city, or town.

POBLADORES: The original Hispanic village settlers.

POBLANOS: Inhabitants of an Hispanic village.

POLITICO: A politican, one who is in complete sympathy with the current government.

POLYCHROME: Literally, decorated with several colors.

PORTAL: A doorway, gate, or entrance.

PRESIDIO: A fortified military outpost generally comprising barracks, workshops, a chapel, and stables; forts strategically positioned to protect Spanish holdings on the Alta California frontier.

PUEBLO: A small village or town; in Alta California a non-Indian community.

PULPIT: A raised and railed platform used in preaching a worship service.

QUADRANGLE: A four-sided enclosure with gardens, fountains, and areas for both work and recreation, and enclosing various subsidiary buildings.

RANCHERÍA: An Indian village.

RANCHO: A large Hispanic agricultural establishment.

RECTORY: The residence for the clergy.

REFECTORY: A dining area in a mission.

RELIQUARY: A sealed metal and glass receptacle for displaying sacred relics.

REPLICA: A reasonably close copy of an original.

REREDOS: A screen placed on the rear of the altar table and against the wall which is usually subdivided into painted panels and nichos for bultos representing holy persons.

RIVER OF LIFE DESIGN: A deeply carved pattern consisting of vertical parallel serpentine lines, used primarily to decorate Alta California mission church doors.

SACRISTY: A room in the church opening on the sanctuary for storage of various articles utilized in the church service.

SAGRADA CORAZÓN: Sacred Heart.

SALA: A formal reception room; in the Alta California missions it was an area for receiving guests and visitors.

SANCTUARY: The most sacred part of the church building in which the mass altar is placed.

SANCTUS BELLS: Holy bells rung during the most solemn part of the Mass; in the Alta California missions a number of small bells were attached to a large standing wheel which was rotated.

SANTO: Literally, "holy one"—a saint, an angel or a divine person.

SECULARIZATION: Bylaws enacted by the Mexican Congress in 1828, ratified in 1833, and enforced in 1834, in which the Mexican government removed the mission lands from the jurisdiction of the Franciscans, who were replaced by secular priests. Mission properties were to be turned over to the Indians but mainly fell into the hands of land speculators and corrupt politicians. Mission buildings then fell into ruins and were plundered.

SOLDADO DE CUERO: A "leather-Jacket" soldier dressed in a reinforced deer- skin jacket designed to stop an Indian arrow.

TABERNACLE: An ornamental receptacle placed on the center of the altar to hold the consecrated wavers of the Eucharist.

TERRA-COTTA: A brownish-orange fired clay utilized for roofing tiles, decorative ornamentation, and statues.

THIRD ORDER OF ST. FRANCIS: An organization of lay people who emulate and follow the teachings of St. Francis, but who do not give up marriage or worldly possessions.

TRANSEPT: The part of a cruciform church that crosses at right angles between the nave and the apse.

TROMPE 'OEIL: Literally, "cheat the eye": a style of painting where the objects are portrayed with photographically realistic detail.

TULES: A strong wild reed or sedge, growing in wetlands, and utilized in thatching the roofs of buildings.

VALANCE: A drapery hung along the top edge of an altar; in the Alta California missions they were generally painted decorations on the interior church walls.

VIA CRUCIS: The Way of the Cross; Stations of the Cross.

VIGA: A ceiling beam; generally a long tree trunk from which the bark and branches had been removed, and which offered the primary support for the roof of a building.

VOUSSIORS: Wedge-shaped stone pieces that form an arch or vault.

REFERENCES

Abbott, Mamie Goulet, 1951, Santa Inés Hermosa: The Journal of the Padre's Niece; Sunwise Press, Montecito, Santa Barbara, California, 262 p.

Baer, Kurt, 1955, Painting and sculpture at Mission Santa Barbara; American Franciscan Hist., Washington, D. C., Mon. Ser., v. 3, 244p.

Bannon, John Francis, 1974, The Spanish Borderlands Frontier 1513-1821; Univ. New Mexico Press, Albuquerque, 308p.

Barrow, Clare, S., (Ed.), 1998, Mission San Luís Rey de España; Bicentennial Publ., Clare Vista Co., Inc., & Franciscans of Mission San Luís Rey de España, 30p.

Benton, Lisa M., 1998, The Presidio, From Army Post to National Park; Northeastern Univ. Press, Boston, Massachusetts, 277p.

Blackmer, Frank, W., Spanish Institutions of the Southwest; The Rio Grande Press, Inc., Glorieta, New Mexico (Reprint of the 1891 Edition), 353p.

Bolton, Herbert, Eugene, 1979, The Mission as a Frontier Institution in the Spanish American Colonies. IN: New Spain's Far Northern Frontier, Weber, David J. (Ed.), Univ. New Mexico Press, Albuquerque, p. 51-65.

Boulé, Mary Null, 1988, The Missions: California's Heritage, A Series of Twenty-One Booklets: Mission San Diego de Alcalá, Mission San Carlos Borromeo de Carmelo, Mission San Antonio de Padua, Mission San Gabriel Arcángel, Mission San Luís Obispo de Tolosa, Mission San Francisco de Asís, Mission San Juan Capistrano, Mission Santa Clara de Asís, Mission San Buenaventura, Mission Santa Bárbara, Mission La Purisima Concepción, Mission Santa Cruz, Mission Nuestra de La Soledad, Mission San José, Mission San Juan Bautista, Mission San Miguel Arcángel, Mission San Fernando Rey de España, Mission San Luís Rey de Francia, Mission Santa Inés, Mission San Rafael Arcángel, Mission San Francisco Solano; Merryant Publ., Vashon, Washington, each 24p.

Brunelle, Mark, 1984, Fray Junípero Serra: This Most Unworthy Priest; Dobronte Publs., Carmel, California, 78p

Casey, Beatrice, 1976, Padres and People of Old Mission San Antonio; 2nd. ed., Casey Newspapers, King City, California, 140p.

Castillo, Edward, 1995, Indians, Franciscans, and Spanish Colonization: The Impact of the Mission System on California Indians; Univ. New Mexico Press, Albuquerque, 214p.

Clark, David, E. (Ed.), 1986, The California Missions: A Pictorial History; 4th print., A Sunset Book, Lane Publ. Co., Menlo Park, California, 320p.

Connell, Will, 1941, The Missions of California; Hastings House Publs., New York, 105p.

Corle, Edwin, 1949, The Royal Highway (El Camino Real); The Bobbs-Merrlll Co., Inc., New York, 351p.

Costello, J.G., 1991, Documentary evidence for the Spanish Missions of Alta California. IN: Spanish Borderlands Sourcebooks, v. 14, Garland Publ., Inc., New York & London, 541p.

Costo, Rupert & Jeannette Henry Costo (Eds.), 1987, The Missions of California: A legacy of Genocide; Indian Heritage Press, San Francisco, California, 233p.

Cutter, Donald C., 1995, The Writings of Mariano Payeras; Bellerophon Books, Santa Barbara, California, 384p.

Demarest, Donald, 1963, The First Californian: The Story of Fray Junípero Serra; Guild Press, New York, 176p.

De Nevi, Don, & Moholy, Noel, Francis, 1985, Junípero Serra: The Illustrated Story of the Franciscan Founder of California's Missions; 3rd. print., Harper & Row, New York, 224p.

Drain, Thomas, A., & Wakely, David, 1994, A Sense of Mission: Historic Churches of the Southwest; Chronicle Books, San Francisco, California, 133p.

Eagen, I., Brent, n.d., A History of Mission San Diego de Alcalá the First Church of California Founded by the Venerable Junípero Serra July 16, 1769; San Diego, California, 24p.

Englebert, Omer, 1956, The Last of the Conquistadors: Junípero Serra (1713-1784); Harcourt, Brace & Co., New York, 368p.

Engelhardt, Zephyrin, 1921, San Luís Rey: The King of the Missions; The James H. Barry Co., San Francisco, California, 265p.

Engelhardt, Zephyrin, 1931, Mission San Juan Bautista: A School of Church Music; The Schauer Printing Studio, Inc., Santa Barbara, California, 153p.

Engelhardt, Zephyrin, 1972, San Antonio de Padua: The Mission in the Sierras; Ballena Press, Ramona, California, 140p.

Engelhardt Zephyrin, 1973, San Fernando Rey: The Mission of the Valley; Ballena Press, Ramona, California, 160p.

Engelhardt, Zephyrin, 1986, Mission Santa Inés Virgen & Martir and it's Ecclesiastical Seminary; McNally & Loftin, Publs., Santa Barbara, California, 200p.

Faulk, Odie, B., 1979, The Presidio: Fortress or Farce?; IN: New Spain's Northern Frontier, Weber, David J. (Ed.), Univ. New Mexico Press, Albuquerque, p. 69-76.

Geiger, Maynard, 1969, Franciscan Missionaries in Hispanic California 1769-1848; The Huntington Library, San Marino, California, 304p.

Geiger, Maynard, 1993, Mission Santa Barbara: Queen of the Missions; Legacy Publ., Santa Barbara, California, 34p.

Hageman, Fred, C., & Ewing, Russell, C., 1991, An Archaeological and Restoration Study of Mission La Purisima Concepción;Santa Bárbara Trust for Historic Preservation, Presidio Research Center Publ., Whitehead, Richard S. (Ed.), Santa Bárbara, California, 307p.

Hall, Douglas, Kent, 1990, Frontier Spirit: Early Churches of the Southwest; Abbeville Press, New York, 216p.

Ingold, Ernest, 1950, The House in Mallorca; Paul Elder & Co., San Francisco, California, 48p.

Iversen, Eva C., n.d., California's Mission San Miguel Arcángel; Franciscan Padres, Old San Miguel, California, 24p.

Jackson, Robert H., 1997, The California Missions; Tradicion Revista, Winter, p. 61-63.

Jackson, Robert H., 1998, Missions and California Indians; Tradicion Revista, Spring, p. 53-56.

Jackson, Robert, H., & Castillo, Edward, 1995, Indians, Franciscans, and Spanish Colonization: The Impact of the Mission System on California Indians; Univ. New Mexico Press, Albuquerque, 214p.

James, George, Wharton, 1928, The old Franciscan missions of California, Little, Brown and Company, Boston, 200p.

Johnson, John R., 1997, The Indians of Mission San Fernando; IN: Mission San Fernando, Rey de España, 1797-1997, A Bicentennial Tribute, Hist. Soc. Southern California, Los Angeles, California, p. 249-290.

Johnson, Paul C. (Ed.), 1968, The California Missions: A Pictorial History; A Sunset Book, 3rd. print., Lane Publ. Co., Menlo Park, California, 322p.

Kennedy, Roger, G., 1993, Mission: The History and Architecture of the Missions of North America; Houghton Mifflin Co., New York, 240p.

Langelier, John Phillip, & Daniel B. Rosen, 1992, Historic Resource Study: El Presidio de San Francisco, A History Under Spain and Mexico, 1776-1846, U. S. Dept. Interior, Natl. Park Service, Denver, Colorado, 128p.

Lee, Gregory, 1992, California Missions: A Guide to the State's Spanish Heritage; A Renaissance House Publ., Frederick, Colorado, 48p.

Levick, Melba & Young, Stanley, 1998, The Missions of California; Chronicle Books, San Francisco, California, 135p.

Margolin, Malcolm, 1989, Life in a California Mission: The Journals of Jean Francois de La Pérouse (1786); Heyday Books, Berkeley, California, 112p.

Miller, Henry, 1997, Account of a Tour of the California Missions & Towns 1856: The Journal and Drawings of Henry Miller; Bellerophon Books, Santa Barbara, California, 63p.

Mills, Paul & Cutter, Donald C., 1966, A Gallery of California Mission Paintings by Edwin Deakin; Ruth I. Mahood (Ed.), Los Angeles County Museum of Natural History, The Ward Ritchie Press, Los Angeles, California, 60p.

Morgado, Martin J., 1991, Junípero Serra: A Pictorial Biography, Siempre Adelante Publ., Monterey, California, 137p.

Neuerburg, Norman, 1989, The Decoration of the California Missions; Bellerophon Books, Santa Barbara, California, 80p.

Neuerburg, Norman, 1995, Saints of the California Missions; Bellerophon Books, Santa Barbara, California, 51p.

Neuerburg, Norman, 1997, The Indian Via Crucis from Mission San Fernando: An Historical Exposition; IN: Mission San Fernando, Rey de España, 1797-1997, A Bicentennial Tribute, Historical Society of Southern California, Los Angeles, California, p. 329-382.

Newcomb, Rexford, 1990, Spanish-Colonial Architecture in the United States; Dover Publs. Inc., New York, 169p.

Nunis, Doyce B., Jr. (Ed), 1994, Tales of Mexican California by Antonio Coronel; Bellerophon Books, Santa

Barbara, California, 104p.

Nunis, Doyce B., Jr. 1997, The Franciscan Friars of Mission San Fernando, 1797-1847: IN: Mission San Fernando, Rey de España, 1797-1997, A Bicentennial Tribute, Historical Society of Southern California, Los Angeles, California, p. 217-248.

Oak, Henry L., 1981, A Visit to the Missions of Southern California in February and March 1874; Southwest Museum, Highland Park, Los Angeles, California, 87p.

Olmstead, Cresencia and Dale, 1995, Mission Santa Inés: The Hidden Gem; Cachuma Press, Los Olivos, California, 25p.

Paddison, Joshua (Ed.), 1999, A World Transformed: Firsthand Accounts of California Before the Gold Rush; Heyday Books, Berkeley, California, 344p.

Phillips, George, Harwood, 1979, Indians and the Breakdown of the Spanish Mission System in California; IN: New Spain's Far Northern Frontier, Weber, David J. (Ed.) Univ. New Mexico Press, Albuquerque, p. 259-270.

Pourade, Richard F., 1960, The History of San Diego: The Explorers; Commissioned by James C. Copley, The Union-Tribune Publ. Co., San Diego, California, 203 p.

Pourade, Richard F., 1961, Time of the Bells: The Story of the Mission Period of California; Commissioned by James S. Copley, The Union-Tribune Publ. Co., San Diego, California, 262p.

Priestly, Herbert Ingram (Translator), 1972, A Historical, Political, and Natural Description of California by Pedro Fages, Soldier of Spain, Dutifully Made for the Viceroy in the Year 1775; Ballena Press, Ramona, California, 83p.

Ruscin, Terry, 1999, Mission Memoirs: A Collection of Photographs, Illustrations, and Twentieth-century Reflections on California's Past; Sunbelt Publs., San Diego, California, 205p.

Starr, Kevin, 1973, Americans and the California Dream, 1850-1915; Peregrine Smith, Santa Barbara, California, 128p.

Stern, Jean, Miller, Gerald, J., Hallan-Gibson, Pamela, and Neuerburg, Norman, 1995, Romance of the Bells: The California Missions in Art; The Irvine Museum, Irvine, California, 128p.

Tompkins, Walker A., 1967, Old Spanish Santa Barbara; McNally & Loftin Publs., Santa Barbara, California, 60p.

Weber, David J., (Ed.), 1979, New Spain's Far Northern Frontier: Essays on Spain in the American West 1540-1821; Univ. New Mexico Press, Albuquerque, 321 p.

Weber, Francis J., (Ed.), 1995, The Mission in the Valley: A Documentary History of San Fernando, Rey de España; 3rd print, Saint Francis Historical Society, Mission Hills, California, 136p.

Weber, Francis J., 1997, Memories of an Old Mission: San Fernando, Rey de España; Saint Francis Historical Society, Mission Hills, California, 186p.

Wright, Ralph B., (Ed.), 1964, California's Missions; 5th print., Sterling Press, Los Angeles, California, 95p.

INDEX